Beyond a cry for Tibet, this book is a rema
human compassion and for hope in the fu

This is the stunning story of a nomad boy who escapes the
Chinese Red Army by crossing the Himalayas. Chope Paljor
Tsering becomes an international diplomat for His Holiness the
Dalai Lama, is imprisoned in Nepal, makes a harrowing visit back
to Tibet, and travels the world as an advocate for the Tibetan
people's struggle under Beijing's jackboot, before settling his
family in Australia.

— *Senator Bob Brown*

Chope Paljor Tsering's remarkable story brings to life the warmth
and colour of a traditional, Tibetan, nomadic childhood. The
world that he describes so vividly has almost disappeared in the
face of the twin onslaughts of the Chinese occupation and modern
consumerism — this book is a poignant reminder of how much
has already been lost and of how much we all have to gain by
helping the Tibetans to preserve and develop their unique
Buddhist culture.

— *Alex Butler, former President,*
Australia Tibet Council (ATC)

Chope Paljor Tsering writes his courageous story with simplicity
and humility, yet it is a journey of epic proportions and utterly
engrossing. Those curious about Tibet and its people, their
struggle, strength and faith, would gain much from this book.
I walked each step with him and was enriched and humbled.
A privilege to read.

— *Tracy Mann, actor*

Chope Paljor Tsering is a remarkable man who has lived an extraordinary life. I was moved to tears and laughter by his story which he tells with both humility and compassion. He provides a fascinating account of nomadic life in Tibet, followed by the heartbreaking period he spent as a refugee in Mustang and India. I loved sharing this journey with him and meeting all the interesting characters along the way. An inspiring read.

— *Bunty Avieson, author of*
A Baby in a Backpack to Bhutan

This portrayal of nomadic life is almost unique among refugee stories and his evocation of the stern yet loving family life among the herds is highly memorable.

Despite the exigencies of refugee life and the loss of his country, Chope maintains his sense of balance and commitment to others throughout and the reader is struck by his compassionate and insightful outlook on the life events that shaped him. One cannot but be impressed by the complete absence of the destructive elements of rancour and bitterness, both towards the Chinese and to his situation as a refugee.

Readers will be struck by the fact that the life of this noble and gentle man has become a series of profound Buddhist teachings, something to assist us all in the process of readjusting our own lives.

— *David Templeman, Tibet historian*
and translator of Buddhist history texts

The nature
of all things

*This book is dedicated to all Tibetan children:
to Tibetan children inside Tibet whose right to be
educated freely — especially in their own tongue and
within their cultural environment — has been seriously
infringed by the Chinese occupying authorities;
and to Tibetan children in exile whose right and
freedom to be in Tibet is denied.*

The nature
of all things

The life story of a Tibetan in exile

Chope Paljor Tsering

Lothian
BOOKS

The names or identities of some people in this autobiography
have been changed, shortened or omitted.

Thomas C. Lothian Pty Ltd
132 Albert Road, South Melbourne, Victoria 3205
www.lothian.com.au

Text and illustrations copyright © Chope Paljor Tsering 2004
First published 2004

National Library of Australia
Cataloguing-in-Publication data:

Tsering, Chope Paljor.
The nature of all things.

ISBN 0 7344 0741 6

1. Tsering, Chope Paljor. 2. Refugees — Australia — Biography.
3. Refugees — China — Tibet — Biography. 4. Immigrants —
Australia — Biography. 5. Buddhists — Biography. 6. Tibet (China)
— Biography. 7. Tibet (China) — History — 1951– . I. Title.

305.906914092

Managing Editor: Magnolia Flora
Edited by Stephen Grimwade
Cover illustration by David Brooks
Cover photographs courtesy of Chope Paljor Tsering
Cover design by Michelle Mackintosh
Internal design and typesetting by Caz Brown
Printed in Australia by Griffin Press

Contents

Acknowledgements

One day in 1981 when I was serving in Kathmandu as the Deputy-Secretary at the Tibetan Government-in-Exile's Representative's Office, my five-year-old son Tenzin eagerly rushed back home from the garden where he had been playing with his friends. He looked as if he had something very urgent to tell me. He sat himself firmly down beside me and held my hand. Then looking straight into my eyes, he told me, 'Daddy, don't sit idly like this. Please write down the story of your life. Do it before you get too old!'

I was thirty-three years at the time.

The suddenness and the maturity of Tenzin's remark astonished both my wife Palden and me. Tenzin used to listen to me so intently whenever I talked about Tibet and my family. Since then he and my two younger sons Tenzin Lhadhar and Shenphen Dorje have reminded and urged me repeatedly to write about my life. Palden also often reminded me to write down my story for the sake of the boys.

I began jotting down a few notes here and there during the 1980s but my limited writing skills and my workload at the time prevented me from fully taking on the task. More recently, my

Acknowledgements

son Tenzin Lhadhar not only typed up the collection of my notes, but also transcribed several tapes which I had recorded. My youngest son Shenphen went through the work and helped me in his own way. All along Palden has encouraged and supported me in every way. This book would not have been possible without the sincere and dedicated help and support of my family.

My brothers and sisters have helped to confirm and clarify some memories about which I was uncertain. My friends Roger Catchpole and John Pearce have helped me with their invaluable suggestions and clearer memories of the times I shared with them. My Australian friend Wendy White introduced me to Magnolia Flora and Lothian Books who have been a great pleasure to work with.

I would like to sincerely thank Stephen Grimwade for his skillful editing and the managing editor, Magnolia Flora, for her professionalism, dedication and sincerity. I would also like to sincerely thank Dr Nawang Rabgyal for his support.

While working on this book, I have been repeatedly reminded of the truth of the law of interdependency. Without the efforts of all the people mentioned and many others who have either directly or indirectly contributed in the process, it would have been impossible for this book to have materialised.

Thank you all from the bottom of my heart.

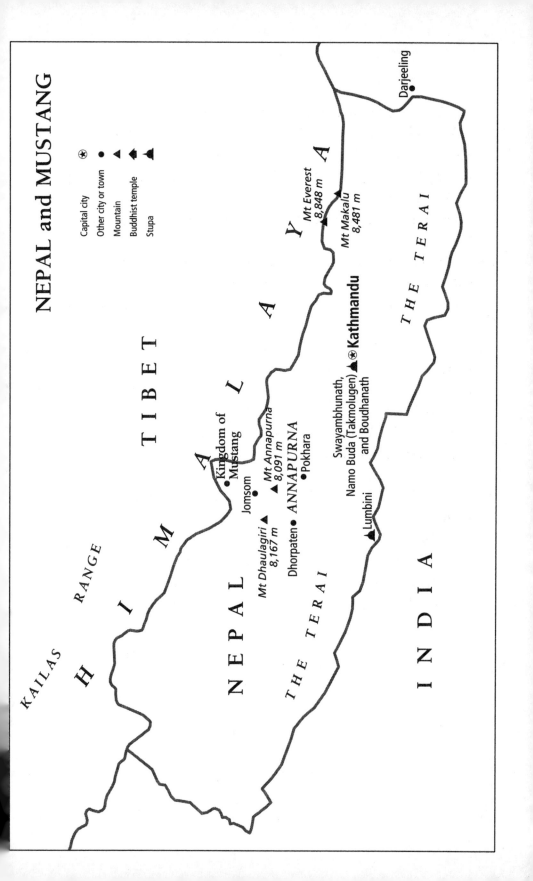

NEPAL and MUSTANG

Capital city ✳
Other city or town ●
Mountain ▲
Buddhist temple ▲
Stupa ▲

KAILAS

H I M A L A Y A

RANGE

TIBET

Kingdom of
Mustang
●

Jomsom
●

Mt Dhaulagiri ▲
8,167 m

Dhorpaten ●

Mt Annapurna ▲
8,091 m

ANNAPURNA

Pokhara ●

Mt Everest
8,848 m

Mt Makalu
8,481 m

▲ ✳ Kathmandu

Swayambhunath,
Namo Buda (Takmolugen)
and Boudhanath

NEPAL

THE TERAI

Lumbini ▲

THE TERAI

INDIA

Darjeeling
●

TIBET

Capital city ✦
Other city or town ●
Mountain ▲
Buddhist temple ♠
Stupa ▲
Country border ▬▬▬

Xinjiang
(CHINA)

KUNLUN MOUNTAINS

CHANG -

Namru

KAILAS
▲ Ghang Rinpoche
(Mt Kailash)

HIMAL RANGE

Jokhang Temple ♠
Lhasa ✦

● Kingdom of
Mustang

Mt Everest
8,848 m
▲

NEPAL
Kathmandu ✦

BHUTA

Darjeeling ● ● Kalimpong

INDIA

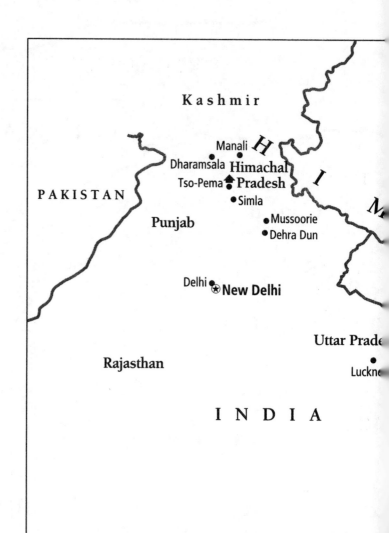

NORTHERN INDIA

Capital city	⊛
Other city or town	●
Mountain	▲
Buddhist temple	♣
Stupa	▲

TIBET

H I M A L A Y A

● Kingdom of
Mustang

NEPAL

▲ Mt Everest
8,848 m

⊛ **Kathmandu**

Sikkim

A

BHUTAN

Darjeeling ●

● Gorakhpur

Bihar

● Patna

● Varanasi
(Benares)

▲ Bodh Gaya

Family tree

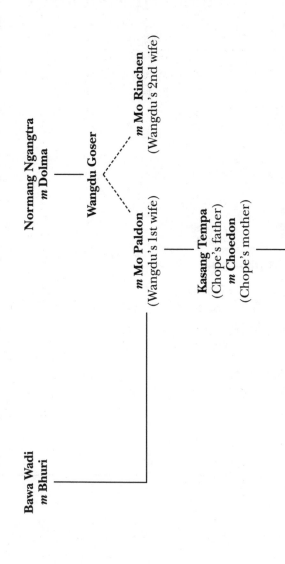

Bawa Wadi
m Bhuri

Normang Ngangtra
m Dolma

Wangdu Goser

m Mo Paldon
(Wangdu's 1st wife)

m Mo Rinchen
(Wangdu's 2nd wife)

Kasang Tempa
(Chope's father)
m Choedon
(Chope's mother)

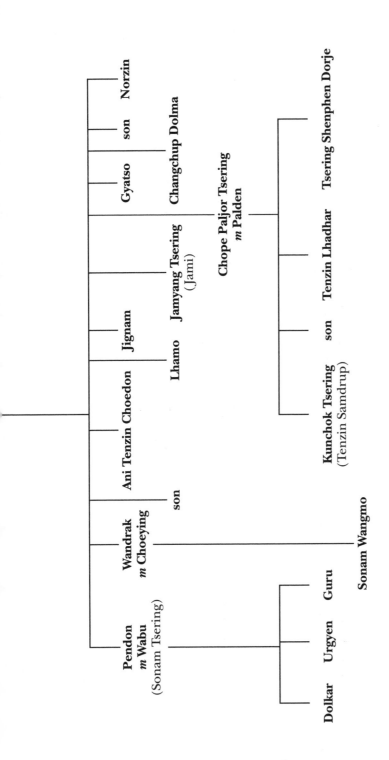

A day with grandmother

A cloudless patch of blue sky filled the circular chimney hole in the middle of the ceiling. A shaft of afternoon sunlight landed on the large carpet on the earthen floor below; light also flooded through the many squares that formed the rectangular south-facing window, revealing a sizeable room. Drifts of smoke wandered through the sunlight, patiently searching for an escape. In one corner a dancing fire warmed the room and heated the pot above it, its contents quietly gurgling and scenting the air with the satisfying aroma of Tibetan tea. A large, earthen bed stood beside the western wall of the room. Within the hollow of the bed, bundles of dry hay and some dry sheep droppings were placed to make it soft and comfortable. On top of it all was a woollen mat with beautiful patterns of many shades and colours.

Sitting comfortably cross-legged on the bed was a grey-haired old woman swaying slightly from side to side as she recited a continuous stream of prayers, one hand turning a large prayer wheel heavy with auspicious decorations, the other counting her prayers with the prayer beads. Within the metal wheel were prayers written on rolled-up pieces of paper, and each time the wheel was turned clockwise it was as if the prayers had been said thousands of times.

The able, attractive and independent woman she had been in her youth had watched herself grow old and ugly as the years piled up like winter snow on mountain slopes. Her face was wrinkled with her seventy-five years. Below her left ear, a large tumour had grown. An operation to remove the tumour, which she had sought against the advice of doctors and family, had gone wrong and had caused her whole face to skew towards the right. The loose skin over her left eye had slid down and now covered that eye, and so a string tied to her head held this loose skin back. She was my grandmother, Mo Rinchen. I was sitting beside her, a little boy with large, inquisitive and attentive eyes. I was three years old.

Grandmother's prayers paused and were replaced by the slurping of buttery Tibetan tea. Then she continued her prayers, putting the wooden cup back on the small table in front of her. After a while her muttering came to an end with the last few words climbing slightly in pitch. Holding the prayer beads in her two hands she joined her palms together in supplication and momentarily closed her eyes to dedicate her prayers and make her wishes for the future. She then put the beads down next to the prayer wheel on a pillow beside her. With a finger she wiped some of the yellow butter floating on the surface of the tea and oiled her palms. Then rubbing her palms together until they were warm, she turned to me and tenderly oiled my face. I shut my eyes tightly to avoid getting butter in them.

'Alright, I have ended my prayers early today, let's go outside,' grandmother told me. 'Now I will tell you your story under the afternoon sunlight.'

This was what I had been waiting for all afternoon and I excitedly gathered Mo Rinchen's sewing kit and an old woollen mat and ran out of the open door into the spring sunshine. Sitting down on the mat I waited for grandmother, who slowly walked out of her room and paused awhile to gaze at the blue mountains in the distance.

I heard the echoing voices of children playing in the hills behind the house and my attention was drawn by their games. Mo Rinchen also heard the voices and turning towards them she sighed with disapproval, 'Why are the children playing alone in the hills? They will hurt themselves. Someone should go and look after them.'

For a few moments she looked slightly troubled as if her own words had convinced her. Then turning to me she said, 'So what was I saying … Oh yes, a story, I was going to tell you your story, yes.'

I fixed my eyes on grandmother's wrinkled face and listened. But even before grandmother began I was engulfed by an almost melancholic feeling. I felt as if I was a traveller in strange lands, as if the trot of a horse swayed me from side to side. Then the feeling reshaped itself and became more vivid, and I now began to feel as if I was in a lonely white tent peering up at the chimney hole. Fragrant smoke curled upwards from an incense holder and I felt as if I was the smoke, slowly rising up out of the tent, leaving behind everything and embarking on a lonesome solitary journey.

Once again, grandmother stared out into the distance as she began her story. 'Many years ago, there were misunderstandings and friction between the central Tibetan government in Lhasa and Tashi Lhunpo, the seat of the Panchen Rinpoche. As you know the Panchen Rinpoche is a very revered lama with many disciples and followers.

'I heard that Tashi Lhunpo had not paid its due tax to the government and so the government had sent collectors. Panchen

Rinpoche feared arrest for tax evasion and had fled to China. Since you had received teachings from and had faith in Panchen Rinpoche, you escorted him to the border. But on your return, you were captured by government soldiers and taken to Lhasa for imprisonment!'

There was so much I wanted to know, but Mo Rinchen did not like being interrupted while telling stories, so I decided to just listen and ask questions later.

'I was so afraid for you, I didn't know what to do. Of course you had escorted Panchen Rinpoche to the border, but there wasn't anything wrong with that. I didn't think that was against the law. So I travelled south to Lhasa for your trial. It was almost unbearable to see you as a prisoner. An investigation and questioning took place, but it was a foregone conclusion that you were guilty because you sided with Panchen Rinpoche and escorted him to the border. For assisting a fugitive you had acted as an accomplice and so you were given a sentence of many years of imprisonment at the Nangtse-shar prison in Lhasa. I thought it was very unfair. I cried but I was helpless. You had acted in accordance with your faith. After all, Panchen Rinpoche had been a lama of yours.'

Grandmother quivered as she cried, 'So, there was I, in Lhasa, away from my home. Far from my family and relatives. I brought food and visited you in prison many times during those years. Seeing you in a dark cell hurt me so much. On special days you were allowed out of the prison and I would walk with you around the city. But the clinking of the iron shackles around your ankles followed us everywhere. The eyes of strangers followed us, some watching in pity, others in scorn. It shamed me. You were chained like a criminal but you had done nothing. And I suffered with you. I suffered because of you and again you will make me suffer ... I am sure. I was so ashamed and lonely in a city where I knew only a few. I would often go and pray for a happier life at the great Jokhang temple in front of the statue of the Lord Buddha and that helped me deal with my pain. Still, life often felt so meaningless, not worth living. I often thought about taking my own life, thinking there couldn't be anyone suffering more than me on earth or in the sky. Why live a life of shame, unjust shame?'

By now tears rolled down grandmother's cheeks. 'That was when I met the Dégé Khandro. A woman who looked very normal, just like the rest of us. But she was actually a lama from the Dégé region of eastern Tibet.'

Grandmother put the palms of her hands together in reverence, 'The Dégé Khandro consoled me, and advised me when I faced difficult times and choices. She taught me how to live through such times and become a survivor. She gave me teachings and they helped me cope with seeing you in the dark prison cell and in shackles; they helped me with the eyes that chased us around the city on the days you were allowed out, and with all of the pain in my mind. I still practise those teachings today. I could never repay her kindness, the Dégé Khandro. I wonder where she is now?'

Grandmother's voice died down and it looked to me as if she was searching for the Dégé Khandro in the distance. Then the barking of dogs broke the silence and she continued, 'Well, eventually you were released and fortunately, I survived through everything. But your dark days in prison scarred you for the rest of your few years. The cold prison floor on which you spent so many years made you weak. Your intestines threatened to come out and you went through so much, so much pain. Confusion gripped me whenever you became ill. I felt sad and sorry for you, why did you have to suffer so? But you were also making me suffer, which made me angry. You were a religious man but your short-tempered personality didn't help me deal with my suffering either. I repeatedly asked myself what I had done to have to go through so much sorrow for you.'

Mo Rinchen looked down at me, almost angrily, from behind the lens of tears, as if she still bore the brunt for the injustices she felt she had suffered. Then calming herself she added, 'But the forces of *karma* indeed work in strange ways.'

'One day you went through acute pain again and you quickly became very weak. We were alone, many furlongs from anywhere and there was no hope of finding a doctor. I tried to help you but there wasn't much I could do. Life left you that day and you left me, all alone in a small white tent, days from anywhere.'

Grandmother now began to sob loudly. In between the weeping and the heavy breathing she moaned, 'I was so shocked and grieved. I didn't know what to do. I never considered you a particularly healthy man, but I never thought you would leave me so soon and so suddenly. I felt helpless and life again ran out of meaning. I couldn't think at all. There was only one thing I could think of doing. I got onto my horse and made for Namru where your son lived. As the horse's pace quickened I looked back one last time at the white tent in the middle of an endless plain. The last thing I saw was the incense smoke rising out through the smoke hole in the tent. I can still see it, faint and light, a wisp of white rising into the evening sky.

'I rode the horse for much of the night without stopping. I just wanted to get away from everything. The feeling of loss, the dry, empty feeling that stirs the dust inside of you and makes you cough, this is the worse feeling there is. It is a thief. It steals your hope, energy, reason, and can easily rob you of sanity. That night it robbed me of everything, and almost my life, but again the words of the Dégé Khandro came back to my mind like fresh droplets of rain on a barren wasteland. Memories of her and her teachings brought some sense and energy back into me. They turned the flood of tears from my swollen, red eyes to a trickle. With the sky above and the galloping horse beneath I travelled for days before reaching Namru and your son. I told him of your death and he at once set out for you, and he found the white tent as I had left it. He held a proper funeral for you at the site and spent much for your departed soul, on the prayers and ceremonies that followed. I sold most of our animals and I paid for many days of prayers and other things the lama recommended we carry out. You have seen the huge pile of stones with *mani* carvings near the house?'

I nodded.

'They were all carved for you. I knew that a sinful man like you, someone who loved hunting as much as you did, would go to hell. But all the prayers and meritorious things we did for you and the few virtuous things you did in your life must have saved you.

'Many years before your imprisonment, we went on pilgrimages to Ghang Rinpoche (Mount Kailash). Altogether we were able to do thirteen circumambulations of the mountain. It is not an easy pilgrimage to Ghang Rinpoche and we faced snow, treacherous passes and other dangers. But we also had many happy times together during those trips. Once we stopped at a beautiful village called Cerva, the "gold mine village". Like other pilgrims, we stayed there for a few weeks and panned for gold. We found a bit of gold and then went on. After all, pilgrimages are to earn merit not to find wealth.

'There is also a lovely, very colourful market near the great mountain. There Indian merchants and pilgrims brought sweets, caramel, fabrics, wooden cups and other items to sell to the Tibetans, and the Tibetans brought wool and other local things to sell to the Indians. You know, we could get things for just a handful of wool!

'Each journey to Ghang Rinpoche took many months,' continued Mo Rinchen, 'but in the end we completed thirteen circumambulations and the merit of it must have been immense. Each circumambulation took a few days, although faster, very youthful legs can complete it within a long day. Treading on the ancient worn-out paths, we were blessed by the mountain. It is such a sacred site. Do you know that holy deities reside at that mountain? Those were happy days when we were fit and able. How I long to see the majestic mountain again and receive the blessings of the deities. But this old body of mine …

'Anyway, when we returned from our pilgrimages we were always filled with a sense of fulfilment and fortune. Instead of being tired out by such a long trek, we would be rejuvenated. Ghang Rinpoche, the snow-covered peak, its ancient bare sides almost blue with slate; so grand, so majestic, so auspicious, the very sight of it will fill anyone with awe. May the deities of Ghang Rinpoche bless and protect you again, my child.'

1

The history of a name

I was born in 1948 into a Tibetan family who lived in the very heart of the great and remote Chang-Thang plains of northern Tibet. I was the eighth child of my parents, and my early childhood was very different from that of my siblings. I was particularly lucky, and due to one belief I was shown more love and care by everyone.

A few months after I was born, a member of one of the eminent Sakya families came to Namru — they had been especially requested to go on a teaching trip and were on their way north. Members of this great, noble family are highly venerated and the throne holder of this family is considered one of the highest lamas in Tibet — the head of the Sakya branch of Tibetan Buddhism. As it is a common practice among Tibetans to ask a lama to name a child, my parents decided it was a wonderful opportunity to ask this visiting Rinpoche to name their newborn son.

When my parents found some time between the teachings the Rinpoche was bestowing, they carried me before him and asked him to name me. But when he conferred a name, my parents looked very surprised, even troubled. The name he gave me was Wangdu Tsering — exactly the same name as my late grandfather, my father's father — and it had only been a few years since the old Wangdu Tsering, known by most as Wangdu Goser, had passed away. My father was particularly troubled by the new name of his little son. It was customary in our community that a family would not use the name of any deceased family members. My father asked the Rinpoche for another name, but the Rinpoche repeated the name 'Wangdu Tsering', emphatically adding that that was his own son's name.

The following day the teachings concluded, the Rinpoche left and we went home. But the new morning was unable to wash away my father's unease with my appointed name. At that time Genphel Rinpoche, who was a very well-known and well-respected lama, was staying with our family for a few months. He asked father if he had requested a name for me. My father replied that the eminent Sakya Rinpoche had indeed named his son but that the name was unusable. Then my father requested that Genphel Rinpoche bestow another name. In astonishment Genphel Rinpoche asked why. He wondered why the name bestowed by such a great lama was unusable. My father told Rinpoche that the name given to me was Wangdu Tsering, the name of his late father. 'That is why I am so uncomfortable with the name,' he told the lama.

'Perhaps he is your father, reborn,' said the old lama, 'But since you are uncomfortable with the name, from henceforth your little son will be called Paljor Tsering.'

And so I became Paljor Tsering, which means 'glorious treasure long life'. Only later did I become 'Chope', after an English teacher misspelt a childhood nickname without grasping its true meaning. During my early childhood my niece Dolkar was my closest playmate, as she was only a few months younger than me. Somehow I had always thought that she was my brother and

I used to call her JoDol, while she called me JoPal. *Jo* in our local dialect means brother, while Dol is short for Dolkar and Pal stands for Paljor. So I became Brother Pal and she became Brother Dol. My teacher then misspelt Jopal as Jopay, which has since become Chope!

The conversation my father had with old Genphel Rinpoche rekindled suspicions that my father had held since my naming by the Sakya Rinpoche. Could this little son of his really be his old father reborn? Indeed, he had paid many monks and monasteries to pray and carry out other religious practices for his father when he had passed away. He had paid for the printing of the mani prayer (the mantra of compassion) onto thousands of stones. He had carried out all of the numerous acts that lamas had advised him to do following *divinations* which they had carried out. (Divinations are means of consulting divine deities on a particular matter.) My father was known to have spent all of the family's wealth for his deceased father's sake. All this for the *rebirth* of his late father into his own family.

So my father repeatedly asked himself, 'Now could this little child really be Wangdu Goser?' Despite his very deep and stable faith in the lamas who had hinted at the possibility, a part of him was still very doubtful. He had done much on his father's behalf, following Wangdu Goser's death, but his father was far from a perfect man and was very fond of guns. Still, it seemed very improbable that he had regained a meaningful, precious human life once again.

Even though I was too young to remember those days, my family later told me that once I was old enough to talk I kept calling my father, 'my son'. Whenever anyone called me by my name, Paljor, I would say, 'I am Wangdu, not Paljor.' I also recognised many people and objects the late Wangdu Goser had known, including my Auntie Pentso. Apparently, Wangdu Goser was very fond of his niece Pentso and in his last years, after returning from imprisonment and detention in the Lhasa–Yangpachen area, he always enjoyed 'butter and *pak*' at Auntie Pentso's house. (Pak is the general term for *tsampa* which is flour made from roasted barley, kneaded into a dough. Pak can be made either with butter and tea, or with any liquid since it is made by kneading. Tibetans normally make pak with a little bit of dried cheese dust, a lump of butter and some Tibetan tea. A very rich pak can be made with just cheese dust and butter added to the tsampa.)

My older siblings and family members can still remember me often saying, 'I am off to Pentso's house for some butter and pak.' Those words were particularly strange coming from me because all of the children would say 'Auntie' and never just 'Pentso'.

My family members also recollected another day when Wangdu Goser's youngest brother, our Grand Uncle Tserun, had visited our home to meet my father. That was the first time that I had ever met our Grand Uncle Tserun but upon seeing him, I ran out ecstatically to welcome him. To Grand Uncle Tserun I was just another child among many in our household, so he didn't pay any special attention to me. But I suddenly began to sob inconsolably, muttering, 'It was brother Tserun but he didn't speak to me, didn't even notice me!' When Grand Uncle Tserun heard what I was saying, he is said to have run to me and enveloped me in his big, teary embrace. He was certain that he had once again met his brother.

Soon everyone in my family became convinced beyond doubt that I was indeed Wangdu and they began to accept me as our grandfather reborn. Therefore I enjoyed a privileged status within my family and was given much respect and even more love by all. Our grandmother, Mo Rinchen, who was Wangdu Goser's wife, always took special care of me and often told me stories of when she and Wangdu had been together. She would often talk to me as if I was an adult and could remember everything Wangdu had done. But occasionally some of my siblings and cousins teased me about being our grandfather and would not let me join them in their games.

Our homeland was the Chang-Thang plains and there we lived the life of the Tibetan *drogpa*, which literally means 'animal farmer' or 'nomad'. Like our family, most of the families in the region permanently lived in the same place, although the animals were seasonally moved around for better pasture.

Wealth in the land of drogpas was measured by how many domestic animals each family had, and economically we were modest. We only had about forty yaks, the male *nor*, and only ten to fifteen *dri*, the female nor. We also had some two hundred sheep, another fifty or so goats, over twenty horses and one mule. There were twenty or so people in our family and we had many visitors every day, so it must have been very difficult for our elders to accumulate enough to feed and clothe everyone throughout the four seasons. But we never had any worries over food or clothing. Meat was more abundant during the winter and dairy products were plentiful in the summer, and there was always plenty of tsampa. Nevertheless, I do remember my mother complaining that the tsampa was running out and on a few occasions several yak loads of barley had to be borrowed from our aunt who was very rich. It was believed that her family had enough stock of barley to last at least a couple of years.

As the domestic animals were the main source of livelihood, ours was indeed modest. But the modesty of our family was only in the form of making ends meet, and the family enjoyed tremendous social status due to the popularity of my father, Kasang Tempa. His name was heard not only in our own district, Namru, but throughout northern Tibet. He was elected the Nam-ru *Garpon*, the local district leader, at a relatively young age and managed to hold on to that post until we lost our country to the Chinese. The garpon was elected by the *dharokhas*, who were themselves directly elected by the community members of each *tsowa*; a tsowa was a sub-grouping of the district, rather like a village. Once elected the garpon was validated by the Tibetan government.

My father was a man who commanded a great amount of respect and affection. He was hardly ever at home, having to spend most months travelling on official duties. Whenever he was at home, there was an extraordinarily warm and lively atmosphere around our home, even though he had to spend much of his time listening and mediating different 'court cases'.

These cases meant that there were always different people around us. Those who had their own means would pitch their tent nearby our home and those who didn't would come and stay with us. This had long been the tradition, so such individuals wouldn't even ask if they could stay. Fuel for fires would always be provided for those who camped nearby.

Those people arguing in front of my father, putting their cases forward as they felt right, never failed to fascinate me. The majority of them would talk in so much metaphor and stories of old while making their point that several hours were engaged by each person. The general public would view such articulate people with some degree of admiration. The great orators were considered clever for being able to make almost poetic verses from their arguments, or for being able to remember such clever examples to put their points across. Tales told in court cases sometimes became public talk for years. In contrast my father never had those wonderful exemplifying stories to tell, and people used to be amused by his straightforwardness and lack of what we call *tam* (tales of examples). In my homeland well-known public figures were expected to know or talk with a great deal of tam.

This was not a handicap for my father. He never minced words. His words were to the point and precise. He was greatly admired as a man of truth and justice. It was customary to offer such leaders a white scarf and some specially shaped butter and a little dust of dry Tibetan cheese, or some dry meat. Any gift more than that would be considered a bribe. I remember my father getting up and walking away from one such session when someone tried to give him some silver coins along with the usual gifts. As my father refused to hear his case, the case had to be heard at the district headquarters when all leaders would be present. More serious cases were usually fought at the district headquarters, where sometimes severe punishments such as flogging were carried out.

Whenever time permitted my father would read biographies and stories of the wise and fools, the *Dho Zanglun*. There were several such books advising the common person to lead a happy and virtuous life. Many of these books tell stories of wise people leading virtuous, happy lives and fools leading greedy and miserable lives. My father would also listen to others reading and singing the great Tibetan epic King Gesar stories. Back then I used to think my father was an old man, but he was only in his late forties.

All those who gave him the customary gift also received a gift of similar nature from my father, usually without the scarf. He was a very kind and gentle person. I hardly ever recall him losing his temper or uttering offensive words. He was deeply religious and he told his beads day and night, muttering some barely audible mantras. He would tell his beads even when he was hearing a case or listening to Gesar stories. He often took snuff but he would tell us that taking snuff was a great sin and would advise us not to.

He was of medium height, dark skinned, thin and he didn't enjoy good health. One evening, just as the stars had begun climbing the night sky, I asked my mother why our father was darker, thinner and unhealthier than the rest of us. It was one of those quiet winter evenings when my father was away and my mother had some time to rest and tell us stories. My mother never had a moment of rest until late in the night, except on rare winter evenings when my father was away and we had no visitors. This evening was one of those rare evenings. My unusual question drew giggles among the other family members who were gathered but my mother took it seriously and told us the whole story. It made us all feel very sad and angry. It also brought us a great deal of pride.

My mother looked very disturbed as she began her account. She held back tears and the power of integrity rang in each word she spoke. And as she spoke every line on her face drew a vivid picture of what had happened. I was lying on my mother's lap as she began her recollection while stroking my head.

'Your father was not always dark skinned, nor thin and frail. He was a very handsome and healthy young man until that tragedy took place. It all happened the year after he was elected and appointed Namru Garpon. A batch of national Tibetan soldiers was on its way from Lhasa to Kham. There were about two hundred of them and it would take them several days to travel to Namru by horse. The government issued a decree in advance of their arrival ordering all districts on their way to provide them with three basic facilities: tents, water and firewood for their overnight sojourn. Several days before their arrival, stories of their misbehaviour reached our ears. We heard that the three basic facilities were not appreciated and that the soldiers demanded meat, butter and even horses. The day they arrived at our district your father purposely prepared only the basic facilities. Of course there were people to receive them and to attend to any further requirements and wishes. Your father planned to pay his courtesy call to the commander after they had settled. He was prepared for some trouble but not to that scale.

'As soon as they had arrived at the prepared site, it was understood that the commander was infuriated for only receiving the basic facilities and that the garpon had not been there to receive them. The Namru Garpon's rank was fourth, which was equal to that of a cabinet minister. It would have been improper with his official rank for your father to receive the soldiers. As soon as your father arrived to greet the troops, the commander rebuked him for giving them such a mean reception and ordered his men to beat him.

'He was beaten so severely with rifle butts and boots that he fainted and had to be carried off on a makeshift stretcher. The beating did not stop until your father stopped breathing, even when all the local leaders pleaded for mercy. Several of his ribs were broken and he vomited blood. But his willpower not only kept him alive but gave him strength enough to ask his colleagues and countrymen to carry him on a stretcher to Lhasa by day and night. He did not return home for months and we did not know what had happened to him.

'The soldiers did not proceed further, remaining in our district for several months. There was no news of your father at all. They, the soldiers, became completely undisciplined, like a pack of wolves let loose on a flock of sheep. Once, some of them even came to our gate and shouted at us saying that the dead body of the garpon had already been fed to the vultures. They even warned us to leave our home saying that they wanted the warmth and comfort of our house and the large tents. Their contempt was such that at one stage I nearly had to take up arms against them. All the men including Wangdrak were away with your father.' Wangdrak, my oldest brother, must have been in his teens at the time.

Mother continued, pointing at my sister Tenzin Choedon, 'My only companion was this one. She was only four years old then. But she was such a brave child and was never afraid. When those men were shouting at us, abusing us from our gate, I couldn't bear it and I went to grab a sword. She also grabbed a stick and went straight to the gate and banged it. Oh! Was she brave! Those few lonely months were very bad indeed. Your father disappeared for several months completely. And no one knew where he was or indeed whether he was alive at all. There were so many rumours that nothing could be believed. Some even suggested that your father had died of the beatings and that Wangdrak had gone into the mountains, forming a local group to fight the soldiers. Such were the rumours that there seemed nothing good left.

'As if a miracle had happened, one evening a messenger came from the district headquarters and broke the news that a senior government official had arrived from Lhasa, and orders were posted on the gate proclaiming the de-ranking of the commander for his misbehaviour. The government's order also went further and said that henceforth the basic facility should only be fuel enough for cooking the tea. Even this should not be imposed if the local people have shortages of fuel.'

With a sparkle of old triumph in her eyes, my mother went on to say, 'Only then did I know that not only was your father alive but he was in Lhasa winning a case. After that the batch of soldiers were like balloons without air. It was such a relief. But the price that your dad had to pay was heavy. He did not recover from the broken ribs for over a year. Even when he could finally reach home I had to nurse him for almost another whole year with a physician permanently at our home. Not only were the ribs broken, the whole of his blood circulation system became poor. Since then he has been dark skinned and thin.'

2

The same cup

'Come to your mother little calf, come to your mother. She will shield you from the winter winds, and her milk is sweet in the summer,' sang Choedon, my mother, in her gentle, caring voice. In time with the song she lifted me high into the air with her arms stretched out. Then she lowered and cuddled me. I could feel the warmth of her unconditional love, as the deep-blue sky spun behind her and the sunlight dazzled my eyes.

My mother was almost illiterate but she could recite many popular verses from the *Dho Zanglun*, the books of the wise and the fools. She had also memorised many nice prayers and her prayer recitations were sung in very sweet melodies, like a gentle song. The sound of churning butter and those comforting prayer melodies were the first sounds we heard each morning, as the first fresh rays of dawn ushered in the day. We learnt most of her prayers off by heart just by waking up to them and falling asleep with them at night.

My mother married my father when she was only eighteen years old, and my father was only three years older. My mother was born in the neighbouring district of Dholwa, which was about one-and-a-half day's journey by horse from our home.

As her family had come to Dholwa from the district of Yakpa, their family was called Yakpa-Ru-sar, 'the new family from Yakpa'. This seemed to have become their unofficial family name.

My mother had many sisters and two brothers. The daughters of Yakparusar were admired by many in the locality, and it seems that all of them married into wealthy or respectable families. In those days parents arranged most of the marriages. Because my mother's family was quite wealthy, and with her sisters married off to rich families, I had several aunts and two uncles who were all much better off than us — in terms of the number of domestic animals they had. But our family had much wealth in the form of ornaments of gold and silver, studded with precious stones. Typical middle-class housewives would have dozens of corals and silver coins attached to their braided hair. These ornaments covered them from their shoulders to their heels. My mother had several sets of these.

My mother had a reputation for not only looking after her own twelve children but also for looking after those who depended on our household. She was extremely hardworking, efficient and very kind. Without someone like her at home, I don't think my father would have been able to devote all of his life to his duty, which brought nothing tangible that could benefit the family. She was a great, caring mother with an enormous capacity for putting up with difficulties.

A typical day for her would be getting up at dawn before everyone else and churning yoghurt to make butter. Yoghurt butter was more solid and considered to be of a higher quality than butter made directly from milk. She would then prepare tea and breakfast for all and she also made the tsampa, which required a great deal of work and energy. Between serving tea and meals to all the unexpected guests we always seemed to have, she made lunch and dinner. Mother also milked the dri in the evenings throughout the seasons. During the summer, she milked the sheep twice a day, once at about ten in the morning and again at around four in the afternoon. Most of the family helped her milk the animals, but without her expertise and practical direction everything was more difficult.

I remember when my mother went on a pilgrimage to Lhasa and other holy places for several months. My eldest sister and a maid took over my mother's daily routine. They could hardly cope with it all. Sometimes there wasn't enough dinner, and sometimes the smaller ones even missed dinner when it was being served. I remember one evening when my sister and our maid Ani-Dolkar forgot to serve me and I was too embarrassed to say that my dinner was missing. They only noticed when my brother Jamyang saw that I was weeping quietly. There were twenty-one of us in the family back then and with a few uninvited guests who had come from distant places someone could easily be left out.

In our custom each person had his or her own bowl or cup and one always ate from the same bowl and drank from the same cup. We even carried our cups with us whenever we went to herd the sheep. We had a saying and kept our tradition true to it:

> *Always bear your dagger at your side,*
> *One never knows where enemies might be,*
> *Always bear your cup in your amdrak,*
> *One never knows where a friend might be.*

Except for guests of high social status, the moment a guest sat on the mattress they would be asked to produce their cup, as tea was ever ready. For a guest of very high social status with a servant, the servant would be asked to produce the master's cup. For important guests a cup would be provided but most would say, 'I have my cup' and would then present their cup from their *amdrak*. An 'amdrak' is the chest pocket created by the overlapping of the *chupa* cloak when it is tied up around the waist. 'Chupas' are the Tibetan national dress worn by both men and women, although the styles are different for each.

My mother taught us many things, very often quoting from the *Khache Phalu*, one of the popular books of the wise and the fools, purportedly written by a Muslim. One of her favourite quotations was, 'If mothers keep their mouths locked, the children might open the gate of disaster.' When we did something naughty, she would say this and then tell us where we were wrong. Some of my mother's advice still seems very appropriate for today's generations. She would tell us that plucking one blade of green grass would cause a great sin, a sin equivalent to that of killing a three-year-old goat. This advice seemed incomprehensible in those days; killing a little three-year-old goat was unthinkable but grass was almost infinitely abundant. I can now appreciate that she was teaching us the basics of the fragile ecosystem in a way that would make an impact.

Even now, as I recollect memories of those days, I feel so much of my parents' kindness and presence that I find myself missing them beyond expression. I know how lucky we were to have had such wonderful, loving parents who devoted their whole lives to our upbringing. My siblings and I were born during the most difficult period in the history of the Tibetan people and yet we managed to escape the holocaust caused by the Chinese occupation. We suffered the acute agony of the passing away of our beloved parents in exile, under the most difficult circumstances, yet we managed to survive with hope and dignity. I believe that this was only possible because of the internal strength that both of our parents had given us. Their every word and deed made us stronger.

My oldest sister, Pendon, was the first child of my parents. My mother gave birth to her when she was only nineteen years old. By the time I was born Pendon had already grown up and married, and her first child is just six months younger than me. My sister Pendon was a second mother to me and to all of my younger brothers and sisters.

Pendon's husband was affectionately called Wabu, although his real name was Sonam Tsering. He was a very hardy, animal farmer who did all the family business. One might even call him 'a typical man of our locality'. He was a man who quietly carried out his duties without any grudge or fear; someone who knew exactly when was the best time to collect salt from the northern lakes, and where to go for the next grain-purchasing business trip. In between the long journeys he would engage himself in preparing for the journeys ahead by mending bags, sewing saddle cushions for the yaks and carrying out numerous other tasks.

He had a reputation for being very straightforward and never being able to say anything other than what he thought. Once a travelling monk, who had been on pilgrimage to almost all the sacred places in central Tibet, came to our home and stayed for a whole winter. He was undoubtedly a worthy monk and it used to be said that truly pious monks possess a particular fragrance called *tsultrim drima*, the scent of unfaltering morality. One day, when all of us were present, the monk asked Wabu if he could smell anything on his shirt and gave it to him to sniff.

'It smells like dirt,' was the reply. The monk then presented his cup to my brother-in-law and asked him to smell it. He got a whiff of it and said, 'It smells of tobacco.' It was true that the pilgrim monk snuffed and it might indeed have smelt of tobacco. Everyone else had a hearty laugh, but Wabu was still unmoved.

The monk also had a good laugh and admitted that some people told him that they smelled tsultrim drima on his clothes.

Wabu never differentiated between his own children and us. We all impatiently looked forward to his return whenever he went on a journey. He always brought back presents for all of us. He was unquestionably one of the pillars of our family.

My brother Wangdrak was the second eldest child in the family. He was only two years younger than my sister Pendon and always accompanied my father on his travels, acting as his personal attendant. He was very handsome and always very well dressed. Unlike the rest of us he also had a good voice. He had learnt to read and write and was also good at accounting in our traditional system. He read and sang book after book of the King Gesar epics. He was incredibly good at training race-horses and 'reading' the horses — my father owned a book on horses and how to treat them if they were sick; brother Wangdrak seemed to have learnt the entire contents off by heart.

Unlike our parents, Wangdrak was not very religious in his youth, but he was especially talented at shooting and twice he was the district champion. I remember him shooting through a thin bamboo target, which could not have been more than three centimetres wide and fifteen centimetres tall, from a distance of a hundred paces. I envied him and wanted to become like him in riding and shooting. His position as the son of the Namru Garpon, his physical attractiveness, his wonderful qualities as a person, and his sportsmanship with horses and guns made him the most respected and popular young man in our *zong* (district) and beyond.

The third child of my parents, a son, had died before I was born. My mother used to say that he had many extraordinary qualities and that my parents had not had enough fortune to have such a son living.

My sister Tenzin Choedon was the fourth child. She was very intelligent as a child and extraordinarily sensitive towards the feelings of others. She decided to become a nun when she was sixteen years old. She had warned my parents that she would disappear from our home if they did not allow her to become a nun. Although there were already some well-to-do and well-known families asking for sister Tenzin Choedon's hand in marriage, my parents gave in to her wish. Once she had become a nun she was known as Ani Tenzin Choedon (*ani* meaning 'nun').

Her nunnery was in Tolung, which was not too far from Lhasa but very far from home. She was excited and eager to be able to leave and become a nun but the rest of the family was very sad. We missed her dearly. We missed her ability to look after the animals. We missed the love with which she cared for her younger brothers, sisters, nephews and nieces, and her endless stories about good and evil, and heaven and hell. She seemed to know so much about everything, that I too believed she was someone special.

The fifth child was my sister Lhamo and she was always quiet, soft-spoken and very calm. She was the nanny who looked after all the younger children of the family. After sister Tenzin Choedon became a nun, sister Lhamo took on her responsibility of herding the sheep during the day. I used to be very happy if my sisters would take me along as a helper when they went sheep herding, but they would rather take my brother Jamyang Tsering who was three years older than me. I was too sensitive and easily frightened. I would beg to go home as soon as thunder rang in the distance beneath the dark summer rain clouds.

Lhamo's caring and kind nature attracted every child to her and she had the most difficult time as she quietly bore all the shouts and cries of all the young children.

The sixth child was my brother Jignam. He was also a quiet

and unassuming child. He did not rush and jump about like the rest of us, although he was very good at riding horses and I used to envy his ability. He won awards on two occasions, coming first at our local, annual horserace and third at the district-level horserace, which used to take place once every three years. He was thirteen years old when he became the youngest district-level jockey and was praised for his sense of timing, knowing exactly when to gallop and when to ride more slowly. Then he decided to become a monk; my parents were pleased with his decision and my mother was particularly happy.

Jignam left with my father during one of his yearly visits to Lhasa and did not return with my father. We were told that he had been ordained in the Nalanda monastery in Phenpo, which is not so far from Lhasa but again was very far from our home. He became a pupil of a tall, bearded, middle-aged monk called Jinpa-la, who was once a student of our old *genla*, our resident teacher. On my father's return from Lhasa he brought a photograph of my brother together with himself and Jinpa-la. That was the first photograph I had ever seen. The photograph awoke an indescribably melancholic feeling within me. All sorts of thoughts rushed into my mind. I wondered how my brother could possibly live in a different place with complete strangers. I thought he was so very brave. Back then I could not even imagine living in this world without my parents. It was enough just to be without two of our older brothers and sisters. But we had one consolation, we could avidly await their homecoming each summer.

When Jignam returned after a year he had changed a great deal. He had a shaved head and was wearing brown and yellow robes, although not the complete monk's attire. He had grown taller and the thing that struck me the most was that his accent had changed. This change of accent, along with the robes and the shaved head, made him seem like a new person. But his personality had not changed; he was the same quiet, confident and gentle person. There were so many questions to ask and so many things to tell him, that when he returned the children slept on the roof of our house and talked the whole night long. There was some difficulty in understanding some of his newly acquired terms and expressions at first, but we soon got used to them. I can never forget those summer nights under the twinkling stars talking, laughing, playing and sleeping.

My parents' seventh child was Jamyang Tsering, who we often called 'Jami'. He was two years younger than brother Jignam and three years older than me. As a child he was the most introverted of all of us, but he was very playful and I spent much of my childhood with him. He used to play with my psychology very effectively. If we had an argument he would not be able to match me with words, so he would sit down, look right into my eyes and pull funny faces at me while making repulsive noises, as if to say that I looked and sounded like that. This always infuriated me and I would jump on him, punching him with my fists. He would just sit with his head covered until I became exhausted and then laugh at me or pull faces again. Jamyang and I usually played and fought while herding the nor in the wilderness.

As youngsters we had heard a number of stories about local spirits leading children away from their home and turning them into their servants for months. Such local spirits were believed to reside in mountains, rocks and even lakes. Children were told not to mention their names lest they were to be invoked to come and take us away. There was one such mountain nearby our home called Tsegu, meaning 'Nine-peaked Mountain', and a lake called Zeling Du Tso, meaning 'The Demon Lake of Zeling'. Both the mountain and the lake were believed to be the residences of wrathful non-Buddhist spirits and we were advised never to mention their names or fall asleep near these fearful areas. I was extremely afraid of them and any mention of their names would send shivers down my spine.

Brother Jamyang would recite the names of these places and pretend that he was being possessed. That brought me to my knees, begging him to stop and I would promise to give him whatever he demanded. But when it was lunchtime he would always give me extra cream or butter to go with our tsampa, and he would always take genuine care of me. Sometimes, as Jamyang and I ate alone on little green hilltops, he would eat very little and give me most of his lunch.

My younger brother Gyatso was the ninth child in our family. He was two years my junior and was very active, playful, clever and fearless. His feelings were never easily hurt but once hurt, his ears would go red before he lost his temper. Eventually this became known by all those who came to our home, which practically meant everyone in our tsowa, and a local saying soon developed, 'Never let Gyatso's ears become red!'

The tenth child was my younger sister Changchup Dolma. She was a very cute little child with an extraordinarily fair and round face. She had incredibly black, gleaming hair and unlike other girls, her hair was cut short. She was very quick in imitating the adults, although she was too small to be playing and running about with us in the Chang-Thang.

My parents' eleventh child, a boy, and their twelfth child, a girl, both died young. The boy died when he was not even one year old and his death was the first of a person in my memory. It was a very sad time. He caught some sudden ache and died within two days. Prayers were said day and night for his recovery, but when death is imminent nothing seems to prevent it.

There were neither hospitals nor child specialists in the

modern sense. But there were several physicians trained in our own Tibetan medical system. Some of these physicians were extremely skilful and effective. One such old physician was called Razi Amche who lived two days away from us. He was the best-known physician in our locality although there were two other physicians within half a day's journey from our home. Our brother-in-law Wabu went to call Razi Amche that day while our old family priest administered some medicine. Unfortunately my little brother died before old Razi Amche could reach us.

It was a late autumn morning when he died, and monks from nearby Dinga Garba monastery were called to perform the funeral rites. Many people came to console my parents, particularly my mum. Everyone who came brought tsampa for the rituals; meat was also brought because no domestic animals were butchered within the forty-nine day period while the consciousness of the deceased is believed to be in the *bardo*, intermediary, state. The bardo state is that between death and rebirth, during which the consciousness of the deceased takes a 'mental' body which is projected by the person's previous karmic tendencies. It is believed that within this period consciousness takes its rebirth in one of the six realms — in one of the realms of hells, hungry ghosts, animals, humans, demi-gods or gods. The family of the deceased try to refrain from committing any negative deeds during this mourning period, so as not to harm the dead in their pursuit for a better rebirth.

My mother wept every time someone close came to console her. However, she bore the loss of her youngest son very bravely. She worked as usual, but her face betrayed her tremendous grief. The little body was kept for one whole week in our chapel in accordance with astrological calculations, while religious ceremonies took place. Towards the end of each day, my mother held a thin stick with a piece of paper attached to it, like a small banner with some mantras printed on it. Mother held the stick between her folded hands and prostrated several times towards the altar while the monks chanted prayers. With her hands folded she touched her forehead, throat and heart, in a mark of respect to the Buddha's body, speech and mind, before lowering herself to the ground. When she had finished prostrating, the priest would perform the *phowa*, a special religious rite to free the consciousness of a person from the dead body to a higher rebirth. He would then burn the piece of paper over a butter lamp, and this daily ceremony always brought tears to my mother's eyes. This stirred a terrible sorrow within me, yet I was too curious and fascinated by this rite not to watch. Apart from those ceremonies, the presence of many monks reading prayers, the endless stream of relatives and friends who came to console my parents, and the burning of so many butter lamps made the whole atmosphere seem rather festive in my young mind.

On the seventh day after my brother's death, a lama accompanied by my brother-in-law took the little corpse to a previously chosen site. In our Tibetan tradition, lamas conducted the funeral services, although most Tibetan funerals were very different from those of other countries. We usually fed the corpse to the vultures as a final act of charity. Only in rare cases, such as a death caused by a dangerous epidemic disease, were the corpses buried. In such cases, family members and relatives would lament that nothing of charity could be made out of the body of the deceased. Cremation was also carried out, but this was usually only done for high lamas.

The lama and Wabu proceeded towards the west. My brothers Jamyang and Jignam were to look after the nor that day and I pleaded with them to take me along too. After securing their permission, I had to get my mother's permission, which she granted and she also gave us extra food for lunch. We went southwards and in the early afternoon we could hear the steady beat of a drum and the intermittent ring of a bell from the northwest. This was the direction where the lama had taken our little brother's body, so we gathered that the funeral was taking place. A little later, we saw a number of vultures flying in that direction.

For much of that day we played; we also took quite some time to cook our lunch, all the while forgetting about our nor. After lunch we found that the nor had gone towards the site of our little brother's funeral. I was very curious but fear and sadness were even stronger emotions while we looked towards that site. So I was too afraid to go to collect the nor lest I come across some remains of the little body. That meant that one of my brothers had to stay with me while the other went to fetch the animals. So, following a hesitant pause, brother Jignam left alone rather reluctantly. We were anxious yet impatient for Jignam to come back and tell us what he had seen. Once back, Jignam told us that there was nothing left except for the cloth that had wrapped the body. The several dozen hungry vultures, summoned by the drum and the bell, had consumed every bit of his little body. Finding out that nothing remained was an unforgettably difficult experience.

3

At home on the Chang-Thang

Our forefathers built their home in a green valley formed by four small mountains with grass and protruding rocks. At the eastern foot of one of these mountains two sparkling white streams flowed around either side of our home before uniting in the distance. This small river then flowed into the north-east where it joined a greater river in a vast open vale. This vale was about ten to fifteen kilometres from our house, and the soft, sandy earth in between was covered with long, soft grasses that swayed with the warm, summer breeze. Wildflowers of countless hues grew amid the grass under the bright summer sun, and our sheep and goats loved this grass.

From our home, the land rose towards the south to the peaks of Narding and Tsegu, which were around twenty kilometres away. Thick grasses grew on this hard ascending ground and they turned golden yellow as autumn set in. When golden the grass was so dry and crisp that it came off the ground easily when trampled upon. Our nor preferred this type of grass, which they could easily lick off the ground with their tough tongues. If strong winds blew the grass off the ground and carried it into sheltered mountain curves, the children were sent to gather it in sacks and bring it back home for storage. Our house was perfectly located for a drogpa family.

If we were to look down upon our house from the east it looked like an upside-down 'L'. The large central room was our family *lhakhang*, the chapel. Our lhakhang was the envy of many people in the area. A huge window formed the southern wall of the room, keeping the room bright and sunny the whole day. The whole of the northern wall was fitted with a huge altar with a display in the centre, in which there were gilded statues of the Buddha and his two main disciples, Sariputra and Mogul Putra. The rest of the altar had small square holes that held the 108 volumes of the Buddha's teachings and many other religious books. The two other walls were completely covered by *thangkas* (Tibetan scroll paintings depicting Buddhist images of deities and enlightened or compassionate beings called *bodhisattvas*). Some figures in the thangkas smiled down at us with eyelids lowered and eyes fixed in deep contemplation, while others had fiery wrathful faces and bore lethal invincible weapons, ready to destroy the enemy — ignorance.

Our resident monk, affectionately called Genla (meaning *guru* or master), stayed in the lhakhang on a high bed and studied, practised and prayed day and night. In a way Genla was also our resident teacher, teaching the children to read and write in Tibetan. I must have started learning at quite an early age as I could read quite well by the time I was eight years old. Many of us young boys also slept in this room. None of us had any beds and we slept on woollen mattresses that could be rolled up during the day and put under the bed of our old Genla. Besides the water offering which we changed every morning, a huge butter lamp burnt twenty-four hours a day. At bedtime, the vision of the flickering flame of the butter lamp, the sound of Genla turning his prayer wheels and the clicking of his prayer beads comforted us to sleep. The kind old monk hardly slept. He went to bed very late and woke up before dawn. He would not talk during his prayer time and there was always a serene peaceful silence in this room.

A high wall stood around the property, forming a large court-yard in front of the lhakhang. In the centre of the courtyard stood our family tent. The tent covered approximately twenty-five square metres and had an enormous three-cornered, pol-ished stove in the centre. The tent was made of woven black cloth produced from yak hair, but from within it felt like a very large and cosy house with walls on all sides and built-in shelves. As was customary, the entrance faced the east. If one peered in from the door, one would see the women working and talking on the left while the men were on the right, chatting or readying themselves for long business journeys.

Within the courtyard we had a sizeable stable in which about five of the strongest horses were kept during the winter. To the right of the main gate and outside the courtyard our fierce mastiff dogs were usually chained to very tall, stone pillars watch-ing out for any unwelcome strangers.

About fifty metres outside the main entrance stood a huge heap of ashes. This was the remnants of the dry dung fuel that cooked meals for the family and kept them warm for genera-tions. Several times a day we used to pour ashes onto that pile. Some fifty or so metres further south there was quite a high semicircular wall, maybe a metre or so tall. It could hold three hundred to five hundred sheep during the winter months.

At the foot of a rather rocky mountain stood our tent–hall, sheep-yard, doghouses and our white house with colourful flags flying over it. Several small tents were usually pitched close by for shepherds and travellers on business journeys, or even for professional beggars who had come to camp for the night. Just behind the main tent a tall flagpole was set. Attached to it was a large, rectangular, white cloth printed with prayers on it — this flapped day and night printing prayers on the wind and blessing the very air our family breathed. The house was whitewashed every few years, but about half a metre of the top of the family chapel was painted reddish brown. Four banners were erected at the four corners of the roof of the family chapel, which were all connected by colourful prayer flags. Our home always looked so warm and impressive when we spotted it from distant mountaintops, and we were all very proud of it.

The large tent in the centre of the courtyard was the hall where our family gathered in the evenings. At the southern corner of the tent was a small altar and some offerings. In this corner my mother and her helpers cooked and tirelessly did all the seemingly perpetual housework. My father used to sit at the northern corner on a thick mattress with a carpet on top. Stretching from either side of this bed to the other ends of the tent–hall were two very long mattresses covered with equally long carpets. Guests and travellers sat on them drinking end-less cups of Tibetan butter tea. Work and talk never ceased here, and words were accompanied by the slurping of the tea being churned, the click of prayer beads being counted, the laughter of children, and the puffing of strong men spinning the tough yak hair to make bags for long business trips. It is in this tent that the warmth of our elders' love, together with that of the central fire, was shared by all. Where stories of bygone days were told, where tales of adventures of travellers were heard, where biographies of great masters such as Milarepa were read, and above all, where the great Tibetan epic stories of King Gesar were sung day and night.

As a curious child I used to ask our resident monk Genla where the centre of the earth was. He would say, 'It is wherever you are.' In those young happy days the centre of the earth definitely seemed to be at home on the Chang-Thang.

4

Two means for two ends

During my childhood the nation of Tibet was a vast territory covering around 2.5 million square kilometres in the centre of Asia. Tibet's mountain ranges formed its natural boundary for many centuries, allowing its people to live in peace and harmony with their natural surroundings. Following the introduction of Buddhism to the ancient kingdom, the Tibetan people seemed to have set their goal as the enhancement and protection of the practice of *Dharma*, the teachings of the Buddha. The 'Three Jewels' of Buddhism are the Buddha — the teacher, the Dharma — the teachings and the *Sangha* — the community of those who practise the teachings.

My father used to often say that the goal of this life, either collectively or individually, was to gain 'two means for two ends'. The two means are religion (*choe*) and wealth (*nor*). Here, it's interesting to note that nor means 'wealth' and not 'yak'. The two ends are wish fulfilling (*dhod*) and reaching enlightenment (*thar*). So the phrase, so often repeated was, 'choe, nor, dhod, thar'. The philosophy behind the phrase is that one's material desires cannot be fulfilled without wealth, and so wealth is necessary for a wish-fulfilling life. But wealth should not be the sole aim of life. For both wealth, which is necessary to create a physically comfortable life, and life itself are impermanent. Therefore, choe must necessarily be practised as a part of life, as the means to lead oneself to nirvana — the permanent state of complete peace and knowing, a state of existence free from the heavy, iron shackles of suffering. Thus, even the instruments of government were geared in realising these two simple, yet deep goals.

As its undisputed supreme Head of State, Tibet had the Dalai Lama. He is believed to be a manifestation of Avalokiteshvara, the bodhisattva of compassion — the embodiment of the compassion of all buddhas. This in a way symbolises the ultimate wish of the Tibetan people, to be led to nirvana through compassion. All other levels of officialdom were dualistic — each post was held by both a monk and a lay person.

The vast territory of Tibet was naturally divided into several districts and each district was administered by two *zongpons* (district commissioners) — one a lay person and the other a monk. The district commissioners were directly appointed by the government, usually for a period of three years. As the government of Tibet was decentralised and, in spite of the fact that most district commissioners were appointed by the government, the actual administration of each district seemed to differ from area to area.

In the district of Namru there were several levels of local leaders including the Namru Garpon. The garpon was the highest local authority who was indirectly elected by the people of Namru, and it was a post my father enjoyed from a young age until the Chinese invasion. During his tenure the garpon enjoyed the rank of a cabinet minister of the Tibetan government. As such, he had all the official dresses and ornaments of this rank and these items were handed over from the old to the new incumbent. One of his privileges included an audience with the Dalai Lama every year, or with the regent if the country was under the rule of a regent. (When a Dalai Lama passed away a regent ruled the country until the new Dalai Lama reached an age of maturity, which was usually eighteen years of age.)

The district commissioners sat in equal status with the garpon during their sessions in the summer months when they were in the field, which created a very interesting system of checks and balances. The main function of the commissioners was to collect taxes and settle disputes, so they had to act as judges as well as tax officers. They normally enjoyed very high respect and had the full co-operation of the local leaders. But sometimes the district commissioners abused their authority, imposing taxes for their own personal benefit and taking bribes while settling disputes. It was difficult to fight a case against such an abuse of power, as some of the highest-ranking aristocrats in the country could be in collusion with them. However, a deterrent to such abuses was the yearly audience with the Dalai Lama or the regent. This was effective because it was an opportunity for the local leadership to bring any grievances to the direct attention of the highest authority in the land. If the local garpon had enough nerve and wisdom to report any misconduct by the district commissioners, it brought immediate results and the corrupt officials were removed.

The Namru drogpas always paid their taxes in the form of butter and wool. This proportional taxation was levied on the basis of the number of domestic animals each family owned. Every three years there were livestock counting sessions and district officials, together with local leaders, would travel to every family and do the tallying. The local and district officials would stand on two sides. Then the shepherds and yak herder would force the animals between the two groups of officials, as they recorded their tallies. After having concluded this rough counting, the officials would compare their respective results. They would usually stick to an average because the local leaders usually ended up with a smaller total than the government officials.

The drogpas of Namru were very proud and, in a way, honoured if they could pay their tax in the form of butter. The reason was simple. Unlike *meeser* (subjects) they were *tralwa* (taxpayers). The meesers had to pay their tax to one of the monasteries or even directly to aristocrats in Lhasa. Although the actual quantity of taxation may not have differed greatly, the tralwa's tax was received directly by the government headed by the Dalai Lama. There was very strong belief among the locals that the tax butter was used to burn butter lamps in the Jokhang temple, and to make tea for the thousands of monks and nuns gathered during the annual prayer festival of Monlam. Therefore the drogpas considered their tax payment an act of great spiritual benefit.

The Namru Garpon and all local leaders had tax exemptions in accordance with their ranks. As we did not have many animals, my father's tax exemption could almost cover the tax due from our whole tsowa. There were thirteen tsowas in the district of Namru and each tsowa had its own name. My family's tsowa was called Ringpa; it was one of the poorest tsowas of Namru.

The richest family in the Namru district was the Kakya family of the Sewa tsowa. The last 'headcount' recorded over a thousand nor and over ten thousand sheep in their possession. They also had many horses. They had houses with several rooms and an immense quantity of stored food. Their wealth in gold, silver, precious gems and stones was also well known. Although the Head of the Kakya family was subject to a large tax exemption as Dharokha (tsowa leader) of Sewa, his family paid the largest tax in the Namru district.

Taxation could also be paid in the form of work done for the government, for the local district or even for one's own tsowa. An assembly of accounting used to be held every year at the tsowa level and every third year for the whole district, and this was known as the 'the black and confusing meeting'! Such a meeting usually lasted for about a week when it was at tsowa level, and around a month for the whole district. While a member of every family attended the tsowa accounting meetings, only the leaders of each tsowa attended the district level meetings.

During these accounting meetings all the work done by people, horses and yaks, and even the use of utensils, were recorded, and the values deducted from the tax they owed. In many ways it was a very fair society. For those who were attending the meetings it must have been very boring, but for a young curious child like me it was a true spectacle.

5

In praise of mountains

During the midsummer of each year the locals used to hold a one-day festival called *Risol*. Since *ri* means 'mountain' and *sol* means 'to praise', Risol was literally 'the ceremony to praise the mountains'. This special festival was dedicated chiefly to Nyenchen Thangla.

Tibetans revere Mount Nyenchen Thangla as the residence of the great protective deity known by the same name. As a protective deity, Nyenchen Thangla is believed to be committed to protecting the Buddhadharma and practitioners of the Dharma. Nyenchen Thangla is one of the main protective deities of Tibet known as the Nine Deities of Existence, which are believed to have existed since the birth of the Tibetan land. Nyenchen Thangla is depicted as a handsome young man riding a white horse and wearing white apparel, including a white woollen hat. With his right hand he clasps a horsewhip high in the air, while his left hand bears a spear with a white banner attached to it. His turquoise hair is divided into five portions on his head and he is said to have three hundred and sixty attendants. Nyenchen Thangla is thought to have received teachings from Lord Buddha himself and to have taken a vow before the Buddha to protect the Lord's teachings when they arrived in Tibet.

A high lama would be invited to conduct the prayers for the Risol, which usually included putting up prayer flags on the top of a particular mountain and the burning of incenses. The lama and his monks would invoke and praise the deities, reminding them to protect the Buddhist teachings, and the people and animals of Tibet, in particular those of the local district. After the completion of this religious ceremony the young men on their horses trotted to the top of that mountain, from where the glistening snowy peak of Nyenchen Thangla could be seen. There they dismounted from their horses and adorned the tall prayer-flag posts with new flags before trotting back down to their encampment where the lama and the local dignitaries were seated in their very colourful tents.

Riding down the mountain slope was an opportunity for the youth to show off their horsemanship and the ability of their horses. In fact, this was always considered an informal trotting competition and the best horse and rider were admired. As soon as the horses and riders had returned, a shooting competition was held and the best shots were also commended. If a particular young man happened to be the champion of both the trotting and the shooting competitions, his fame spread far beyond the local district. The champion received some silk scarves from the local elders in recognition of his victory, no other prizes were awarded. However, the galloping competitions held at the tsowa- and district-level horseraces had much higher stakes.

The young riders in the yearly tsowa-level horseraces knew that they had to compete well if they wished to qualify for the district race. After all, only the best five from each tsowa qualified for the district race which took place once every three years. As the five fastest horses galloped past the finish line, judges rushed to the jockeys to place white scarves around each of their necks. Later, at an awards ceremony, the first place winner was then awarded what was commonly known as *ngatsen* ('the five'). Ngatsen comprised a yak, a sword, a sheep, silver coins and a box of Tibetan tea blocks. (Tibetan tea leaves were compacted into tea bricks that were then packed in dozens to be boxed.) The other top four jockeys also won smaller prizes, and five differently coloured 'congratulations scarves' were placed around the necks of all five riders. Apart from the fastest five, the last horse also received a white scarf! Those were the official prizes, but the young riders were presented with gifts from the district commissioners as well as the Namru Garpon. Traditionally, these gifts were envelopes of cash accompanied by white scarves.

There were competitions for other sports such as weightlifting, wrestling, archery and shooting, and the festivals lasted several days. As always, such events were combined with religious activities. Putting up prayer flags preceded the horserace, and a locally respected lama would usually give teachings and a long-life initiation during such gatherings.

These festivals were also occasions for young men and women to get lost in their worldly attachments and sing and dance for several nights under the bright moonlight of Tibet. It was also an occasion for the elders to look for prospective life partners for their sons and daughters. These were social gatherings of great merriment and joy.

I must have been five or six years old when I first attended the district horserace. I remember my brother training his horse for two or three weeks at our home before setting off for the district headquarters several days before the race. For a drogpa child, who had never been to such a grand gathering, it was very exciting.

The *zongkhang*, district house, looked enormous and beautiful and consisted of a lhakhang (chapel), a courthouse, the assembly house and the residences of the district commissioners and their personnel. There were hundreds of tents pitched in an orderly fashion in the meadow near the zongkhang. All the tents of the people from each tsowa were arranged around a larger central tent that served as the main tent for meetings of their tsowa. In the centre of all the different groups of tents there was one large, carefully and beautifully decorated tent. This tent was for my father to both rest in and to conduct meetings of the Namru leaders.

There were hundreds of horses of every colour in the lush valley and on the green slopes of nearby hills. The site was ablaze with life and colour. That year I went with my father and his retinue, while the rest of our family would come later. As we entered the valley and approached the entrance to this tent town, incense was burnt to welcome us. The leaders of Namru, together with representatives of the district commissioners, were waiting to receive my father. After this brief ceremony we were led to the main tent. From the main entrance to the central tent a path with the eight auspicious symbols drawn in white chalky dust had been created, and was bordered by lines of white stones. In front of this tent, a small platform was raised and this was covered with a white woollen cloth. My father would use this platform to dismount from his horse.

I had earlier seen such paths of white stones, auspicious symbols and similar platforms for dismounting from horses used to welcome high lamas visiting our tsowa. I had never imagined that people would do the same to welcome a layman like my father. He was the same frail-looking man — except for the funny red hat with tassels and an ornamental coral top the size of a table-tennis ball, and the yellow silk he was wearing on top of his usual lamb-skin cloak. He was also wearing large earrings, which I had never seen before. His horse was decorated with red tassels at the neck as well as over its heart. I have since learnt that this peculiar attire was a part of the official raiment of the Namru Garpon, and was only worn during official functions.

These district assemblages were not merely an occasion for horseracing. They were also the time for discussing and settling taxation issues, criminal cases, disputes between different tsowas over grazing rights, and divorces which could not be settled by the tsowa leaders. These official businesses were conducted after the horseracing festivity. I now understand that my father was there to conduct his official duties and thus the local community had received him in this capacity.

Every day streams of people poured into our tent. Many of them never seemed to leave. They talked day and night. I had begged my father to take me with him to the races, even though my mother and other members of our family were to join us a day or two later. Uncle Ajig, a distant relative of ours, a bachelor who used to stay with us for many months at a time, was a part of my father's retinue that year and he was to take care of me. There were about five people in the retinue including my brother Wangdrak and myself. My brother was always busy with his horses and also had to attend some of the official meetings, as he was the dharokha of our tsowa. He did not have much time or interest in taking care of me.

On the first day Uncle Ajig took me for a walk. I was delighted that there was so much to see. I was especially excited to find several tents acting as shops. There were tents filled with guns, tents full of coloured woollen clothes and tents filled with

Tibetan tea, some of which was imported from China and India. There were tents where only sweets were sold, others selling soaps, others with cosmetics and yet others with women's wear such as traditional aprons. In the fresh breeze of the Tibetan highlands the sweets, the soaps, in fact everything in the different tent–shops seemed to emit a hundred different delightful fragrances. I had seen the lone tents of business people who came to our locality during the summer and I had seen many of the goods which were being sold at this market, but I had never seen so many differing types and in such quantity. The excitement of seeing a tiny part of the greater world for the first time was an experience beyond words.

The drogpa shoppers could buy goods in exchange for wool, yak hair, goat hair, lamb skin, yak, sheep or with cash. Trading was always brisk and the hustle and bustle of shopkeepers and buyers buzzed in the air. Somehow many of the business people seemed to know who I was and they gave me sweets. I was embarrassed to take them and show them to my father, but I enjoyed them all the same. It certainly was a very happy time.

That night and for the next couple of nights until my mother arrived, I had a rare experience of witnessing the funfair of the youth of Namru. Uncle Ajig carried me in his cloak to groups of young people singing and dancing in the moonlit night. There was no kissing or hugging as one commonly sees in the West, but there was a fair bit of pulling, pushing, pinching, whispering and eventual disappearances of pairs into the distance. Singing and dancing continued late into the night. Uncle Ajig must have been in his early twenties back then and he was a well-built, slightly dark-skinned, quiet man. He was never a good singer or dancer. Having to carry me around all the time, he did not have the chance to act as he would have liked.

Just before midnight he would take me to my bed beside my

father. As there were many people seeking my father's advice or briefing him on the various cases that were to come before him and the district commissioners, he had very long working hours. Sometimes he worked well past midnight. As he was leaving, Uncle Ajig would tell me not to tell father where we had been. My father did not notice me much as his full attention was drawn to the people talking to him.

On the third day at the festival when my father's sessions with the district commissioners in the courthouse began I was deeply shocked. I was very frightened by the menacing whips, feet- and handcuffs which were hung beside the entrance to the courthouse. Then, within the courtyard of the zongkhang, I saw a ragged young man sitting on the bare ground. As I looked closer I found that his legs were actually shackled. I was very saddened by the sight and I felt that it was completely unfair to chain a person while everyone else was enjoying themselves outside the courthouse. I was frightened of going further into the zongkhang. I wanted to go back to our tent, but I did not have the courage to tell my father that I wanted to run away.

This was a very bad day for me in stark contrast to the joys of the previous couple of days. I did not feel like going near the zongkhang again. But I was taken there to circumambulate the district chapel every evening. The chapel contained all the volumes of the teachings of the Buddha and many other books, and there was, of course, a statue of the Buddha and many thangka paintings. The chapel was large and beautifully decorated and people circumambulated this building, as we always do around temples and monasteries, to show reverence to the Buddha and his teachings, as this is believed to bring spiritual merit. It was that evening, after seeing the prisoner and the chains, as the reddening sun slowly set in the west, that I became homesick, although we had only been at the tent town for three days.

That evening I told my father how homesick I was and how disgusted I was with what I had seen that day at the zongkhang. My father explained to me as he always did when asked questions — in a gentle and straightforward fashion. He explained that the 'punishing' equipment hung at the entrance of the zongkhang was not used, and that they were just there to show the authority of the courthouse. Smaller devices were used against people who had committed crimes like the lone man we had seen that day.

The lone prisoner was a young man who had strangled a young girl to death. The young girl was his neighbour. He had been attempting to kill a two-year-old yak, but when the girl pleaded with him to not kill the yak, he had strangled her to death instead. As she was dying the murderer was heard saying, 'If you would rather die than this animal ...' The younger brother of this unfortunate girl was reported to have been with them and had called their family while the girl was being strangled. This was a very rare and horrific story. This prisoner was kept there until the district leaders and the district commissioners could decide whether he should be sent for a longer imprisonment term in Lhasa, or if he should be kept at the zongkhang for a shorter term. He had already had a few lashes of flogging as punishment.

My mother arrived on the fourth day and I was overjoyed to be with her again. Although everyone had treated me with care and much respect, as if I was a prince of some sort, I missed the warmth of my mother's love and the comfort of knowing and understanding everything in that little world of our home in the valley. But my brother Wangdrak thoroughly enjoyed every moment of those days. He met old acquaintances, made new friends, entered shooting competitions and readied the horses for the big race.

Meanwhile, I could see horsemen trotting and galloping about from dawn till dusk in every direction. Every tsowa was training their horses for the big day. There were also clever businessmen trotting their horses in a bid to show them off, hoping to fetch high prices if anyone wished to buy them.

On the day of the horserace we all had an early breakfast, as the race ground was a few miles away from the district head-quarters. The start of the race was fixed at 'well after sunrise' — which happened to be at about nine o'clock in the morning. The trainers, jockeys and horse owners were in a frenzy of last-minute preparations. The mane and tail of each horse was neatly tied with different coloured ribbons. Each tsowa wore chupas of different colours and matching hats.

The five riders from the Ringpa tsowa wore white chupas and white hats and the manes and tails of their horses were adorned with white ribbons and cloths. The jockeys wore only a thin, cloth chupa and they did not use saddles — the riders had quite a rough ride. The horses were impatient and irritable, any sound made them dance and jump. Once the preparations were over everything quietened at the starting line. The men and their horses stared towards the finish line, all breathing heavily.

The spectators had trickled in from early in the morning to find the best place to watch the race from start to finish. A while before the race, the district commissioners, the garpon and the leaders of tsowas rode off in a grand procession, each of them wearing their official attire. They headed for a tent near the finish line to watch the race. Meanwhile, some local elders had gone to a small hill in advance to carry out Risol (the ceremony to praise the mountain), by putting up prayer flags and burning incense to honour the local protective deities. As soon as the leaders had arrived and had taken their seats, the tsowa elders burnt the different incenses and erected prayer flags.

The small hill where the prayer flags were erected and the incense burnt was situated at about halfway between the race's starting point and the finish line. Earlier on, in that vast flat race ground, I had watched the racehorses and their escorts slowly disappear out of sight towards the starting line. A calm settled as the crowds quietened in anticipation.

Suddenly the quiet was shattered by the shouts of '*Lha-gyalo!*' from the elders who had gone for Risol. Besides meaning 'Victory to the gods!', these shouts meant the race had begun. After a few minutes I could see the horses racing towards us in front of a cloud of dust. The crowds around helplessly broke into shouts in support of their own tsowas. At the finishing point a local leader waved a white scarf against the dark-blue sky, summoning the riders and their horses and encouraging them to gallop even faster. Everyone watched with great excitement, some with binoculars, others without. Some horses were galloping without a jockey and others were thundering off course.

Soon, sizeable gaps had grown between individuals and groups of competitors. The fastest horse thundered past the finish line, with the second horse around a hundred metres behind. This large gap was due to the large distance over which the race was run. The race for third, fourth and fifth places was much closer, with many horses finishing within a metre or two of each other. All spectators praised the winners but waited until the last horse crossed the finish line.

That year, the winner was a yellowish horse belonging to the wealthy Kakya family. Mr Kakya, as a dharokha, was seated in the leaders' tent, but he rushed out to cheer his jockey and his horse as they snatched the white winner's scarf signalling their victory. One of our own horses came fifth, which was also a prize-winning position. After the last horse had been awarded his scarf, the much-awaited race was over and everyone returned to the encampment. Even returning to the camp was an opportunity for those with good horses to show how well they could trot.

That afternoon the award ceremony of the big race was held. There the names of the families who owned the horses, the names of the horses, the jockeys and the prizes they had won were announced aloud by the secretary of the district commissioners. Then the official prizes were presented. The winners were all presented with five different coloured silk cloths and a white scarf. All the jockeys were very proud to be wearing them. They also received an envelope containing cash along with all the other official prizes, and these prizes were followed by the endless private gifts of scarves and cash envelopes to the five winners.

Over the next three days running races for young men, wrestling, weightlifting, shooting and archery competitions were also held. As with the horserace, prizes were awarded to all top five competitors in these events. I was always very partisan. I remember how I could not even bear to watch a distant uncle of ours taking part in the men's running race. I am sure that I would have cried if he had not won a prize. Luckily Uncle Lhawang won a prize in the race and I was able to enjoy the rest of the tournaments. Another distant uncle, Uncle Tamding, then a young man in his early thirties, once again won the weightlifting competition for our Ringpa tsowa. Uncle Tamding was also a champion wrestler and he had won both events a number of times over the years. I was especially happy that year as Uncle Ajig also won one of the wrestling competitions unexpectedly.

Inspired by the abilities of the jockeys at the district race, I dearly wanted to become a good horseman and to jockey at a horserace. A few years later that opportunity arose.

One summer's day when I was eight years old, father went to wash his favourite old horse, a very beautiful white horse, in a small dam near our home where the two clear streams met to form a small river. We, the children, flocked to the dam to watch the beautiful horse swim and be washed. After washing his horse, father challenged us boys — daring us to ride the horse and gallop back home. We were perhaps about one-and-a-half kilometres away from home and there was only soft green meadow the whole way. My elder brothers and cousins giggled and were too polite to take on the challenge. But I jumped around saying, 'I dare to gallop back home!'

Father picked me up and put me on the horse. There wasn't a saddle so I rode bareback. Father told me to pull the reins if the horse galloped too fast. Father then gently lashed a whip on the horse's back telling it to set off. At the same time all other children cheered loudly, which seemed to make it gallop rather quickly. I did not want to look too nervous on the horse so I did not pull the reins, but at the same time I was finding it really difficult to stay on, and I was getting quite afraid that I might fall off. So I patted its neck and said, *'sho, sho!'* meaning for it to slow down. Unfortunately the horse did not slow down at all but my desperate 'sho, sho' was heard by quite a few people, including mother and others at home who had rushed out to see what had happened. By then I was already quite close to our house. Poor mother anticipated me falling off the horse, ran towards me and grabbed the reins. I did not fall off and everyone at home had a good laugh. After that day, I used to become extremely embarrassed whenever my siblings teased me by saying 'sho, sho'. I had thought that I was only whispering to my horse but obviously it had come out as a loud cry. Since that day I was determined to become a jockey to prove to everyone that my 'sho, sho' was nothing and that I was really an able horseman.

Two years later, my father allowed me to be a jockey at our tsowa-level horserace. Three horses from my family were trained and my brothers Jignam, Jami and I were to ride them. We had to get up at dawn for about three weeks, training the horses for about an hour on the first day — letting them trot gently and only trying short gallops. As the days went by the lengths of these training sessions, and the distances galloped, were increased. By the final sessions of the three-week training period, we would have galloped almost the full length of the racecourse a few times. The horses' diet was carefully monitored and we washed them every day, sometimes in the early mornings before dawn and sometimes late at night, giving them a full cover of warm rugs after each wash.

By the day of the race, the horses' coats looked very smooth and sleek, and they had become very alert and excitable. Brother Wangdrak had trained the horses and he was happy with the way the training had gone. All three of us jockeys had very sore bottoms that hurt awfully for the first few minutes every time we rode the horses. Then towards the day of the tsowa horserace, the people of our Ringpa tsowa came to camp near our home for a few days of festivities. For me it was an opportunity to show off my ability by having become a jockey at the young age of ten. In fact, I was the youngest of all the jockeys that year.

The whole time, mother was very worried lest I should fall off my horse and be killed. I rode a particularly big horse which father had bought a few years earlier. About thirty horses took part in the race that year and my horse and I came fifth, which was a prize-winning position. At the awards ceremony that afternoon the five-coloured cloths were put around my neck, a mark of recognition. But the cloths were too long and I had to fold the ends up and carry them in my arms so that I wouldn't trip over. I was so happy and proud that I had actually won a prize and had been able to ride a racehorse. Besides the official prizes, I also received a great deal of money in envelopes as presents from relatives and family friends. It was one of the happiest and proudest days of my childhood.

6

Omens, prophecies and prayers

The drogpas of Namru have a saying: 'Six is the age of crawling after horses, at toothless eight one goes after nor'. True to this saying I would volunteer to herd our nor and sheep with my elder sisters when I was eight. Whenever they rejected my offer I would become terribly upset, but when that happened I would be comforted by my grandmother. She used to take a group of us children to nearby hilltops to spot horses. The sight of grazing horses in the distance, tiny against the endless green plains and the towering blue mountains in the horizon, never failed to take my breath away. Our own horses grazed alongside the many wild horses that roamed freely in the Chang-Thang. On those hilltops grandma would tell us stories about the various spirits residing in the different mountains, and how the wild animals belonged to them in the same way that our animals belonged to us.

From the patterns formed by the wild animals and the direction in which they were grazing in the green plains below, grandmother formed an opinion as to whether they were good or bad omens. She also used to make forecasts for our own animals for the rest of the year. I don't think anyone took her forecasts and omens very seriously, but her introduction to the mountains and the local deities fascinated our young minds.

If a crow happened to make any unusual sound, she would tell us to find out where the crow was standing and in which direction it was facing. She would then bring out her *Book of Crow Language* to foretell whether it was bringing us any messages. She could tell whether a distant traveller was arriving within a given number of days, whether a mishap had taken place with our animals, such as wolves attacking them, or if there was going to be a thunderstorm or snowfall soon, depending on the season. Sometimes, her readings were amazingly accurate and she used to boast that her readings were therefore prophetic. But if her readings proved untrue, she would blame us and tell us that we had given her false information on which way the crow was facing and in which direction it flew off.

Of all my grandmother's prayers, one in particular used to upset me deeply. Padmasambhava, the great Indian Buddhist master who helped bring Buddhism to Tibet during the eighth century, wrote this prayer in the form of an autobiography. It was then hidden away — as is common practice among great sages — and was only unearthed a few centuries later by Ugyen Lingpa, another great master. Mo Rinchen recited it aloud every day, and although I loathed hearing it there was no escape, and I unwillingly memorised it.

That prayer is called 'Kathang Duepa', which means 'concise Kathang'. The Kathang are biographical books on Padmasambhava. There is one particular passage in this prayer that troubled me the most, and that unfortunately proved to be prophetic. It says, 'One with a mole on the face will take the capital of Tibet. Sun of happiness shines through chimney holes. In the years of the Horse, the Sheep and the Monkey, the Chinese army arrives. In the year of the male Monkey, a military formation takes place in Yarlung. Ultimately this country, Tibet, falls under China. Fraternity and brothers fight each other as if on the back of an untamed horse ...'

There wasn't a single Chinese in sight back then, and the idea of the Chinese invading Tibet was beyond imagination. However, the prophetic words of this particular prayer gave me good reason to look back into my own culture once we were in exile, when the Chinese had indeed taken over Tibet.

The people of Namru considered themselves very fortunate to be blessed with two of the most revered landmarks in the country. To the south of our home was Mount Nyenchen Thangla, and next to this, closer to our home, was Lake Namtso Chugmo. This lake is believed to be the home of one of the twelve most important female protective deities of Tibet, Dorje Kundrakma. It is also considered to be very holy as it bears the handprint of Padmasambhava, and because of this many small and sizeable monasteries used to surround the lake. No wildlife was hunted here so it was possible to see wild Tibetan blue sheep roaming into the monasteries to lick the salt given to them by the monks and pilgrims.

There are said to be eighteen islands on or leading into Lake Namtso Chugmo, and each one of them hosts great stories of outstanding masters who have meditated there. Apart from Padmasambhava, these masters include the first Karmapa. The Karmapa is another one of the highest lamas in Tibet, and is the head of the Kagyu branch of Tibetan Buddhism.

From time to time such high lamas visited our region on trips to the north and I can still remember the Karmapa visiting the neighbouring district of Dholwa. He arrived with his grand entourage at the designated site where the teachings were to be held. He was amazingly handsome and imposing.

During the teachings my father requested the Karmapa to perform 'the Black Crown Adornment' ceremony for my health and fortune. During this ceremony the Karmapa put on his re-nowned 'Black Crown' and held it with his right hand. With his left hand, he slowly counted the sparkling crystal prayer beads while reciting a mantra in deep meditation. As a benefactor I received all of the gifts that were presented to benefactors, including blessed strings to wear around my neck and blessed pills. Blessed pills are small pills usually made out of several hundred medicinal herbs that have been blessed with the reci-tation of several hundred-thousand or several million mantras. The 'mani rilbu', a blessed pill given by His Holiness the Dalai Lama, is made out of one hundred and eight medicinal herbs and is blessed with the recitation of ten million mani mantras. Blessed threads are specially knotted threads which have been blessed in a similar way. They are believed to protect the wearer from harm and evil.

Although any offerings made in return for the performance of the ceremony were purely voluntary, most people offered a large benefaction consisting of some nors, or money of a simi-lar value. It must have been expensive for my parents but for us drogpas wealth meant nothing in comparison to *sonam*, posi-tive karma. Wealth is understood to be impermanent and is exhaustible, even in this short life. Sonam is believed to be the seed for eternal happiness, leading eventually to enlightenment. A person with sonam is believed to be naturally endowed with wealth, since wealth too is a by-product of virtuous deeds.

Following Dholwa, the Karmapa was going to give teachings to our tsowa at Nyilung. Nyilung, or 'Sunny Vale' as its name is translated, was the usual site chosen for such teachings due to its gentle geography and its central location. On the Karmapa's way to Nyilung he visited our home, probably at the request of my father. When the Karmapa and his entourage arrived, amid the great horses and strong mules was a young, wild ass. Apparently it had joined the company as they were travelling in the vicinity of the Mount Nyenchen Thangla. People said that it was an offering from the protective deity of our region to the great Karmapa.

For some time the Karmapa rested under a great, white tent. He then entered our tent–hall through an entrance at the back of the tent; this had been created so that he would not be contaminated by having to enter through the front entrance, which everyone else used. This was an expression of deep reverence.

That day was cloudless and sunny, but as the Karmapa entered our tent–hall a little, dark cloud formed and our home was filled with the sound of the light pattering of rain. The rain grew stronger and soon the heavy downpour cleaned the whole area. As far as the eye could see, our home and the immediate vicinity was the only place where it rained on that otherwise bright and clear day. Indeed it seemed like a miracle, as we regarded rainfall on special occasions as a very good omen.

The visit from a lama that I can remember most clearly was the visit to Namru by Chogye Trichen Rinpoche of the Nalanda monastery. He was a very handsome young man wearing grand headgear and unforgettable red and gold robes. He rode a huge, proud and most majestic horse, and as Chogye Trichen Rinpoche and his retinue came into the view of the awaiting masses, a welcoming group galloped off to meet them. The riders dismounted and prostrated before Rinpoche. Then they got back onto their horses shouting, 'Victory to the gods!' and thrice circled Rinpoche and his entourage before trotting back to us ahead of Rinpoche's retinue.

Chogye Trichen Rinpoche gave a short teaching on the Four Noble Truths and bestowed a long-life initiation. After all the teachings had been held and the lively festivities were over, Chogye Trichen Rinpoche and his retinue slowly rode away as the locals farewelled them. When Rinpoche had travelled a short distance he turned his horse around to see a local elder waving a white khata (a ceremonial scarf) — this expressed the mutual wish that Rinpoche would be able to visit Namru many times in the future. Rinpoche never had the opportunity to visit Namru again, but my own future would often intersect with his and he continued to play an important role in my life. Chogye Trichen Rinpoche rode on before turning towards the locals once again, at which time the khata was raised again. A while later Rinpoche turned his horse around for the final time, now small between the vast green plains and the endless blue sky. The white khata waved one last time as the wind tried to pull it from the steady hand that held it aloft. Only the flapping of the khata could be heard as the silent crowd watched Chogye Trichen Rinpoche's entourage fade into the horizon, everyone with their hands folded in supplication, their eyes wet with tears of farewell.

7

The invasion

In the evening of a warm summer's day in 1953, Grandma Rinchen and I were sitting in our tent in a great, green valley. Suddenly the whole earth began to shiver, shudder and shake violently. My grandmother grabbed a handful of earth, put it into her pocket and cried, 'Take me to a happy place!' The fierce tremor lasted for only a few seconds and when it was over we joined our neighbours outside. I was shocked by the power of the first earthquake I had ever experienced. Of course my grandmother soon had her books out and was asking our neighbours about the direction from which the quake originated and where it finally subsided, to see whether it was a good or a bad omen.

Ours was a society where superstition and wild tales played significant roles in affecting people's lives. Such tales usually originated from ordinary people, some of whom do seem to have abnormal gifts in sight and hearing. Rumour soon started that the earthquake was indeed a bad omen. Parts of the revered Nyenchen Thangla mountain had cracked and many took it as a sign that our local protective deity had lost a battle against a dark power. The rumour also said that 'the dark power will run over Tibet and no wealth will be of any worth. Those who have stocks of clothing and food should make good use of them now or a time will come when the right to use them is denied. The nation will be turned into a state of hungry ghosts.' *Hungry ghosts* are one of the six types of beings of the six realms, and have taken rebirth in the realm of hungry ghosts as their karma was strongly affected by their miserliness and greed. The rumour continued, 'Those who have faith in the teachings of the Buddha, and particularly in Guru Rinpoche, should now start their journey in search of Ugyen Beyul to escape the onslaught of the dark and evil forces.' The 'Guru Rinpoche' was Padmasambhava and Ugyen Beyul is believed to be a hidden valley for Buddhist practitioners to take refuge in when they are persecuted in Tibet by non-believers. These hidden valleys were prophesised by Padmasambhava.

It seemed that omens were ripe and a change was coming. Our old Genla — the resident priest, my grandmother and many other elderly people who came to visit us had either heard, seen or sensed that something very bad was going to happen to Tibet. Many of them quoted from books of prophecies by Padmasambhava. Others uttered their own versions of prophecies, which they had received directly from their lamas.

Evenings were usually a time that all of us children looked forward to each day. Everyone sat in a large circle around the fireplace and the adults would tell us old folktales and stories of their experiences. Sometimes a lodging traveller might tell us of their travels to many parts of Tibet, India and Nepal. But now a change had arrived. Something alien, even fearful, replaced the warm and happy atmosphere. Adults ceased to tell stories of the past. Now their conversations became dominated by horrific events that had engulfed faraway regions of Tibet.

During these very disturbing times came the news that the Chinese army had entered Tibet and that it would reach Lhasa and our district at any moment. In remote parts of Tibet such as ours, no radio or electronic communication media existed at all and information could only reach us through travellers or from government decrees. We had only come to learn of the fall of Chamdho and the Chinese capture of its governor through word of mouth from travellers and pilgrims. Chamdho was the administrative headquarters for the government in eastern Tibet and also the headquarters of that region's security force. Its fall was worrying news and this news spread quickly in our region. The people of Namru fully realised what was happening to the country when government messengers under Chinese pressure came to the district to proclaim, 'China and Tibet would now co-exist like the sun and the moon to dispel the darkness over Tibet. The Chinese People's Liberation Army has come to Tibet to protect and develop the nation. Not even a thread and needle will be demanded by the Chinese and a great dawn of prosperity will prevail in the Land of Snow.'

We heard about how the Chinese military had marched into Tibet. Entire families were murdered, monasteries had been burnt down, many high lamas had either been killed or invited to China and afterwards mysteriously disappeared, never to be seen again. Tales of terror and destruction about the Mongol Junggars' incursion into Tibet centuries earlier were recounted. Some even said that lesser local deities fled when the Junggars swept across our region, massacring Tibetans and looting their properties during their brief incursion. The news was that the Chinese were even worse than the Mongols, because they were coming 'specifically to destroy the Dharma'.

With each traveller, there was more news of Chinese atrocities in eastern Tibet and of course, more disturbing signs and omens. Each day at dusk, as the troubled sun set in the west, we dreaded what the growing darkness in the east might bring. The evenings felt hollow, the people felt hollow. We were fearful of losing our parents, fearful of losing our old Genla, fearful of losing our white home in the green valley, fearful of an uncertain future.

We had never seen a Chinese person. I could hardly imagine what they might look like. The image I constructed in my mind was built from the abominable accounts I had heard. I could only picture blurred images of frightful people grasping guns and long swords, suddenly emerging to slaughter everyone who practised religion. Beyond this blurry image my imagination failed.

Somehow my father always seemed to be away in Lhasa or in different parts of the district. I only felt comfort and warmth when he was home. With all the dreadful news, I had many sleepless nights.

One night we were all asleep and only the distant noises of our animals disturbed the steady silence. Suddenly, a haunting long call shattered the still air. *'Jaaaaar-Lo——ong-ngo!'*, followed by another, then another. The call of this human voice was not usual. It was an emergency call from a messenger from the district headquarters. It meant 'Receive this message!'

The dogs barked fiercely and the elders returned the call by shouting, 'We are coming, we are coming!' Everyone got up and Wabu, my brother-in-law, went to receive the news. This emergency call meant that something bad had happened that required the attention of my father as the leader of the district. That was the second such call I had heard in my childhood. The first time, some bandits had robbed one family of all of their nor and I remember how my father and brother-in-law left immediately. That was another fearful night. Several days later my father came back having recaptured all the nor. After chasing the robbers for several days they had had a brief encounter in which there were exchanges of gunfire. The bandits finally gave up and ran away after having lost their leader, leaving all of the nor behind.

This time my brother-in-law disappeared into the night to meet the messenger. When he returned, he brought back the news that the Chinese army had arrived at our district headquarters. Although my father was away the district officers wanted my brother-in-law to let our tsowa know about the arrival, adding that the Chinese were all friendly and humane and that they do not demand any services from the public. 'However, no hostilities may be aimed against them and their safety must be guaranteed if some of them should happen to pass through our tsowa,' Wabu was told.

I was extremely afraid at the prospect of actually coming face-to-face with Chinese soldiers. I desperately wanted never to meet one. This fear became worse and worse as the adults talked about how these 'destroyers of the Dharma' loathed all those believing in the Buddha's teachings. I hoped that my father had all the answers and was looking forward to his homecoming more than ever before.

When my father finally arrived from his official trip he brought more bad news. My father spoke of how more and more Chinese soldiers had arrived in Lhasa. He suspected the validity of rumours that some aristocrats were collaborating with the Chinese army. He was also of the opinion that a dark era for Tibetans was imminent.

Father also brought many new things with him. Things that had come to Tibet as a result of the Chinese arrival: many colourful magazines in Tibetan, packets of cigarettes and badges of Mao

Tse-tung. These were given to my father by Chinese military offi-cials he had met. The Mao badges were golden in colour with red rims and yellow stars in the background. I looked at one of them and asked my father who the person on the badge was, thinking he might have been a lama of some sort. Father told me that he was Mao Tse-tung, the new king of China. I looked at my father questioningly and said, 'But he isn't red! Po Urgyen told us that Mao was completely red!'

Indeed, I was very startled to find that he was not red as I had imagined him to be. I did not know that I had misunder-stood Po Urgyen, an old distant cousin of my mother, taking his words at face value. Despite the embarrassment it caused me, I was happy that because of my comment everyone broke into a chorus of laughter, a glimmer of joy during anxious days of uncertainty.

8

Opposing paths

Everyone talked about what a nuisance it was to have the Chinese building a road in our region. The animals of Tibet were not used to the noise of motors and engines, let alone the explosions carried out by the Chinese while building the road. The continuous flow of military trucks and the occasional blasting of rocks frightened off many yaks and horses.

After the arrival of the Chinese, drogpas could easily sell animals and animal products for a hundred times more than they used to fetch, but it was of no use. Other food commodities now cost even more too. It may have been the first time in the history of Tibet that such extreme inflation had ever occurred. The poor drogpas were helpless and did not understand the causes of this new economic dilemma.

Some new items such as alcohol and cigarettes appeared in large quantities and were sold at very low prices. Even young children like me started smoking. The value of the currency, the Tibetan *sang*, had virtually vanished. Amid this scene the government decree — that the Chinese had come to help Tibet — had very little meaning, but there was a slight sense of optimism. Most of the people who had come into contact with the

Chinese soldiers praised them for their discipline and courtesy. But while there was some sense of relief, everyone was still very unsure about the future. If the Chinese had come to help Tibet why did they send so many soldiers and so much military equipment?

We children always listened to the conversations of our adults and somehow shared the anxiety of our country. Even though things were superficially quite normal, there were many new and unusual phenomena, both natural and man-made. One year a terribly bleak winter descended upon us with an extremely heavy snowfall. None of the adults, not even my grandma, could recall such a snowfall in our region. Elderly people of my grandmother's age had heard about a natural disaster known as the Great Snowfall of the Year of Fire Rabbit, when they were children. Thousands of animals had died then and even more animals died during this awful winter.

The people of Namru blamed the Chinese and somehow believed that the constant blasting of rocks from sacred mountains had displeased the local protective deities. Not only did most of the animals die but the few which survived were too weak for a long time to produce proper milk, wool and other products.

The Chinese began to mine borax at a site not too far from our home, in one of the most desolate areas in our locality. This place served as a mining encampment as well as a huge military reserve centre. Thousands of people were brought here from many parts of Tibet. Makeshift structures were built for the Chinese military and other personnel while thousands of tents were pitched by 'Tibetan proletariats'. The Tibetans who were either forced to go there or who were attracted there were mainly the poorest members of our society, or criminals who had found a safe-haven under the protection of the Chinese forces. While the law was still in the hands of the Tibetan government, any criminal who went to the Chinese encampment and confessed their crime to the Chinese authority was pardoned. In fact, if a crime was committed against the rich or against the so-called 'upper-class society', the criminals even received some political training, and later jobs, as a reward. This situation created law-lessness and many weekend raids on local drogpas occurred.

The only contact between the local Tibetans and the Chinese remained almost exclusively between the local leaders and the Chinese military officers. Obviously, there was a huge cultural gap between the two sides. The Chinese looked down on the Tibetans as dirty due to the fact that the Tibetans, particularly people of my region, rarely washed. The climatic condition and high altitude meant that constant bathing and washing was not needed. On the other hand, the Tibetans believed the Chinese to be spiritually dirty because they seemed to kill everything that moved, and because they would eat any animal, including dogs and monkeys. The cultural and linguistic differences kept the two sides far apart.

The devastatingly bleak winter of scarcity and the hyper-inflation rendered the local drogpas poorer and poorer. The Chinese attempted to use these natural and economic disasters to gain political support. They brought several truckloads of white flour and a few truckloads of rice for distribution among the Tibetans. The Chinese military officials summoned the leaders of every tsowa in our district and offered this relief aid.

I have a vivid memory of these meetings and they lasted for several days. As it was near the end of the winter there were no district officials from Lhasa and the meetings were presided over by my father. I was not present during my father's meetings with the Chinese during the day, but the meetings of tsowa leaders lasted well into the night, and I sat in my father's warm cloak and listened to these discussions.

It was evident that our community did not want to accept the relief aid. In fact, many viewed the offer as an insult.

'They have caused all these disasters and now they try to give us a little food, as if we are all beggars,' declared some.

'How can we eat food from the hands of these dirty sinners? We would all go to hell without doubt.'

'How can we accept food without our government's consent?'

'They should feed themselves first rather than eating horses and dogs.'

One remark, I do not recall by whom, caused a great chorus of laughter and lifted the atmosphere for a short while; I have ever since remembered it. The remark was, 'No, I don't want such a big present as that of last year; neither do I want *mii-hoho* nor *showp-pala*.'

I later learnt the meaning of this saying. It was based on an old story. Once, a servant of an aristocrat was given an old horse (mii-hoho) as a gift from his master. After spending all of his wages feeding and caring for the horse, it died. 'Showp-pala' is the expression used by the servant in the story when helping his old dying horse to get up; it's an expression used when lifting heavy objects. So when the servant was offered another gift the next year he is said to have used the expression. It was just one of those many expressions that our people used while making a point, and it seemed to sum up our fate with the Chinese.

My father listened to everyone and I do not recall him making any suggestions or remarks. But as the Namru Garpon he had to convey the feelings of our community leaders to the Chinese. The offer of relief assistance was completely rejected. At their final meeting with our community leaders and my father, the Chinese officers conveyed the message that they 'were very happy that the drogpa brothers could feed themselves'. After a pause, trying unsuccessfully to cover up the hidden anger within, the leading officer added, 'When a flood sweeps the world, no one can expect to remain dry.' The local leaders nodded, conveying their comprehension of the true meaning of those words, and my father replied, 'We will see when the flood comes.'

Although my father was mostly quiet during these discussions, it was obvious that he fully supported the locals' position. It may have been likely that he had intimated his position to some of the tsowa leaders who then came out strongly against accepting the Chinese aid. I know that he strongly believed the presence of the Chinese was contaminating the whole country both externally and spiritually. I had overheard many conversations between my father and visitors, and between my parents, and their paramount concern was the gradual erosion of spiritual belief among the younger people, and that we might all become merciless in taking lives like the Chinese.

Ironically, my father bought rifles and swords for all of us and then taught us how to use them. My cousins, the sons of my father's only sister, my brothers and myself all had to wear swords on our belts during the day. And at night we had to keep them under our pillows while sleeping. He would tell us that we should not hesitate to use them if the Chinese attacked us. During the process of our shooting exercises I was praised quite often for being a good shot at still targets. But my father always told us that a live animal is far more difficult to shoot than a still target. To prove his point he let me and my older brother Jamyang shoot at a rabbit, expecting us to miss. Unfortunately, I didn't. I shot the poor animal, blasting one side of the lower part of its body. There were several people about, including all the children, watching us shoot. We all rushed to see the rabbit but it was not dead — it was dying. It was squirming and obviously in great pain. When I think about it now, the agony of the rabbit still deeply stirs my conscience.

My father had taken a Buddhist vow not to take life or to let others under his order take the lives of other living beings. This incidence caused a breach in his vow and he was visibly disturbed. When we went home my mother was extremely unhappy and started to speak sternly with my father. She was saddened by the fact that we all blamed the Chinese for killing and eating every animal they saw. Yet my father, who was believed to be morally strong and spiritually pious, was now teaching his children to shoot innocent animals, just like the Chinese. My father told me to go to our family chapel to light a butter lamp and he read his prayer books. My mother carried on for a while but he didn't argue with her, and after that we were not allowed to shoot at any wildlife.

It was the beginning of spring then, when the curving landscape begins to turn golden green. Countless flowers bloom in the wild with only the sun and the mountain streams to tend to them, and birds of diverse forms and colours begin to arrive in Namru. For us drogpas, and particularly for the shepherds, even though it was a time of scarcity, this was an exciting season of rejuvenation. However, it turned out to be an anxious summer.

My father was away for meetings at the district headquarters. Unlike in previous years, the Chinese military officials showed up for a few days during these meetings. The Tibetan government jointly gave new orders in conjunction with the Chinese authorities. Even though these orders bore the name of the Tibetan government, I am certain that only the Chinese were responsible for them. One of these orders, I can still remember, said, 'Everyone should co-operate to catch or kill reactionaries.'

The word 'reactionary', *log-choe*, must have existed in the Tibetan language before this time, although it was the first time our locals had heard it. We thought it was a funny catchphrase as the use of this compound word, in that order, was particularly ironic, almost humorous. My parents would tell us not to do *choe-log*, which is just like saying 'don't misbehave'. *Choelam*, the word from which 'choe' comes from, means conduct, behaviour or manner, while *log* is to miss, to get wrong, to do something in the opposite way from which it should be done.

This political terminology according to the Chinese was aimed at our countrymen of the east, the Khampas and Amdowas, who had revolted against the Chinese, and many of whom were pouring into central Tibet as refugees, bearing horrible stories of Chinese atrocities. Indeed for the Tibetans, the Chinese were the real log-choe in the true sense of the word. Everything they did was our opposite. Dogs and horses, which we adored as friends and companions, were eaten by them. The Dharma that we held in the highest esteem was denounced by them as poison. And the environment, which Tibetans have preserved and respected for generations, was ruthlessly exploited.

The new joint orders were read by the Tibetan district commissioners in the presence of the Chinese officials and their interpreters. There were further orders from the district commissioners and the Chinese military officials that any group of people passing through the district should be immediately reported to the Chinese camp. Those tsowas who failed to report to the Chinese would have to bear the consequences.

The local community had already indicated their non-cooperation with the Chinese when they had come to give relief aid. There was no question of turning over any refugees to the Chinese. But the locals were very suspicious of their own government representatives, the district commissioners, one of whom began dressing like the Chinese and had even learnt the Chinese language.

There were more orders, some directly from the Chinese leadership from the borax mining camp, while others came jointly from the district commissioners and the Chinese authorities. One such order was that many people must be sent to Dhamshung, a valley to the south of the Nyenchen Thangla mountain range, as labourers for the construction of a new airport. For us drogpas of the region, where men had to be constantly on the move for trade and to look after animals, this order was almost impossible to fulfil.

The district meeting that year took the whole summer, as the local leaders, led by father, resisted this order. Finally the number of people who had to be sent was reduced to only thirteen, one from each tsowa. This was a great victory for the locals.

The group of locals who were sent to work as labourers with the Chinese were called the 'voluntary force'. Each tsowa collected food for their 'voluntary force' member and the Chinese paid the workers some silver coins as their salary. They worked at the Dhamshung airport site for about a year.

My father appointed an elderly man called Samphel Norbu from Namchen tsowa as the leader of our labour force. He was a respected and trustworthy elderly man, without any distinctly special characteristics. After a year, when they finally returned home, Samphel Norbu came to our house to report to my father. He told us about his experiences during the construction and how he saw an aeroplane actually land after the airport was built. We, the children, listened to those stories as if they were fairytales.

9

The wedding feast

Even as the noose of the Chinese army was tightening around our people, our family had the opportunity to enjoy a special type of happiness. In the autumn of 1957 our eldest brother Wang-drak got married. The soon-to-be couple had been lovers for quite a few years, and the families had not 'arranged' the marriage. The wedding preparations took almost an entire year. For most of that year, two medium-sized tents were pitched near our home to house a tailor and a silversmith. The silversmith crafted the jewellery for the womenfolk of our household and the new bride in particular. The tailor sewed beautiful new clothes for our large family and the couple to wear on the important day.

In the life of a drogpa family, a wedding is one of the happiest and most important days, but it is also one of the costliest and most demanding. Both families wished the event to be modest, but looking back I think the renown and social status of my father as the Namru Garpon meant that the marriage celebrations had to befit the status of the families, which accounted for the lengthy preparations.

As advised by astrologers the marriage was to take place on a certain autumn day, the season when the plains near our home turn a golden colour. The tradition of the region meant that if we sent five horsemen to receive the bride, the bride's family would send twice the number of horsemen to accompany her to our home. So more than a week before the wedding day five horsemen departed from our home. The leader of this company is the *nyampo* and he has to be a good orator. Upon arrival at the bride's home, he must eloquently speak of the bride-to-be's family. This usually consisted of praises but also included witty questions and comments — some of which were even derogatory.

The receiving company sent by our family spent a couple of days with the bride's family enjoying the festivities and celebrations there before heading back with the bride and her ten companions from her family. They included their own nyampo, an uncle from the bride's mother's side, a brother and a bridesmaid. The uncle had to accompany the bride until she had been introduced to the care of the protective deity of the new family. The belief is that as the mother and the uncle are of the same family line, the protective deity of the uncle looks over the bride during the journey to her new home.

Just past noon on the wedding day, as prescribed by the astrologer, the company of sixteen arrived at our home. All the guests were sitting in their proper places inside our tent–hall, a number of other tents and within our house. Only members of our family and some friends were there to witness their arrival.

In the distance we could see our nyampo — the one we had sent to the bride's home — leading the horse ridden by the bride. The horse was completely covered in green cloth and all the specially prepared lamb-skin and silk clothes the bride was wearing were covered by a white cotton chupa, as advised by the astrologer. As the group neared our home, we could hear our nyampo singing customary songs which were laced with improvised wit and eloquence. We were all very excited at the opportunity of glimpsing our brother's new bride but her face was covered up. She may have been embarrassed at the prospect of meeting so many people or this could have been the fashion for young women at the time.

As the bride reached the newly created northward-facing door to our tent–hall, also prescribed by the astrologer, mother greeted her in her best new clothes and her prized headgear made of corals and precious stones. Then mother presented the bride with a wooden bucket full of dri milk and a rope used to tie the legs of the dri together while milking. This act not only has an auspicious meaning in that the bride enters the home with a full bucket, but also symbolises the mother's introduction of the responsibilities which lie ahead. Meanwhile, the nyampos and other members of the arriving company went to sit down in their arranged places. Then someone took the rope and the bucket from the bride and she was led past the many guests and onlookers to the other side of the hall where my brother was sitting. Once she had sat down beside my brother, with her bridesmaid beside her, the religious aspect of the marriage ceremony began.

During the ceremony the celebrant who officiates at weddings symbolically tied one end of a multi-coloured string to my brother's ring finger and the end of another string to the bride's ring finger. Then the celebrant tied the other ends of both strings together and held it in his hands as he recited the ceremonial prayers. This ceremony constituted the main religious act of marriage and from that moment on the two — my brother Wangdrak and his bride Choeying — were united in marriage. The celebrant continued with the ceremonial prayers as he bestowed the protection of our family's protective deities on the new bride. That was the end of the ceremony for the day, but the festivities had just begun.

The second day was the day for the main public marriage ceremony. Well into the day, as deemed appropriate by astrology, our family sat in our tent–hall. Father and mother sat at the head, with our family members, including brother Wangdrak, Choeying and her bridesmaid on one side, sitting in the order of seniority. This meant that I was quite far from my parents towards the end of the line with my younger brother and sisters even further down. On the other side sat the nyampos and the bride's companions. Then all the guests queued up to offer gifts and the usual white ceremonial scarves to each of us as we sat there. Most of the gifts consisted of cash in envelopes. I was very happy to find that I was quite rich by the end of this ceremony. I also somehow felt proud to be wearing so many scarves, as if I had won the district horserace.

Our family had prepared celebrations for over eighty people. Our home had become a village as guests sojourned in the many tents that we erected for them. Even our stable yard was covered with a yak-hair tent roof and converted into a huge kitchen and entertaining area. We borrowed great pots and pans from the district headquarters, and banquets and feasts were cooked for everyone for a whole week around the day of the wedding. For that week our home was filled with the buzz and laughter of people. Everywhere I looked there were people eating, singing, playing games such as dominoes and dice, participating in shooting and horse-trotting competitions and of course drinking some *arak*, Tibetan home-brewed whisky, and vast amounts of *chang*, Tibetan barley wine.

One individual who tried his best not to drink too much chang during weddings was the nyampo from the bride's family. This was because our maids tried to get him drunk so that they could merrily mock him. After all, the nyampo had to be alert and ever ready to eloquently point out and criticise any deficiencies in hospitality — be it too much or too little food served, or a small mistake in the manner in which they were served. But to counter his critiques was the *nyampo taknon* — which literally means 'the one who bears down upon the nyampo' — who was usually a respected and eloquent local elder. He always sat right next to the nyampo on a slightly higher cushion. He artfully countered any unfriendly remarks by the nyampo. Usually, they both ended up drunk amid the festivities. Unfortunately, in certain extreme cases, I have heard stories of the nyampo and the nyampo taknon becoming so drawn into their arguments that it led to unpleasant events. But during my brother and his bride's marriage celebrations, there was much jest and laughter and nothing disagreeable.

In the days following the wedding, neighbours and relatives arrived from surrounding areas to congratulate the newlyweds, and stayed for days as some of the other guests returned to their homes. For one wonderful week, I forgot about the strange and uncertain times we were living in. For one week in our age-old family home, we all got lost in the joy of the competitions, gifts, songs, and stories as we celebrated the marriage of brother Wangdrak and his beautiful young bride Choeying.

10

The raw yak-skin hat

Despite the joy of the wedding, the atmosphere in our locality deteriorated month by month. We could see the huge Chinese military encampment from the hills surrounding our house, and the roar of hundreds of green trucks transporting the People's Liberation Army and their military equipment caused animals to flee in all directions.

Food was scarce. Although selling a yak or a sheep fetched enormous sums of money there was nowhere to buy the traditional barley to make the famous tsampa. And we Tibetans could not live without tsampa. Going about business had become dangerous as crime had risen dramatically. Some robbers were desperate, starving Khampa refugees while others were Chinese disguised as Khampas. The sole purpose of the latter was to create rifts between the Tibetans. Even the weather had become abnormal, as if it too was colluding with the Chinese invaders.

Our home was situated on the border of two districts. The district of Namru, to which we belonged, paid taxes directly to the central Tibetan government. The neighbouring district was Dholwa. The people of this particular district were subjects of the Tashi Lhunpo monastery, the seat of the Panchen Lamas, so their tax went to that monastery. As the Chinese camp with borax mines fell in the Dholwa district, the Chinese started to manipulate this difference by giving special treatment to Dholwa's subjects. They invited the leaders of Dholwa for meetings in their camp and paid them large amounts of silver coins as a salary.

We hardly had any close relatives in Namru, but we had many close relatives in Dholwa. In fact, my mother came from Dholwa and our grandma, Mo Rinchen, was a meeser (subject) of Dholwa herself. Although she was very much a respected member of the family, our grandma always considered herself to belong to Dholwa and therefore was a meeser of Tashi Lhunpo. Our grandma was called to the meetings by the Chinese officers through the Dholwa leaders and received a monthly allowance of silver coins. The Chinese managed to persuade the people of Dholwa that they had come to help Tibet at the invitation of the Panchen Lama, who was the head of the Tashi Lhunpo monastery. The people of Namru refused to take anything from the Chinese, even in the face of famine. A new front of tension was building between those who received silver coins from the Chinese and those who refused to co-operate with them. It was a subtle and clever plot by the Chinese designed to divide the people of the region and, unfortunately, they were succeeding.

At the mining camp in Dholwa there were two sections, a Chinese section which consisted of several newly built houses and a Tibetan section which was a large village of tents. The miners included quite a few Chinese and Tibetans from Kham and Amdo who were prisoners. Other Tibetan miners included the paupers from our community who were the ones the Chinese really wanted to attract. As they were paid very highly with pure silver coins and with promises of large shares of animals from better-off families, some even slaughtered the few animals they possessed in order to become 'model revolutionaries' and to earn more coins.

My own Auntie Manee, her husband Orok and their son Buchung were a classic example. Auntie Manee's family had lived a comfortable life. They had fifteen nors, of which three were dri, while the rest were of a very good breed. They had a few sheep, enough to provide them with the wool, milk, butter and meat they needed. They had all the basic necessities of a drogpa's life. Auntie Manee was the youngest of my mother's sisters and my mum was very fond of her, often visiting her home. Like most of my close relatives they belonged to Dholwa. Uncle Orok used to go to the Chinese camp quite often and one day he decided to kill all of his animals except for six yaks to carry their load to Tsalakha, the Chinese mine. They would move into the camp once and for all. Auntie Manee came to say goodbye to us on the way. Uncle Orok was praised by the Chinese for his revolutionary spirit and was even given some provisions upon arriving at the camp. There were rumours that Uncle Orok even knew how many yaks and sheep he was going to get from the stock of one of the wealthiest families in Dholwa, 'after democratic reforms had taken place'. Of course, this political terminology was completely new to us simple animal farmers. To us drogpas, taking someone else's animals forcefully and dividing them up among others was sheer robbery.

Unfortunately, poor Uncle Orok did not live to see the 'democratic reforms' he was promised. Even though the mining camp was loaded with silver coins and full of new political terminology, there was an acute scarcity of food. The Chinese provided them with a bit of white flour that was simply not enough. For a family who was used to having plenty of meat and dairy products, the new food could not have come close to being adequate. We soon heard that Auntie Manee and her son had both become very weak and that Uncle Orok had died of starvation. The Chinese camp area was so barren, over grazed and over mined that his remaining six yaks were reported to have died too.

When mum heard the sad news of Uncle Orok's death, she desperately tried to get someone to go to Tsalakha and send her youngest sister, Auntie Manee, some meat and butter. But all in vain. Everyone was too afraid to go there in case they should catch the contagious fatal disease that plagued the camp.

Finally, following pleas from the locals, Rah Lama, a distant uncle related to my father, offered to visit the mining camp. Rah Lama was the lama of the local Rah monastery and someone very well revered. Despite being a lama of a monastery he was a layman and was married. Unfortunately, while at the camp both the lama and his wife passed away. They had caught the fatal disease. Following Rah Lama's death, contact between the local community and the starving inhabitants of the mining camp completely ceased for a long time.

Uncle Orok's death was an early indication of what was to come. Foolish Tibetans who considered themselves 'revolutionary proletariats' died, lured by empty promises of wealth and ideology, while other Tibetans were forced into the camps.

After the 1959 uprising against the Chinese, this camp became one of the largest and most infamous Chinese concentration camps in Tibet. It is widely suspected that over 100,000 Tibetan prisoners died in that concentration camp alone. My brother Jignam later met one of the very few survivors of the camp in 1981 when he visited Tibet. This survivor told Jignam how hundreds of thousands of Tibetans from all over Tibet were sent to work at the mine. They were forced to work from before dawn until late into the night with only two watery cans of soup each day. Each prisoner was forced to work until they could no longer get up onto their feet. When that day came, they were left to starve to death. This particular prisoner had survived only by crawling to where he had seen a crow eating something in the distance. There he had found the remains of the head of a wild ass. Only by biting off and scraping off bits of flesh and skin with sharp stones, and hiding it from the Chinese camp authorities in his chupa, had he survived.

Just when new diseases were spreading quicker than gossip and many families were facing food shortages, the Chinese became increasingly lordly. A few years earlier not a single Chinese could be seen at the annual district meetings, but suddenly there were more and more Chinese leaders attending, and they were grow-ing more and more demanding.

They kept repeating their calls for the Namru leaders not to allow any Tibetan refugees, mainly from Kham in eastern Tibet, to pass through our lands. They told us that anyone pass-ing through must be either killed or captured and handed over to the Chinese soldiers. They also demanded that my eldest brother Wangdrak lead the youths from the prominent fami-lies of Namru to China for 'education'. When the local Tibetans utterly refused to comply with this demand, they were forced to listen to the same repeated reasons why the youths should be sent to China. Threats against the locals ensued and thus Namru was forced to send thirteen youths to China after lengthy negotia-tions. Only one volunteer from each tsowa went to China.

When the youths finally returned from a year in China they came back wearing Chinese clothes, with their hair cut short. The traditional Tibetan hairstyle for boys and men was to have their long hair braided with a string which had a long red tassel at the end. This ponytail was then tied around the head with the tassel dangling over one of the ears. Women also had long hair, but it was usually braided into many strands which were let down. Ornaments were also worn towards the tips of the women's hair.

The youths had learnt a little Chinese but apart from that, they had not received any apparent education. They returned having travelled on 'air, land and sea' and had been taken to the most modern and beautiful places in the country, in an attempt to make them think that China was astonishingly great. But the only result was to make them incredibly homesick. The youths told everyone that China was very powerful, with cars, trucks, huge boats and aeroplanes, but that they were immoral, unkind and violent. The youths said they dearly missed their parents and tsampa, and that the Chinese food had been not at all to their liking. One youth, the son of an old man who had once been the Namru Garpon, did not return. The Chinese would not even tell the boy's family where he was, or even if he was alive.

Every day and every night the fierce roar of Chinese military trucks shattered the peace. Many pairs of bright lights could be seen heading to or coming from Lhasa during the night. This filled the locals with a sense of great apprehension and their sleep turned to nightmares. The Chinese noose around the neck of Namru was tightening, just as an old local saying tells of how a raw yak-skin hat tightens around the wearer's head as it shrinks while it dries.

More Khampas, whom the Chinese called 'reactionaries', were flooding into Lhasa and our region, and the Chinese were ordering the locals even more sternly to capture or kill the refugees, threatening to impose very harsh punishments if the orders were not complied with. Even worse was the fact that there were official proclamations from Lhasa through the district commissioners to the same effect. This left the people of Namru facing a difficult dilemma. If they defied the order, they would suffer gravely. If they obeyed they would have to fight fellow Tibetans — their brothers and sisters.

The local leaders found it almost impossible to believe that the Tibetan government would issue such a proclamation, so my father sent a group of leaders to Lhasa to investigate whether it was genuine or something that the local district commissioners, in whom the local community had already lost trust, had cooked up. When the party sent to investigate the matter finally returned to Namru, they informed my father that the proclamation was genuine, but that the Lord Chamberlain had intimated that the Tibetan government had been forced to issue the order under immense military pressure from the Chinese. Whether the order was acted upon was up to the local Tibetan authorities.

After the party from Lhasa reached home the Namru leaders decided on a temporary solution. My father made friends with the Khampas, and a Khampa group from Dégé, in eastern Tibet, then agreed to split up and stay with different tsowas in Namru. When the time was ripe it was agreed that everyone could escape Tibet together. Meanwhile my father told the Chinese that he had convinced the Khampas to not escape abroad and that they were going to settle in Namru.

11

The escape

Many years before I was born there was a venerated lama from Nangchen in eastern Tibet called Bagyo Rinpoche. Decades ago, when he was returning from a pilgrimage to Mount Kailash, he sojourned in Namru. He was well known for his clairvoyance and predictions, and during his stay he gave many forecasts for the people of Namru. While he was visiting our Ringpa tsowa my great grandfather, Bawa Wadi, took my father — at that time a young boy — to see the Rinpoche. My great grandfather asked the Rinpoche what the future held for this young great-grandson of his. The old, wrinkled Rinpoche was sitting outside, wearing a sheep-skin robe and warming his old knees in the sun.

The Rinpoche slowly opened his eyes and momentarily stared at my father before lowering his eyelids saying, 'There will come a time when smoke-belching, evil beings will live at the place called the Seven Thirang Siblings.' From the hilltops near our home we could see seven vertical pinnacles of rock behind a vast green meadow; these were called the Seven Thirang Siblings, and this was the place where the Chinese borax mines were later erected.

'At that time, this child, your grandson, will be the leader of this land. I will be travelling south of here. I will be travelling with a large company. If he is able to meet me then, together we will be able to escape the smoke belchers.'

Many years later, once my father had become the Namru Garpon, Bagyo Rinpoche once again was passing through Namru on his way to Mount Kailash. Bagyo Rinpoche was by then an extremely old man and, sadly, he passed away in Dholwa. Later his reincarnation was discovered and enthroned in his monastery. Thus my father did not lose faith in the prophecy, even after the Chinese had arrived, and he patiently waited for Bagyo Rinpoche's reincarnation to lead us all to safety.

In readiness to escape, we cleaned and whitewashed our house and put up new prayer flags. Leaving everything and taking nothing more than what we needed to herd the animals, we went to the green Narding plateau beside Mount Tsegu, not far from our home. It was the spring of 1959 and there we set up a little camp. From Narding we had an unobstructed view of the region and we could even see the smoky Chinese camp at the Tsalakha mine in the distance.

We had moved to the Narding plateau to decrease the chance of raising suspicion among the Chinese. If they heard that our whole family was leaving home they were bound to pursue us and capture us soon. Setting up a camp at Narding was not unusual and every year, usually during the spring and autumn, members of our family would go there as the pasture was better for the animals. At home there were still a few people such as our Genla and our grandmother, so such a move was unlikely to raise any alarms. Not even our grandmother Mo Rinchen suspected anything unusual. After all, being a meeser of Dholwa, she was receiving silver coins from the Chinese camp.

Around this time word had reached us that the palaces of His

Holiness the Dalai Lama had been shelled and that Lhasa had been captured by the Chinese. These were the days of uprising when Lhasa was raging in turmoil. There was also an unprecedented level of movement of Chinese military vehicles around the borax mine at Tsalakha.

One evening on the Narding plateau two horsemen rode out of the shadows to the south and came riding straight towards us. We were all very afraid lest they should be Chinese agents or people bringing more bad news. Before dawn my father and my eldest brother Wangdrak rode off with the two strangers. They had gone to seek divinations from a lama called Sarjey Rinpoche, a highly respected spiritual master who was accompanying Bagyo Rinpoche. Sarjey Rinpoche's divinations were very negative for my father and my brother Wangdrak and he told them they must leave the area immediately. The divinations for the women and children were good if they also left, but they weren't extremely bad if they chose to stay either.

When my father returned he immediately told my mother about the divinations and said, 'Wangdrak and I must leave soon. It's all up to you. You can come if you wish to; there are many women and children in Bagyo Rinpoche's company already. We will be able to spend however many days or months we have left, together. If you don't want to leave, then we must part now. I don't know when or if I will ever see you again. If you decide to stay then once we are ready, I will try to gather men and fight the Chinese, and destroy the military camp at Tsalakha.'

She looked around at us all, her children, then turned back to her husband and eldest son, 'If we were to stay behind you would come back and try to fight the Chinese. Soon, you two will be dead, and then what? All the other children will follow. One after another, dying under Chinese guns and swords. I am coming.'

We hurriedly packed up and my parents sent Wangdrak and

my sister Ani Tenzin Choedon to call our old grandmother and Genla at the last minute. They soon joined us, although grandmother Mo Rinchen was loudly cursing and complaining because she could not farewell her relatives in Dholwa.

We sent word out to our relatives and friends in Namru, the leaders of Namru and to every family in our Ringpa tsowa. My father let them know that we were leaving, and if they wanted to come with us then they should hurry.

We set off with a heavy heart. What weighed most heavily on us was that we had no way to reach my brother Jignam, who was still at the Nalanda monastery. None of us knew whether we would ever see him again. Father was particularly worried.

Many families joined us, quickly following us or meeting us along the way. For many tiring days and nights we travelled without pausing to rest. If any of the sheep grew tired or were unable to keep up, we left them behind. Everyone rode and walked endlessly, but the going was slow.

I couldn't help thinking about our home, the home of which we had always been so proud. The white house in the green valley with the many colours of prayer flags flapping over it night and day; our lhakhang, the chapel, with the ancient thangka paintings and gold statues of buddhas and bodhisattvas blinding our eyes as they reflected the sunlight; our large tent–hall in which our family had gathered for countless merry evenings for many generations — I could not imagine them empty, lifeless for the first time.

Around eight days later I was overwhelmed by a sight I had never seen the likes of. Nearing the valley of Shuru in Dholwa, we peered over a ridge at a valley. We were astounded to see the huge plain below rolling on for at least thirty or forty kilometres, and completely full of hundreds of thousands of sheep and nor, and hundreds of tents.

Upon hearing of the garpon's escape many entire tsowas in Namru had immediately set off, leaving their homes but unable to part from their animals. It looked as if the whole green valley had been painted white, brown and black. When we climbed down into the valley, the people were overjoyed upon meeting us.

I will never forget the size of the wealthy Kakya family's herd. We met a shepherd looking after hundreds of sheep belonging to the family. Then after travelling for another half an hour, past countless sheep, we met another shepherd. When we asked him whose animals he was herding, he replied, 'The Kakya family herd.' Then again, yet another and then another, all shepherding animals belonging to the Kakya family of the Sewa tsowa. Their wealth in animals was indeed great beyond comparison, as was legendary in our region. But in such times of hardship, many animals were only obstacles to escape.

When the people camping in the valley found out about our arrival, the leaders came and held a meeting with my father. The next morning we set off to the south past a mountain ridge, while all the people who were camped in the valley set off north. It was indeed a strange experience to watch that disorderly sea of people, sheep and nor slowly cross the valley into the north. They had headed north because the daughter of one of their leaders was married into a family in the Nagtsang area. Her father wanted to call her so that they could escape together. Another reason they were travelling north was that most of the inhabitants to the south were subjects of Tashi Lhunpo, headed by the Panchen Lama. On the whole these meesers were more co-operative towards the Chinese. Whereas the locals to the north of the valley were friendly tralwas, taxpayers to the Tibetan government in Lhasa. The night before my father spoke to the gathering to explain that his group must head south.

'From now on, every family must make their own decisions and attempt to survive. There is little use in gathering to fight the Chinese after the sun of Lhasa has already set. We must all go our own ways. But if another country should mediate and help settle this invasion, then we may meet again.'

Four days after parting from us the large group of north-bound escapees were ambushed by the Chinese army. The defenceless women and children seemed to have been keenly targeted by the soldiers, and many of them were killed. Most of the survivors were badly wounded. The wealthy Mr Kakya was among the casualties, barely able to hang on to dear life. After the ambush, those who were still alive were herded back to their homes in Namru.

Nearly two weeks after leaving our home we finally caught up with Bagyo Rinpoche's company. In the company were three lamas. Bagyo Rinpoche was a very energetic sixteen-year-old when we met him. He was a very handsome and playful monk. Sarjey Rinpoche was the most revered and senior of the three. Sarjey Rinpoche was a grey-haired, softly spoken and very saintly old monk. He was always turning a prayer wheel, even on horse-back. Nyima Rinpoche, the third lama, was a very learned and humble middle-aged monk. He was a son of the old Bagyo Rin-poche. Everyone was very happy to be travelling with such great lamas on such a dangerous journey.

We soon met the Khampas from Dégé who had stayed with us in Namru and had escaped before us. All the leaders had a meeting and decided that we would travel as a large company. We always sent a few horsemen ahead and left a few behind to look out for pursuers and the Chinese military. There were around twenty-one families in our group from Namru, around forty families in the group who had travelled from eastern Tibet with the lamas, and another forty or fifty families from Dégé.

The escape

A few days later, the Dégé group diverged from the main company and, sadly, they did not fare as well as our group.

Most evenings our escaping company gathered to decide the course of action for the next day. Sarjey Rinpoche performed divinations on which direction we should head. We also took heed of what our scouts had to say. Some days we would head east, other days south or west. In such a way, led by the divinations of Rinpoche and the knowledge of the scouts, we went in all directions. This made our journey very long. But it all proved worthwhile, as against many odds the Chinese army was unable to find, kill or capture us. After all, it was a well-known fact that the Chinese army pursued every last family who tried to escape the occupation.

Sometimes we stayed put in one place for over a week. At other times, if there were indications of danger, we would all get up before dawn and hurry into the darkness without stopping for several days. I remember falling asleep on my feet many times. As I followed the sound of the nors' feet steadily thumping the ground, my eyelids would weigh down until I could not keep them open any longer. Suddenly I would fall on my knees and by the time I had opened my eyes again, everyone would be far away. I would cry loudly and run after them. I was always afraid of getting left behind and being captured by the Chinese. I also rode a horse from time to time during the journey. But even on horseback I fell asleep with the rhythmic swaying and would wake up bruised, having fallen off the horse's back.

During the whole journey my parents constantly worried over the fate of my brother Jignam. But one miraculous day in the beautiful valley of the Chakthak River, in the western district of Saga and quite close to the Nepalese border, brother Jignam and a group of monks from the Nalanda monastery led by Gen-Jinpa, the student of our old Genla, suddenly reached us.

It was about a year after we had left Namru. We were all happy beyond expression. To be with brother Jignam once again, when we had not had news of him for so long, was unbelievable. Our whole family was finally reunited and we could all hope to survive together. We then proceeded closer to the border with Nepal where we remained for a number of months.

It was while we were camped close to the Nepalese border that my father received a letter proclaiming the setting up of a temporary Tibetan government at Lhuntse in southern Tibet. This was accompanied by the news of His Holiness the Dalai Lama's safe arrival in India. My father placed that letter on his head and wept for a few minutes, then said with complete conviction, 'The sun of happiness will shine over Tibet again.'

We finally crossed the Nepalese border into Mustang, into freedom in exile, in 1961. A journey that would have taken just a few months in happier times had taken over a year.

12

The horseman disappears

Mustang is a small princely state of Nepal ruled by a king who enjoys patronage both from Nepal and Tibet. People of this tiny Himalayan kingdom are of Tibetan origin, yet the landscape looks bare and stony compared to the highlands of Namru. After a few days' stay at Tinkar, near the summer palace of the king of Mustang, we trekked further into the kingdom to a temple called Gekar Gompa. I do not recall how many families of our tsowa followed us into Mustang, but I can recall that many decided to stay behind closer to the border. The *gompa* (temple) was situated amid a thick wood of bushes and tall juniper trees on an isolated slope not too far from the main caravan trail. There was a clear, sparkling spring nearby and Gekar Gompa looked very old and sacred, but rather run-down.

My parents liked this place for two reasons. Firstly, Gekar Gompa is a famed, sacred site for Tibetan pilgrims because this very gompa was mentioned in several ancient Tibetan religious texts. It is believed to be one of the few built in the eighth century, prior to the building of the great Samye monastery in southern Tibet. The second reason was because the mountain slope was brimming with grass and there was enough space for us to camp.

While we camped nearby, my father decided to stay in the temple for some days to make a special ritual offering, a *tsog-gya* (one hundred offerings of *tsog* — tsampa cakes). He spent seven days in the temple and we could only meet him at certain hours. The dark rooms of the temple and the images of wrathful deities frightened some of us who had not seen such things before. But I enjoyed circumambulating the temple with my brothers and sisters. The day's offering of the tsog was brought home in the evenings and distributed among everyone. The children looked forward to having this delicacy, thinking more of the taste than the religious merit of this food which had been blessed at the gompa.

During those few days, my brother-in-law Wabu went to Marang, the closest village, to try to acquaint himself with the people there and to trade some of our animals for some desperately needed barley, wheat and beans. He was successful in his mission and he returned with several loads of these commodities. At my constant request Wabu took me with him to the village one day. Although this village comprised only thirty or forty families, to me it looked like a city. I was astonished to see so many houses so close together, with very narrow alleyways leading from one house to another. Dogs were tied to long poles at the entrance of the houses and they barked ferociously, which somewhat frightened me.

Back in Tibet there was a cluster of houses in a place called Mendang Ragzi just a few miles from our home. There were roughly ten to fifteen houses in that hamlet. But this excursion to Marang was my first encounter with a village in the true sense, and it gave me a strange feeling of being enclosed. As I walked through the narrow alleys I could hear the shouts and cries of people and the barking of dogs but often, all I could see were these stone walls crowned with thorny bushes of firewood. It made me long for the freedom of the endless windswept grass-lands of the Chang-Thang, the freedom of the untamed wilder-ness, the freedom of belonging, and the freedom of knowing that there is a home to return to. Little did I know that this feeling of being enclosed was in a way the first crack, as the dusty hinges squeaked and the heavy door to the rest of the world grudgingly swung open for me, a boy from beyond the mountains.

After having completed his week-long retreat in Gekar Gompa, my father told us how fortunate we were to be at this very sacred place. He explained how fortunate it had been for him to have had the opportunity to carry out his retreat. He then turned to our mother and thanked her for her love and her work in support of him throughout their life together. As my father paused everyone fell completely silent, unsure of where these words were leading. He then disclosed that there were clear signs that he would die within that year but told us all that none of us should be sad or disheartened. He cited three reasons for his premonition.

While practising certain Tantric practices under the guid-ance of a lama in Lhasa, he had once had a vision of measuring fifty-one white woollen cloths. (*Tantra* is often referred to as the 'secret doctrine' of the Buddha's teachings.) His lama interpreted that vision to be the length of his life, meaning he would only live to be fifty-one. Also, he had a prediction done for him by another lama once. This lama also counted fifty-one and a half. More recently, he had vivid dreams that his life was coming to an end during his retreat at Gekar Gompa.

He told us that every life is a mission and that he had suc-cessfully completed his life's mission by being able to lead all those who trusted him to safety. He advised my mother to lead us to India or wherever His Holiness the Dalai Lama might be. He urged us all to put every effort into becoming learned.

'Those who have the precious quality of being learned need no home to protect them. Such a person is revered more in the land of others than in one's own home. One who has such quality need not strive for wealth. For being learned will bring wealth.'

I can still remember the tone of complete confidence in his voice as his gentle glance pierced each of us in turn. It was a very sad evening. We stared down at the dusty floor, with our heads held low as we did not even dare to look up at father. Our throats felt dry and sore all of a sudden. I felt very empty, as if behind all the skin and bones there was nothing inside me. My father did not seem at all anxious even though he believed death was approaching.

My mother reacted sharply. She wept and utterly refused to accept all these claims by father about his life coming to an end. She told him that if he was so wise as to foresee death, then he should do special long-life pujas to prolong it.

'Don't dare to think of deserting us when the need for your wisdom and guidance has never been greater,' mother said. The words diminished into an uneasy silence, intermittently disturbed by quiet sobs as we children joined our mother in tears. But my father was unmoved.

The cheerless hush prevailed until our father broke it. He reminded us all that before our departure from Namru, Mending Drawa (the monk of the Mending family) was invited to our home to perform a special divination.

During this divination, the diviner performs some religious rites and looks into a mirror, often made of zinc, placed on an altar made for the occasion. Then the person who is consulting the diviner can either ask aloud what they want to know, or just toss some grains of barley towards the mirror mentally asking the question. The diviner then sees images in the mirror, which are meant to answer the question. Gazing into the mirror, Mending Drawa said, 'I can see a white horseman crossing a great pass between snow-peaked mountains. Now he takes his hat off and looks back, and I can hear him shout, "Lhagyal-lo!", "My wish is fulfilled!" Now I can only see a country that I have never seen before but the horseman is not in sight. He's gone.'

We had all crowded behind the Mending Drawa, trying to see something in the mirror but in vain. Finally, after trying very hard, I thought I saw something. What I saw was the reflection of the butter lamp flickering in the mirror. I immediately exclaimed, 'I can see a lamp!' Everyone broke into laughter while I was left blushing with embarrassment.

Now, as we sat weeping in our tent in Mustang, my father explained that the horseman symbolised him and the snow-peaked mountain pass matched Tsokar Pass, the crossing point to Mustang from Tibet. His wish was now fulfilled as he had successfully led all that followed him into safety. The horseman disappearing from sight in a new land, which Mending Drawa had not seen before, indicates that he would not remain in the new land much longer.

From the Gekar Gompa we moved to Rikhug, a beautiful, wide valley just a few miles further into lower Mustang, where there was plenty of space for the animals to graze and rest. From this valley we could see a large village called Tsarang with its red monastery looming over the village. Rikhug was so well located that apart from Tsarang, another two large villages, Marang and Drakmar, were both within a day's return journey. It was essential for us to be near the villages so that we could purchase food and other necessities.

Here my father called a meeting of all the heads of the families of our tsowa for the last time. He suggested that we sell all of our domestic animals for cash and set off for India immediately.

The price he had roughly negotiated was 2.5 rupees per sheep or goat, and a little more for each nor. It was not the best price but at least we would have some money if we were to proceed to India. But our community urged him to stay where we were, 'until the United Nations helped resolve the invasion of Tibet', as some community members suggested. More realistically, they added that it would be difficult for any of us to survive if we went further into Nepal or India. They believed it was just too hot and the heat was sure to overwhelm us. It was autumn, the season when the animals were in their best shape.

My father gave in to the wishes of our people and decided to stay in Mustang, at least until spring. He soon set off to contact the village leaders of Marang, Tsarang and Drakmar. The village leaders from those villages also came to visit us and we got their approval to use their pasture. Somehow, despite our grave poverty, we managed to welcome the village leaders. We did not have the comfort of a home and the great wealth of ancient thangkas, scriptures, clothing, gold and silver accumulated over many generations, but at least we now had a daily routine, and most importantly we did not fear being killed or separated from our family by the Chinese. We were lucky in that we were some of the first Tibetan refugees to enter Mustang and were able to make good friends with the locals. We had some relatively happy months there and Bagyo Rinpoche and all of his followers also joined us in this valley.

In those days the situation on the Nepal border was still relatively calm. But the following spring we had a visit by two men from a six-family unit that had parted from us during our escape to take another route. Their families were stuck near the Nepal–Tibet border, and had come to seek help. They lacked armed men to force their way through to Dolpo in Nepal if the Chinese army had already sealed off the border. After hesitating for several days, my brothers Wangdrak and Jignam and five other men, armed with the best rifles our group had, stealthily left one night. They were supposed to return in a month, but there was no news of their whereabouts even after three months. My parents became increasingly anxious.

Meanwhile thousands of Tibetan refugees poured into Mustang having survived the Chinese campaign. Many had lost their entire families, and most of the wounded seemed to be either women or the elderly.

At that time we also received news from Namru. Four brothers from a family of the Gomang tsowa of Namru arrived in Mustang and came to see us. They told us that just a few weeks after we had left, the Chinese had taken full control of each and every tsowa. These soldiers had meetings where they announced that the People's Liberation Army had stamped out all 'reactionary elements' in Lhasa and ordered all locals to co-operate fully with them. They also added that the Tibetans had now been 'liberated' and that they should rejoice. This announcement was followed by an order to surrender all guns and rifles, which the soldiers immediately seized from each family.

Within the next few days another meeting was called. There the Chinese soldiers arrested many of the menfolk except those they considered to be proletarians. This effectively meant fathers, husbands and sons from most families. One day such a batch of soldiers had come to the tsowa of Gomang. After the initial meeting had been held and all guns and rifles seized, the soldiers and their interpreter camped nearby for the night. The people of the Gomang, including the four brothers, knew what had happened in the other tsowas, and the brothers decided to ambush the soldiers that night. They knew that no matter what, they would be arrested the following day if they did nothing. That night was particularly cold and a snow blizzard had engulfed their area.

As the brothers approached the Chinese soldiers, they found them huddled together in a tent. A lamp in the centre of the tent drew shadows which the brothers watched. The brothers had stealthily sneaked near to the tent from all directions and then attacked with their swords. They killed all of the five soldiers in the group before they could use their guns. But the Tibetan translator escaped.

Immediately, the brothers and their family set off to escape the Chinese. But like most Tibetans trying to escape they were ambushed on the way. In the valley at the foot of the great Tako mountain range, they lost many of their family members. Only the brothers had managed to escape the onslaught.

The brothers told us that they were not the only people of Namru to violently resist the Chinese subjugation. The Dhichin tsowa refused to co-operate at all, let alone hand in weapons. In fact, the able folk had formed an armed resistance group of a hundred horsemen and women, who hid up in the mountains around Nyenchen Thangla. Years later we heard that every member of that group except for one had been killed fighting the Chinese army. The sole survivor spent decades in prison.

As time flew by in Mustang we grew increasingly pessimistic about the fate of our eldest brothers. Judging by the numbers of refugees pouring into Mustang and their tales of horror, we had virtually given up hope of ever seeing our brothers alive.

I can clearly recall a particular day during those times — it was the day before a full moon. Due to our Buddhist culture our family performed religious acts and refrained from doing any negative deeds on these auspicious days. That morning my brother-in-law Wabu left for Tsarang with a few bags full of coral, silver and gold head-ornaments belonging to my mother and eldest sister. We were only given a very light watery soup for breakfast and then told to 'enjoy some games' with the other children. My mother told us to come home when Wabu returned. We played hide and seek by the riverside, amid rocks and bushes, until the sun set and the full moon shone brightly above the Himalayan valley.

Wabu was unable to trade any of the jewelleries in exchange for food. We did not know what was really happening until Wabu quietly went to the sheep-yard, brought a sheep near the tent door and killed it. This was the first time in my memory that an animal was intentionally killed during a full moon.

There was stewed mutton for dinner, which was rather late. Many of the younger children were already crying for food by the time dinner was ready. My father started to say the evening prayers aloud and everyone followed him. The prayer went on and on until some of us began to feel uneasy. I suppose we were saying the prayers for the poor sheep, which had to give up its dear life to feed some hungry human beings. My parents and the elders must have felt awful having to butcher this sheep, especially on such a holy day. Somehow, that day imprinted me with a feeling of being loved under sad circumstances.

Amid the deteriorating situation a moment of immense joy arrived. My brothers Wangdrak and Jignam, and all the others who had gone to Tibet to rescue their fellow Tibetans, returned safely one night. It felt as if they had come back from the dead and it was almost unbelievable. We learned that they were intercepted by several thousand Chinese soldiers just a few days from the Nepalese border near Dolpo. They had fought for a whole day and finally managed to escape under the cover of darkness when night set in.

During the day they were fighting the Chinese and escaping

higher into the hills and mountains, two brothers, one called Namlang and the other a monk, mounted their horses and charged at the pursuing Chinese army. Waving their glimmering swords high above them, they cut through the startled soldiers. My brothers saw many Chinese soldiers felled by the two brothers. In confusion, while trying to shoot the two brothers, many more soldiers shot each other. Finally, the two brothers were encircled by hundreds of soldiers bearing automatic rifles. They died in a blaze of Chinese gunfire.

Despite the tragic stories they brought, our brothers' unexpected return was the most joyful event that year. Our family was again reunited.

During this period there was an influx of refugees from all over Tibet. Most groups helped each other and the group leaders contacted one another in order to share campsites and to help find lost animals. Unfortunately, some groups became like bandits after losing everything to the Chinese army. They had no animals, no money and no food. Their only possessions were their weapons and horses and if they wanted to live they had no choice but to help themselves to the belongings of others. Thus the victims of these desperate refugees sometimes included the local people of Mustang, who became increasingly resentful.

In this deteriorating situation my eldest sister, Pendon, gave birth to a girl. Within a month of the birth, Pendon became gravely ill. Many religious rites were carried out and local doctors attended to her but nothing helped, and she died soon after. She had been a second mother to all of us younger children and it was a great loss. She was only twenty-nine years old. Both my parents and Wabu bore the loss very bravely. We could constantly hear them say, 'Although she died young, she was lucky that she died in freedom where we could carry out all the religious rites according to tradition.'

Some lamas were invited to perform a phowa — the transference puja. An elderly religious person was invited to read the *Bardo Thoedrol*, popularly known in English as the *Tibetan Book of the Dead*, which is considered to be a guidebook for the consciousness of the dead person. The belief is that during the bardos (intermediary states), the consciousness of the dead can hear and see things even more clearly than while alive. The length of this period is believed to last for forty-nine days and it is a crucial period for determining the circumstances of the next rebirth.

For the mind of a young child, it was very painful to have to listen to this reading of the *Bardo Thoedrol*. I had many sleepless nights when I imagined my kind, older sister facing all the dilemmas and difficulties described in the book. During this time the family sponsored as much religious activity as possible. This included burning as many butter or oil lamps as possible, so we had to procure oil from somewhere. My father decided to go to Manthang to ask the king to sell us some oil and foodstuffs as the forty-ninth day drew near.

The trip was to take three or four days but he did not return on the expected day. The next day a messenger came from Tsarang saying that my father was severely ill and that we needed to send some strong men to carry him back home. Brothers Wangdrak and Wabu immediately went to Tsarang along with some people from our tsowa. They returned late in the afternoon carrying father on a stretcher. He was suffering from acute stomach pain and bloody diarrhoea. He could hardly speak. A great sense of helplessness descended upon our family and a hollow feeling filled the air we breathed. My mother and sister-in-law Choeying were already crying quietly.

Every elder member of our tsowa came to see father and most of them went home with tears in their eyes. Every time a visitor came, my father tried to hide his agony and told them that he would be better soon. But his extremely weak voice and pale face betrayed his real state. Our community decided to hold a night-long Tara Puja for the quick recovery of my father. This was a prayer in praise of the twenty-one Tara goddesses, which were thought to be the manifestation of the Buddha's compassionate actions. Sarjey Rinpoche was consulted to do a divination, and this predicted no immediate danger but advised that some prayers should be conducted. Some members of the family went with a urine sample to consult the local doctor at Drakmar and came home with a week's medicine.

It seemed as though the medicine had worked and all our prayers had been answered, as my father's condition became slightly better during the next few weeks. Final religious ceremonies for my deceased sister could take place with hundreds of lamps and special religious rites presided over by Sarjey Rinpoche. My father had been able to procure oil and food from the king of Mustang during his last journey, and in spite of all the sad events everyone bore the difficulties with high spirits.

On an evening when everyone was gathered my father told us that he was happy and recovering well, and all of his dreams and predictions had not come true due to the power of prayers performed by our lamas and by the people of our tsowa. He told us that his plan for the coming winter was to proceed to India to be near His Holiness the Dalai Lama. He then told my mother that she should carry out the task of leading us to India should anything happen to him. He told brother Wangdrak that the time had come when one should not rely on a youthful zeal that trusted guns.

'Dying in freedom is far more important than being killed by the enemy of the faith.'

Father distributed his few personal possessions and delegated special duties to most of us, as if he was about to go for a long journey. I was very happy to be receiving two of his most personal and treasured belongings — a prayer book and a ritual dagger. In the back of my mind, however, I had hoped that I would never have to receive them. All I wanted was my father. At that stage I could not imagine a life without either of our parents. That evening, there was an atmosphere of serenity in the tent and no one was crying or sobbing. I presume everyone was optimistic as my father's health was almost normal, and he was talking of leading us all to India before long.

Sarjey Rinpoche and Bagyo Rinpoche often visited our ailing father. It was during one such visit that my father disclosed his spiritual achievements to Sarjey Rinpoche. He sought Rinpoche's advice on whether he should pass away in the upright meditation position. Father and Rinpoche discussed his imminent death as if he was about to go on a journey of his own will. Rinpoche was, in fact, impressed with my father's spiritual achievements and the meditational level he had reached. However, he advised my father to die in the horizontal *parinirvana* position of the Buddha.

I was the only child to be listening to those conversations as I sat beside my father. My sister Ani Tenzin Choedon, brother Wangdrak (both were grown up by then), and mother were also there. It was clear beyond doubt that my father was about to die in the next few days. Again the hollow, empty feeling seized me and I wanted to run away from the tent, from the truth, yet such an interesting, supernatural and secret conversation captivated me and held me there. In the depths of my mind I wanted to grasp everything being said during that conversation between my father and Rinpoche. My father especially asked for the Rinpoche's permission to allow me to be there. Usually such subjects could only be heard and discussed among the initiated. Rinpoche readily gave his permission.

A few more days of meetings followed as my father met old friends and members of our tsowa. One morning I woke up to find an unusual quiet in our tent. Some butter lamps were burning before the altar and one of my elder sisters whispered into my ear that our father was meditating and that we should not disturb him. As she spoke, she carried me out of the tent. The atmosphere was so quiet that it could almost be described as serenely peaceful. We did not speak much but those few words we uttered were in low-toned whispers. I knew then that the unthinkable had happened.

I wanted to run into our tent to see my father for the last time but I could not. Despite all of my father's warnings, nothing could have prepared me for the day when my worst fears came alive. Although endless tears choked me from within, everyone hid their all-defeating sorrows behind brave faces. Although I felt like crying aloud, my sister Ani Tenzin Choedon told me that it would be extremely bad for my father if I cried at all. A few moments later, Sarjey Rinpoche accompanied by Bagyo Rinpoche arrived to perform the phowa. The two Rinpoches went straight into the main tent accompanied by elder members of our family. Some of us children also went in with them. My hope was to see my father's face for the last time. A white blanket covered his whole body from head to toe. There was nothing I could see.

After the phowa had been carried out, the Rinpoches and some monks remained the whole day performing various religious rites. Many people came to console our family and pay their last respects to my father. They all brought the traditional white scarves and many brought butter and food. Everyone quietly talked to my mother and brother Wangdrak. Mum occasionally broke down whenever some very close relative or friend came. But brother Wangdrak did not even shed half a teardrop.

At Sarjey Rinpoche's advice, my father's body was kept for a week before carrying out the funeral according to his wishes. The day of the funeral was unforgettable. Although the funeral ceremony itself was simple, something extraordinary followed.

Sarjey Rinpoche came to our tent home to conduct special religious rites. Our sister-in-law offered Rinpoche his usual preferred tea. Normally Tibetan tea is served as a very rich mixture of churned tea, salt, butter and milk, but Rinpoche always drank his tea without anything else in it. That day, as my sister-in-law poured the dark tea into Rinpoche's glass mug, it immediately turned milky white as if she had poured milk rather than tea.

In astonishment, my sister-in-law exclaimed, 'What has happened to this tea? Sorry Rinpoche!' She bent down to take the mug away, but Rinpoche told her to leave it where it was and then explained with a gentle smile that this might be what he called a *namthik*, 'a drop from the sky'.

'If it is so, then this will be the first time in my life that I have experienced it. I know that my own root lama has experienced such miracles during his lifetime.

'Such things can only happen if there is unbroken trust and faith between the lama and his benefactor. It is said that a drop of real namthik can turn a whole pot of tea completely white. If this really is namthik, then it is indeed a good omen.'

Rinpoche then asked brother Wangdrak to put a small drop of the white liquid from Rinpoche's mug into the pot of tea that was on the stove. To everyone's joy and amazement, the pot full of black tea became completely white.

Seeing this, Rinpoche remarked, 'I myself have no special powers, this phenomenon today is because the late garpon was a man of unwavering faith and a sincere Dharma practitioner.'

We all received a few drops of the namthik as blessings, and this extraordinary phenomenon helped us overcome a great part of our grief and worry. We felt assured that father was indeed spiritually advanced and there was no need for us to worry over his karma.

13

The pilgrims' prayers

The days passed slowly as our leaderless group thought about what to do next. One evening the families discussed their plans and my eldest brother Wangdrak attended on our family's behalf. Some wanted to set off to India to be with His Holiness the Dalai Lama as soon as possible, others wanted to remain in the border regions between Tibet and Nepal. One of my father's friends, Gadun, told of the tragic deaths of scores of refugees in the warmer lands in southern Nepal and India.

'The heat will kill us if we go to India,' he said. 'If it doesn't, famine will. At least here, thanks to the animals, we can survive. If we go, all the animals will perish.'

Another elderly man agreed with Gadun and believed that we could fight the Chinese invaders and raid their camps. After all, there were no signs that the invasion would last long, and we could easily return to Tibet from here once the Chinese were forced back. The old man continued, 'The Zamling Gyalchi [the United Nations] and the international community will do something ... no one on this world could just let one nation carry out such injustices and atrocities against another!'

That evening sealed the fate for many families. Gadun spoke

again, 'I don't know about the Zamling Gyalchi but as far as I can see we are left with two choices, death by hunger or death by the sword. I choose death by the sword, which do you choose?'

An uneasy sleep was just beginning to come over me when brother Wangdrak returned. I was sitting by my mother's side, missing the warmth of my father's evening prayers, while she was grinding some tsampa in our tent. My brother, the young man whose love for and skill with guns and horses was re-nowned, told mother what had been said during the meeting, and how he agreed with Gadun — that he wanted to die by the sword rather than by hunger. My mother was infuriated as she angrily told Wangdrak that he was old enough to make his own choices.

'But,' mother continued, 'I have made a promise to your father. I promised to take my children to His Holiness in India and I will never break that promise. What is the use of fighting the Chinese and eating the animals you manage to raid from them? First you will die, then Jignam, then Jami and then Chope and soon I will lose all of my children to the sinful guns and swords of the Chinese, all for some animals. What is the use of such a pitiful pathetic life? I would rather die by hunger than live such a pointless, sinful life.'

My brother quietly listened to our mother's angry words and then glumly sat for a while, thinking about which path to choose. The next morning he got up having made up his mind and gathered all of our family's guns, ammunition and swords, and left. Brother Wangdrak had gone to spend the day with Gadun and his family and to discuss their plans. Since Gadun and his group were going back to Dolpo, even closer to Tibet, to carry out raids on the Chinese camps and caravans, Wang-drak had gone to give them our weapons. In return, out of the few things he owned, Gadun had given my brother some goat furs, yak tails and some money. Our family could use these to buy food and necessities on our planned journey to India.

From then on our two families parted, never to be together again. Gadun and his family went to Dolpo amid the Himalayas and closer to the border while our family, and other families and individuals who had decided to accompany us, travelled further south, deeper into Nepal.

After a few weeks of travelling our company arrived at a place we called Zong Sarpa, a relatively big town known to the Nepalese as Jomsom. It was situated in a great Himalayan valley just north of the world's deepest gorge between Mount Annapurna and Mount Daulagiri, which are the fourth and third tallest mountains in the world respectively. A large foaming river called the Black Gandagi ran from east to west just north of the main settlement. There were only a few families who lived north of the river and being a drogpa child I was not used to crossing great rivers on wooden bridges, and at first I used to get dizzy. But later I enjoyed running across the bridge carrying paper fans I had made, as the wind made them spin delightfully. Jomsom was an extremely windy place.

On the other side of the bridge there was also a shop, a police checkpoint and a large meadow where the Tibetan refugees had put up prayer flags. The refugee children used to play there, running around and chasing each other with the colourful flags fluttering in the wind above our heads. I was very fond of that meadow. All the prayer flags made it feel like it was a place where we belonged, a little bit of our homeland outside our country. Jomsom could be considered the last outpost of Tibetan culture.

At the time, hundreds of new Tibetan refugees had camped

at Jomsom, and our group also decided to settle there for a while. The Tibetan refugees built the airport that is still in use today, and in return for the work the refugees received food from the Red Cross.

Because of the recent death of our father and not being too far from Kathmandu, the children of our family felt a responsibility to go on a pilgrimage to the capital of Nepal. A number of important Buddhist pilgrimage sites were situated there and we believed that such a journey could burn away the sins of many lifetimes. Our mother and some of the other elders feared we might succumb to the heat in Kathmandu, but they also believed that this pilgrimage was a very fortunate opportunity.

It was decided that sister Lhamo, brother Jignam, brother Jami, my little brother Gyatso and I would be led by our eldest remaining sister, Ani Tenzin Choedon. Upon hearing about our pilgrimage other people, mostly from Namru, decided to travel with us. Most of them wished to go on to India and would part from us at Pokhara.

On a foggy morning, we children parted from our mother with sleepy eyes, assuring her that we would return safely. Each of us carried our personal belongings and necessities in our traditional Tibetan backpacks. Apart from these minor belongings, my siblings only had goat skins and yak tails to sell (which the Nepalese seemed eager to purchase). The goat skins were probably used as mats while the yak tails were used for dusting, particularly for Hindu shrines. We also had twenty-five Nepalese rupees to buy necessities and two lumps of smoked animal fat to sustain us through the long journey.

We arrived at Pokhara over ten days later and those who

intended to go to India said their farewells. Later in the day, the rest of us who were on the pilgrimage to Kathmandu decided to visit the long market of the city.

As we strolled past the colourful shops we met a Tibetan called Buda from the Nangchen region. Back in Tibet, he had been the personal treasurer of a wealthy man. Buda was familiar to us from the time he was in Mustang. He talked with sister Ani Tenzin Choedon for a while and then invited us to where he was staying.

As we sat at his lodging, drinking some tea that we were offered, Buda took a short sip from his cup. Then staring into the distance as if he could see through the walls he said, 'After your father had passed away, I lent your brother Wangdrak twenty-five rupees to pay for butter and oil for the pujas. I am setting off for India tomorrow, so even though I am not demanding the money back, it would be helpful. After all, I am quite old and I don't think I shall ever meet you again, so since it will need to be repaid some day, it will become a karmic debt.' Any sort of debt not paid within this lifetime is believed to become a debt that will influence a person's karma, and would have to be settled in a future lifetime in some way.

Most of us had never heard about the debt and were quite shocked by Buda's sudden claim. Indeed, twenty-five rupees was all we had to pay for the necessities for the rest of our long journey.

That evening, as our siblings gathered for a simple supper, sister Ani Tenzin Choedon explained her thoughts to us. 'You all heard what Buda had to say,' she said to us younger ones, 'I remember brother Wangdrak borrowing some money from him to pay for our father's funeral and the other rites which followed it. As Buda told us, if we are unable to repay the twenty-five rupees, it may well turn into a karmic debt for future lives.

As our very pilgrimage is for the sake of our late father's future life, I cannot bear the burden of such karmic debts. You all know that brother Wangdrak gave me twenty-five rupees for our journey, and I believe we should give it to Buda. What do you think?'

We were convinced by her reasoning and gave nods and sighs of agreement. But already our mouths seemed dry and our throats felt uneasy, knowing that from then on acquiring food for our journey would be more difficult.

The next day, Ani Tenzin Choedon gave the twenty-five rupees to Buda. Then we thought about our situation and the ways of earning some money. Again only Ani Tenzin Choedon had any ideas. She knew that some Tibetan refugees had been earning money by working as porters and carrying salt to distant places. Since Gyatso and I were too young to carry anything, sister Lhamo would have to stay behind and look after us. Ani Tenzin Choedon, Jignam and Jami were going to become porters for a while to earn enough for us to complete our pilgrimage. We didn't dare to think about all that could happen during such trips. Having heard how hard these labours were, we knew that one or more of our siblings could die on such a trip. We also knew how unbearably lonely and difficult it would be for us too, having to stay behind without any guidance or leadership.

Having decided that we would all adhere to Ani's proposition, Ani Tenzin Choedon went to farewell the other members of the company who were travelling to Kathmandu. She told the others to continue by themselves, but they were unhappy and pleaded with Ani Tenzin Choedon to accompany them.

'We need you to lead us for the rest of the journey like you have done until now, we cannot complete the pilgrimage on our own,' cried a man who had been travelling with us since we were in Mustang. 'We could all give you food and lend you some money when you need it, even if we don't have much ourselves.'

He searched inside his backpack. Taking out twelve fifty-paisa coins, each worth half a rupee, he handed them to Ani Tenzin Choedon saying, 'Please accept this small loan as a sign of our sincerity. It will pay for your needs for a short while on our journey.'

The following day, led by Ani Tenzin Choedon, we continued on our pilgrimage with the others. Despite the weight of the pack I was carrying on my back and my legs which were tiring, I was smiling as I watched my feet follow the path to Kathmandu. I was happy that our family did not have to part and that all the unbearably horrible scenarios that had been acted out in my imagination had been averted. I was truly grateful to the other members of our little group for their support.

Every day from then on, our company got up and set off as the calls of the first morning birds woke us. At around ten o'clock in the morning, as the sun brightened in the sky, we halted for breakfast. My older siblings then collected some firewood and set up a small fire on which some water was boiled. A small piece was cut off the shrinking lumps of animal fat and dropped into the boiling water. A few handfuls of crushed corn flour were sprinkled onto the mixture and left to boil. When this watery 'soup' was ready, we would all share it, although the older ones always made sure that the younger ones got more. This was all that we had to keep us on our feet until the next meal. Despite all the hardships that besieged us from all sides, the love and care that our older siblings showed towards us, and the respect and trust that we had for them kept us warm within. We knew that we could depend on each other no matter what.

During these mealtimes, we took off our fur chupas to let the hundreds of lice which infested them scatter under the warm sun. There were always so many lice feeding off us that it seemed these insects were mocking us for our misfortune, stealing the little nutrition our bodies were able to hunt out of the watery meals. We would have another such mealtime at five o'clock in the evening, and after a few more days I began to feel light-headed and dizzy, and my legs and the load on my back seemed heavier. My mouth was dry and foam formed at the edges of my lips, but I continued without complaining. I knew that the others were also growing weak and my older siblings were doing all they could to look after me and the other younger children.

We were also weighed down by a type of claustrophobia. We drogpa children were used to vast open lands where we could see the curving horizon. Here we trekked down steep hillside paths and were often surrounded by dense, dark jungles. Sometimes even breathing felt laborious as if the air had grown heavy, and we felt disquieted as the noise of insects followed us along our journey — in Tibet, insects were almost non-existent. And while the rivers in Namru used to flow calmly around gently sloping mountains, the waters here rushed down the hills, wildly leaping down great falls and onto the protruding rocks below. Here even the rivers seemed to be restless.

On the fifth morning, our company halted at a place where we were surrounded by the satisfied grunts of animals and the lively voices of people talking behind a grey fog that hid them from sight.

'I was hoping that we wouldn't have to beg on this journey,' said Ani Tenzin Choedon to the others in the company, 'but now the children are growing weak, and they might soon die of hunger and exhaustion if we continue further as we are. I think we are in a large settlement, a large village or a town. If the rest of you could settle close to a water source, my siblings and I will have to begin begging.'

The other company members knew that we could not continue any further without a more substantial diet and so agreed, looking visibly downhearted that they were unable to help us avoid resorting to alms — begging for food to survive.

Even though I felt ashamed and disheartened to be forced to resort to such means of survival, the generosity of most of the villagers made me more at ease. As we walked past houses saying prayers, villagers came out and offered us types of tsampa. Within an hour, Ani Tenzin Choedon and I had already filled our little cloth sack with corn and millet tsampa. With our sack full, we returned to our company to find sister Lhamo boiling some water. Soon, Jami and Jignam also returned with their little sack full and together we cooked our usual soup, which to the delight of us younger ones, was followed by a very thick porridge of crushed grains. We were munching the last bits of our porridge when sleep overcame us. Our stomachs, which had been almost empty for so many days, were suddenly full, and this had awakened sleep. The other members of our company rested for a few more hours while we slept soundly without the call of hunger disturbing our dreams.

From that day forth the children of my family begged for food as we continued our pilgrimage towards Kathmandu. This slowed our journey but we now had more to eat to keep our legs in motion, and despite having to beg, we never lost hope in life. I believe we were only able to hold onto hope and to hold our heads high because we had been brought up by loving parents with a formidable sense of right and wrong, and now Ani Tenzin Choedon kept this distinction clear in our minds. We knew that begging, being non-violent, did not harm any other beings and so was not against Buddhist principles. Ani Tenzin Choedon also reminded us that we were begging not because of our own lack of ability and achievement, but because the Chinese had forced us from everything we had ever known and owned.

'Lord Buddha accepted alms himself, it is nothing to be

ashamed of. But we must pray sincerely for the welfare of the benefactors in return for the alms we receive,' Ani Tenzin Choedon would often tell the rest of us. 'And we must keep a clean conscience. Whenever we receive alms, we must never secretly eat anything without sharing it with everyone else. Otherwise, it defeats the whole purpose of this pilgrimage.'

We all kept Ani's words in our hearts and respected her, knowing that we could rely on her love, integrity and wisdom to lead us through anything.

Dignity and some joy always accompanied us, despite the hardship. We felt overjoyed by the fact that we were able to strive with our bodies and go on this pilgrimage to repay our father's and mother's kindness. We also knew that our motivation and our general conduct during the journey were completely sincere and pious. With this knowledge came an unshakeable dignity that never wavered, even when we were at some stranger's doorstep begging for food.

As we begged in many villages I soon learnt that seeking alms would not always be as easy as on the first day. One day I was begging outside a Nepalese country house in which a woman was cooking something on a fire. Upon seeing me begging outside, the enraged woman rushed out wielding a burning log. I ducked as the flaming log came crashing down. Luckily, it hit the wooden rim of my backpack and shattered. I fell forward but managed to quickly get up and run away.

I was shocked. I was only begging for food because I was hungry, why had she suddenly become so angry? I was very upset and kept running until I met our company. When I had my father and my country, I had been treated like a little prince of some sort. Now complete strangers were beating me as I begged for food before their door. Later when Ani Tenzin Choedon finally returned, I tearfully told her about the woman and how she had attacked me. Ani Tenzin Choedon looked very concerned.

'This will not do,' she said, 'It is indeed very unfortunate. Giving us a handful of food would not have made her any poorer. But now, by her rage against you, she will have incurred much negative karma. It is so unfortunate, unfortunate that we pilgrims caused her to act in such a negative way. Poor thing.'

After listening to Ani Tenzin Choedon I also began to feel sorry for her. We later prayed that the woman would not have to face the consequences of her actions. Due to Ani Tenzin Choedon's nightly explanations and stories, I even felt compassion every time I met a relatively rich and conceited individual. Despite my age, I knew the huge changes that my family had been through in less than two years. I had quite quickly turned from someone who felt he had everything to someone who had to beg to fend off starvation. I had lost my country, my home, my father and many other loved ones. I began to comprehend the meaning of impermanence.

As youthful or wealthy people looked down with contempt upon the poor and the weak, I knew that the foundations behind their conceit were also impermanent and that their pride was ill-founded. Although they may not lose their homes and their country as we did, they were doomed to suffer from the agonies of sickness, ageing and in the end, they too would have to face death alone. So what was the use of such irrational conceit and pride? I often wondered how these people would be able to cope with the inevitable turns and falls of this life. When I thought about the consequences of their egotism and ill-founded disdain, I could not help but feel genuine compassion.

As the days and miles passed by, our company steadily progressed towards Kathmandu. On the Tibetan New Year's Day, we reached an elevated ground from where we could see the colourful Kathmandu valley below, not far away. As we eagerly looked out we saw the great white houses around the city centre, many smaller houses and huts spread out across the valley, and isolated far from the city, the great white and gold Boudhanath *stupa*, called Jharungkhashor by Tibetans. (A stupa is a Buddhist monument usually containing relics or other sacred items.) The Boudhanath stupa rose from the fields and was circled by a few houses and woods. We were all overwhelmed by the joy of seeing this great stupa in the distance. Back in Tibet, we had a photo of this stupa and had heard numerous stories about it. Any wish made before the stupa is said to be fulfilled.

That Tibetan New Year's night we found a traveller's shelter in which we slept. We got up early the next day and trekked until we finally reached the city of Kathmandu. Unlike in later times, Kathmandu was unpolluted then. Residents and travellers could breathe the fresh air of the Nepalese capital nestled in a green, woody valley. There were hardly any cars — most people walked or rode bicycles, while a few wealthy people also rode horses.

A couple of days after first seeing the Boudhanath stupa, we reached it on foot. With immeasurable happiness in our hearts, we prostrated before the stupa with complete devotion. Then as we thought more about where we were and what we believed we had achieved, we were filled with even more joy. We believed that we had finally managed to repay a little bit of the kindness of our parents.

We stayed near the Boudhanath stupa for almost a week and every day we woke up early and prostrated around the stupa for the whole day long, taking three steps between each prostration. The great eyes of compassion — the eyes of the Buddha which were painted on each of the four sides of its golden spire — watched over us. Although we would not usually tell each other what we had prayed for, we all hoped to see our mother again. After having lost many loved ones, we were not certain that our mother would survive the few months that we were away.

From the Boudhanath stupa we trekked to the Namo Buda hillside, which is known to all Tibetans as Takmolugen. Takmolugen is believed to be the spot where the Buddha, in one of his previous lives, had sacrificed his body to feed a starving tigress and her four hungry cubs. On the hillside were a stupa and a traveller's shelter. As we were settling down near the shelter, I saw an old, white-haired Tibetan man with large drooping gold earrings and a brown chupa.

He rode a beautiful white horse past our group and halted close by, setting up a small camp. As he settled himself down, he boiled some tea. When it was ready, he poured himself a cup and then poured some of the tea into a bowl full of tsampa and butter. Little white peaks of tsampa rose through the creamy sea of butter and tea that swirled around in his bowl. He skilfully mixed everything and then began his meal.

Water formed in my mouth as the smell of tsampa rose up my nostrils. Usually we were all too embarrassed to beg any Tibetans for food, but that day I could not resist the call of the tsampa. Gathering my courage I slowly crept up to the old man like some frightened mouse and whispered, 'Can I have a little tsampa?'

Upon seeing me standing before him with a sheepish look on my face, he smiled and gave me a generous handful of tsampa from his sack. I was delighted and ran back to our group.

When my little brother Gyatso saw me return with some tsampa, he went to the old man and asked him for some more tsampa. Then my bother Jami and a cousin followed suit. As they approached the old man, we heard his astonished voice exclaim, 'Oh, so many of you!' But the generous old man gave them handfuls of tsampa as well.

Leaving Kathmandu behind we trekked on towards the Swa-yambhunath stupa, which is situated on a hilltop. As we neared the hill, we could see many Tibetans with their white tents pitched on the meadows by the path below the hill. Most of these Tibetans were from parts of Tibet closer to the Nepalese border, and most of them were able to escape with more of their wealth intact. They were still merry as it was only a few days since the celebrations of the Tibetan New Year had begun. The rest of our company trekked on but I slowed my pace and the others didn't notice me fall behind. I halted by a few tents.

Carrying my usual backpack and with my prayer beads in my hand, I began to recite a few prayers. Most of the people quickly took notice of me and looked at me with adoring eyes. A family invited me into their tent and as I sat high on one of their beds, I was offered some sweet Tibetan delicacies which they were having to celebrate the days of the New Year. I had one mouthful and then kept the rest to take back for the others.

As I continued past another tent, an elderly couple invited me inside and gave me pak — lumps of tsampa moistened with tea and butter which has been compressed by hand. When they saw that I wasn't eating, they asked me why. I told them that I didn't want to eat since I had to take the food to my siblings to share.

'Eat boy, I will give you some to take to your siblings,' the old man said. Delighted by his words, I ate the pak. And true to his word, as I was leaving, not only did the old man give me some tsampa but also some dried buffalo meat to take back.

'But before you leave,' added the old woman who was stand-ing beside her husband, 'even though you are young, you look like a religious boy. Please say prayers for us two.' And with that she gave me a fifty-paisa coin. For us children, at the time, that was quite a substantial sum. With that coin we could buy around two kilograms of rice.

I wandered for a while longer amid the tents and some people gave me some chang, Tibetan wine. I drank a bit and then put the rest in my flask. Feeling slightly dizzy due to the wine, I was still walking among the tents when I saw my brother Jignam and cousin Ami coming down the hill. Feeling quite wealthy with some food in my backpack and some money in my pocket, I ran to them. They were very happy to see me as they had begun to fear for me. We started back towards the rest of our group, who were on the hilltop when I saw a Tibetan family camping in the traveller's shelter half-way up the hill. I told my siblings that I would go and beg there.

Staying in the traveller's shelter was a small family — a young father, mother and their little daughter. I went near their door and began to say a few prayers. The man saw me and asked, 'Are you a monk?'

'Not really,' I replied, pausing the prayers to answer his question.

'You look like one, come inside and have a sit,' said the man, with a nudge of his head as his wife braided his hair. 'You're a cute little boy …' Then he paused and smiled playfully, 'Why don't you stay with us? Once you're older, you can marry our daughter.'

I didn't like the idea of getting married, so I quickly lied, 'I am sort of a monk.' The man believed me. After all, I was wearing a brown chupa, and I had my hair cut short. But my hair was cut short because of lice, not because of any monastic vows!

'It's alright,' the man continued. 'At times when all the three great monastic universities of Sera, Ganden and Drepung have been looted and destroyed, what is the point of staying a monk?'

'That is exactly why we lost our country, because we stopped respecting the law of karma,' I returned. 'As the great Padmasambhava said, it is not the times that change but the people.'

Now it was the man's turn to be startled. He became mute for a few moments as he stared at me with a look of astonishment. When he could finally speak, the man said, 'Please sit there,' pointing towards a higher seat deeper within the room. It was a gesture of respect and I did as told.

'You won't become my son-in-law but please take this,' said the man as he handed me a fifty-paisa coin, 'Do pray for us.'

I took the coin and said, 'I don't know many prayers but I will circumambulate around the stupa while prostrating for you.'

When I arrived at our camp near the hilltop I took out all of the food and drinks I had acquired during the day. I gave Ani Tenzin Choedon the two fifty-paisa coins and told her that the elderly couple and the young family with a daughter had asked me to pray for them. Ani Tenzin Choedon was slightly perturbed, 'What prayers? You don't know that many prayers. It is not an easy thing to take money from people and promise to pray for them in return!' My dear elder sister sighed heavily. 'Well ... you will just have to do prostrating circumambulations of the stupa as you promised.'

I spent much of the following day prostrating as I circumambulated the stupa and I prayed for the happiness and well-being of the two families who had been so generous.

The day after, we lifted our backpacks and set off hoping to reach Jomsom as soon as possible. We were all happy in the belief that we had taken part in a very pious and spiritually pure pilgrimage. Our return proved easier and quicker than our journey to Kathmandu. Firstly, we had managed to sell all of the yak tails, goat skins and some of the silver ornaments we owned so we had some money to buy food along our way. We were also more familiar with the road and the surroundings and we knew which villages were likely to be more generous if we had to beg.

During our journey I learnt that the generations of Tibetan pilgrims who had traversed these roads for many centuries must have been very honourable in their conduct. Often villagers would call out, 'Lama-ji, Lama-ji,' as they waved at us and offered food. I not only felt grateful to the generous villagers, but also to the Tibetan pilgrims of old who had conducted themselves in such a pious manner. During our return trip of around a month, we only had to beg once at a village of whitewashed houses. The villagers were very charitable and soon our sacks were full.

Along our return journey, we couldn't wait for each day to pass. Each sunset was taking us closer to our mother and the rest of our family. But in the back of our minds a dark shadow was looming. We knew it was possible that our mother and other family members may have died while we were on our pilgrimage. Nevertheless we dared not speak such dark thoughts aloud.

Back in Tibet whenever members of our family went away on pilgrimage they brought back gifts such as clothes, sweets, bowls and mugs for the ones who stayed behind. But we did not have any presents. All we had left was some brown sugar and some millet. So when we were within a day's journey of Jomsom we set to work, busily baking millet bread over an open fire. When the breads were done, we younger ones spread a little bit of the brown sugar onto some of the breads to make them sweet. This was going to be our present to our mother and our family.

To our enormous relief, when we returned we found our

mother alive. We all ran to hug her as she hurriedly stood up from the floor on which she was sitting and spinning wool. We noticed that she had grown thin and seemed to have aged many years during the few months we had been away. But for now she was alive and that was all that mattered. We were finally with our mother again.

Soon, the rest of our family also returned and we gave everyone the millet breads we had baked the day before. They were much happier to see us again than to be given millet breads. Just as we had feared for their survival, they did not know if we would survive our long journey.

Our mother could not stop weeping. Our cute youngest sister Norzin and our deceased sister Pendon's clever little daughter had both died of measles just a few weeks before our arrival. We were very sad to hear the news but we were also eager to tell mother and the others about our journey. So for the rest of that day and much of that night we recounted our days on the pilgrimage. We told mother about how we had repaid Buda in Pokhara. How we had seen the streets of Pokhara and Kathmandu. We told them about how we had prayed and prostrated at both the Boudhanath and the Swayambhunath stupas and also about the Takmolugen hillside, and how we had met a generous old Tibetan man with a white horse. We told them each and every single thing we could remember. Seeing us all back safe and hearing our many tales seemed to lighten our mother's days.

14

A cupful of rice

Soon after we had returned from our pilgrimage we started work at the dusty airport construction site. We dug up the earth, crushed stones into small pieces and carried rocks on our backs the whole day long. In the evening, with our backs bruised and aching, we lined up for our payment — a cupful of rice and a small piece of cheese. Since we had no money to pay the rent to our landlords, we worked on their land after returning from the construction site.

About one month later the Red Cross staff told us that there was no more rice, and that all the fit youths would have to go to Pokhara to carry back rice and other supplies. During the last month I had become best friends with a boy called Dhondup. Being only twelve at the time, Dhondup and I were the two youngest members of the party who were sent to carry back the rice. Of the hundred that were sent most were in their twenties and early thirties, and most of my older siblings were also with us.

During our pilgrimage to Kathmandu our journey to Pokhara had taken over ten days; this time it only took five as the meals were prepared for us and we did not have any loads to carry. Indeed, this journey to Pokhara was very enjoyable as I had my older brothers and sisters to look after me, and Dhondup to play with. We stayed in Pokhara for a couple of days while the loads were divided among the group. The older people were told to carry back eight kilograms of rice each, while Dhondup and I were each given a four-kilogram pack of DDT (insecticide) to carry back.

Our leader was Pema, a young, impressive and very loud-voiced Bhutanese man in his early twenties. He had been schooled in Darjeeling, India, and spoke good English and Tibetan, as well as fluent Nepalese. He was very well-dressed and usually worked at the camp as an interpreter for the Red Cross. He was very close with the few teenage Tibetan girls and during the trip he camped with them each night.

During our trip back to Jomsom, we got up at around half-past-four when the stars were still twinkling and set off. Except for brief halts for meals, we struggled on until well into the night. Two days into the journey, after having marched down a steep hill, I stared up at the shadowy mountain looming before me and I knew I couldn't go on. My legs were stiff, my skin was wet with sweat and my heart was pounding. I was suffering from a stomach ache and dysentery. My back was also bleeding where the case of insecticide had dug into my skin. I gave up, took my luggage off and rested in the traveller's shelter at the foot of the hill.

A couple of hours passed and the sun was low when I heard footsteps coming down the hill. They belonged to my brothers Jami and Jignam who had come back down to find me. We climbed up the steps together as they took turns to carry my case. A good part of an hour later we finally reached the hilltop village where our group was camping. Just before meeting Pema, I took the case from my brothers and carried it because I wanted to show him how unfair it was.

'What took you so long?' Pema shouted with his usual loud voice.

'What are you talking about?' I retaliated. 'You carry it yourself.' And I took the case off my back and dropped it on the ground in front him. I ignored my two embarrassed siblings who were standing a few metres away. They did not want me to argue with the group leader.

'I am sick, I can hardly go on,' I said, and thinking of the Tibetan girls who stayed with Pema and hardly carried anything I continued, 'You give some people nothing at all to carry and then you make some of us carry things which we can hardly lift! Such a prejudiced person you are.'

'What?' Pema yelled. He handed me some colourful pills and a glass of arak (home-brewed whisky sold by the local inn) and said, 'Sit down, drink this. You'll be alright.'

As I sat down angrily and drank the glass of arak, I could see he was relieved to shut me up. Soon, the anger subsided and my body grew warm. I took the pill after dinner as Pema had advised and I had an undisturbed sleep that night. For the rest of the journey Pema asked others to help Dhondup and me with our luggage and a week later we arrived back in Jomsom.

When the airport construction was complete the Red Cross left. Then there was no aid whatsoever and hundreds of Tibetan families in Jomsom dispersed, most leaving for India. Our landlords asked us to remain and told us that they would allow us to stay where we were, in their small house, and that they would employ us. This way we wouldn't starve, so we agreed and began work.

Our two eldest brothers, Wangdrak and Jignam, were often away for months trying to sell a few of the things we had left, and borrowing money from the local shop owner, Tsakar-singh, they bought goods from some places and sold them in others trying to make a profit. This was our family's main source of income while we were in Jomsom. The rest of us worked diligently the whole day long, usually on our landlords' farm. Whenever we grew tired Ani Tenzin Choedon would remind us that we must keep our word and earn the food we were given for lunch. She would often say, 'We should work even harder when the landlords have their backs turned to us than when they are supervising us. We must be faithful.'

During the autumn we had to carry the rotten leaves from both the courtyards of the landlords' houses and ours to their farm. In the winter we collected firewood from the forests. The next summer Ani Tenzin Choedon and I spent many days on the green slopes near the Annapurna mountain range, looking after our landlords' *dzos* who grazed on the lush grass; dzos are a cross between an ox and the female yak (dri). From these slopes we could see a part of the majestic Annapurna range rising to our south. We were so high up that some mountains even looked as though their sharp peaks were below us.

During our time up there we lived in a small enclosure of stones. It had been erected by the locals to shelter people while they looked after the dzos, and we placed a cloth over the enclosure to provide a roof. This cloth often became damp due to the very heavy mists and sometimes the air was so moist that the firewood became damp and we had to struggle for hours before we could get a fire started. Without a fire it was very difficult, as when the sun fell behind the mountains there was no light at all, and with no fire there was also no source of heat to cook food or boil tea. When it was possible Ani Tenzin Choedon taught me some Tibetan literature and old prayers, and I re-read a Tibetan book by Tharchin Babu that Wangdrak had bought for me, which taught the English alphabet and some basic English words.

When I was back in Jomsom my mother asked me to help an elderly childless couple who lived in the same house as us. For a few months, whenever we went to collect firewood in the mornings, my siblings would take theirs back home while I took what I gathered to the elderly couple. They were very kind and caring towards me.

I remember a particular day during that period with exceptional vividness. It was a cold, early winter morning when there was a knock on our door. When someone opened it, we found the shop owner Tsakar-singh and another man standing outside. Tsakar-singh asked mother to send two children to help him for the day. As my brother Jignam was away with Wangdrak, Jami and I were sent to help Tsakar-singh.

We walked until the day began to warm and then stopped for breakfast at an inn in a village called Marpha. We had porridge and a glass of alcohol each and we felt warm and energised within. Feeling light-headed and light-footed, we followed Tsakar-singh for a few more hours until we reached the village of Tukche.

After talking with some locals, Tsakar-singh had managed to get two loads of cigarette boxes for my brother and the other man to carry and he sent them back straight away. He told me to stay with him to help carry his handbag back, and then he walked into the big house of the person from whom he was purchasing the cigarettes. I waited at the bottom of the steps as servants weren't allowed inside the house. I waited for hours on end but Tsakar-singh did not come out.

Finally, at around four or five, Tsakar-singh reappeared looking quite glad, 'Oi Namru boy, we've been very lucky today,' he said, 'I have managed to get one more load of cigarette packs.'

So I wasn't going back without a load after all. It wasn't intensely heavy but because of its size it was very awkward to carry.

Although Tsakar-singh was quite a young man he put his handbag on top of my load as well. We paused at Marpha again as it was darkening, and Tsakar-singh bought me a glass of alcohol which I duly drank. Then he told me to start off and that he would catch up with me later.

I set off and after a couple of hours Tsakar-singh caught up. By that time, it was almost pitch dark with only a withering crescent moon to show me the way. Tsakar-singh walked ahead at his own pace swinging the torch he was carrying with the rhythm of his feet. Our stony path lay beside the mighty Black Gandagi River and I hurried to keep up and tripped over one of the larger rocks.

Hearing me fall Tsakar-singh turned around and saw that some of the things in his handbag had fallen out. Although the box of cigarette packets had not ruptured, he was furious.

'You blind wanderer, why don't you watch where you're going!'

Not only was I hurt by the fall, his words bit into me. But I tried hard not to retaliate because I feared that my family might be evicted from our home.

'You homeless beggar! You idiot …' he continued. I could not restrain myself any longer.

'What are you calling me "blind" for? How do you expect me to see in the dark when you walk ahead swinging the torch from side to side,' I shouted. 'I'm not carrying this load any more. You bring it.'

Tsakar-singh stared at me, perhaps with shock at seeing his little servant answering back. Then his anger pacified and he walked forward. He picked up the load and put it on my back again. Then without saying anything he walked on towards Jomsom carrying his own handbag. I followed. The sound of our feet, my tired breathing, the calls of nocturnal creatures and the rumble of the speedy Black Gandagi River were undisturbed until we neared Jomsom. The two of us walked together until we reached his house. I put the load of cigarettes where I was told to and then Tsakar-singh's wife, a kind young woman, smiled at me and asked, 'Do you want to eat your dinner here or take it back to your home?'

I was given some tsampa and took it home. I had to cross the bridge across the river which the children used to say was haunted after sunset, but that night I was too tired and angry to be afraid of any ghosts. I reached my anxious family soon after.

While we had stayed behind in Jomsom, our Auntie Pentso, who had escaped with us from Tibet, had gone ahead to Pokhara. On a cold day that winter her son Ami and son-in-law Choptra arrived in Jomsom to let us know that Pokhara was more hospitable. We learnt that there was still aid from the International Red Cross in Pokhara and that a large Tibetan settlement had been set up. Auntie Pentso and her family intended to travel on to India soon. We could stay in Pokhara for a while until we were ready to depart for India, then we could journey together. Otherwise, if we so chose, we could probably join the growing settlement in Pokhara instead.

After meeting our cousins we decided to go to Pokhara. We told our landlords and they were quite devastated; they had hoped we would remain in Jomsom for much longer. They offered us some land of our own and the indefinite use of the house we were living in. We had grown close to our landlords and it was difficult for us to say goodbye, but we had already made up our minds. Our hope had always been to go to India so that we could be close to His Holiness the Dalai Lama, and so that the younger ones might receive some education. We farewelled and thanked our landlords for their kindness and they thanked us for our sincerity and hard work. Then we left Jomsom.

15

An education

For over a week we trod the steep paths and crooked steps on our way to Pokhara. The hillsides were brimming with lush forests, and the wrinkled trees struggled to find enough room for their outspread roots and branches. Our grandmother, Mo Rinchen, found the trek hard and had to be carried all the way by Ani Tenzin Choedon and sister Lhamo. But the younger ones were used to long journeys and heavy loads by now. And while our journey was slow we reached Pokhara without any major difficulties.

The first time I set eyes upon the Tibetan settlement of Tashi Palkhiel I was intoxicated by happiness. Below the cliffs we were standing upon was a settlement beset with innumerable prayer flags: blue, red, green and white, all flapping in unison in the light breeze. There were many bamboo-mat houses and colourful tents, and the sight reminded me of the beautiful days we enjoyed during the district gatherings back in Tibet. North of the settlement, like a grand sparkling backdrop stood the Himalayas. As we neared the settlement the Tibetan voices of the men, women and children, all shouting, crying and laughing, resonated in my heart.

We pitched a white tent and sold the few sheep that my brother Wangdrak had managed to purchase during his trading trips. We saw our auntie and some of our cousins that we hadn't seen for almost two years, and we also met a well-dressed man in his late twenties, around the same age as my eldest brother. He was Sonam Wangyal, an old friend of Wangdrak's, and the younger brother of the last lay district commissioner in Namru. He had been schooled in Kalimpong in India when Tibet was still an independent nation and was well educated in both English and Tibetan. He was now working at the settlement as the interpreter at the camp clinic.

Our family had hoped to stop in Pokhara for only a month or so to meet Auntie Pentso and her family. Then we planned to head for India that same winter, so we would reach India before the lethal summer reigned once more. But just before we hoped to set off, news reached us that the border with India had been sealed. Hundreds of Tibetan refugee families had perished. They had been unable to endure the heat and were easy prey for the diseases that swarmed in the warm lowlands. We decided to postpone our planned journey until the next winter.

After our family decided to join the settlement we had to register our names, the names of our parents and our dates of birth. We had no idea about our birth dates as it wasn't considered very important back in Tibet. We only managed to work out a rough estimate by attempting to convert the Tibetan calendar years into Western years. We were then assigned a number and given a small round metal plate with this number inscribed on it. We had to wear this plate around our necks all the time to show that we belonged to the settlement, and we had to produce it, along with our ration cards, once a week to receive the burghul wheat and beans which were 'donated by America'.

After joining the settlement our family was assigned a bamboo-mat hut, which we moved into from our cloth tent. As camp members the women had to spin wool and the men and the older children were sent to log trees in the nearby forests. I spent about a month helping to cut down trees and bring the wood back to the settlement. During those days there was another boy my age who ran about and played in the woods as we worked. His name was Karma Tsewang Tenzin and he later became a very good friend of mine.

Not long after, I was told that I could enter the settlement school and was overwhelmed with joy. I would no longer have to enviously watch the schoolchildren play and listen to them study. I would become one of them. I could now fulfil my father's hopes.

On the morning of my first day at school, my brother cut my hair with a large pair of scissors. He had been told by the schoolteachers to send the younger children to school looking neat and tidy, and he unsuccessfully attempted to cut my hair in a proper 'Bengali' style. From a distance my hair looked as if someone had put a large bowl on my head and had, rather messily, cut off all the hair not covered by the bowl. Gyatso also got a similar haircut, and we both got a brand new pair of hand-made trousers. Wangdrak and Ani Tenzin Choedon had laughed as they cut the material and sewed the trousers the previous night. I did not know then that they were laughing because they did not know how to sew trousers properly. The trousers looked rather like a large shirt, into the sleeves of which I inserted my legs. I must have looked very comical as I stood there, looking proud in my new, very awkward-looking trousers.

That day in early 1963, I led a group of six consisting of my-self, my two younger siblings, my niece Dolkar, her younger sister Urgyen and their youngest brother Guru. I was about fourteen years old then and as I stepped into the school, I remembered the words my father had spoken to us on that sad evening in Mustang.

'Those who have the precious quality of being learned need no home to protect them. Such a person is revered more in the land of others than in one's own home. One who has such quality need not strive for wealth. For being learned will bring wealth,' he had said.

The camp school was a long bamboo-mat hut that was partitioned into classrooms by bamboo-mat walls. There was no furniture in the classrooms except for a blackboard and a stool for the teacher. Everyone used to sit cross-legged on bamboo mats on the bare ground. Occasionally some classes were also held outdoors.

I was put into year one despite my age and I was slightly disappointed. I had come prepared to learn new things but my classmates were just beginning to learn the English and Tibetan alphabets, and some basic mathematics. I had already learnt the English alphabet and quite a few words, had known the *ka kha*, the Tibetan alphabet, ever since I was six and could read fluently and write well.

After the first day at the school, the teachers found out that I already knew most of what was being taught. So, whenever they were unable to teach for any reason, they would ask me to lead the class. For the first few days, whenever I had to stand up and walk to the front to lead the recitals or to write things on the board, the other children would start giggling. They found my trousers and my hairstyle very funny. The embarrassment I felt was overshadowed by my determination. I used to say to myself, 'They might be laughing at me now, but I will study even harder.'

I studied before the first morning bird sang her first song and late into the night. Every evening I used to beg my older sisters for a little bit of soya oil which I then poured into the middle of a plate. I would tear a small piece from the cloth sacks we received the wheat burgers in, twist it and then dip half of it in the soya oil. Then I would light the other end. This crude lamp lasted for quite a while and radiated just enough light for me to read my school texts and other books. Then when this lamp had burnt out I would carefully put my book down beside me, pull my old chupa over myself and go to sleep on a bamboo mat.

Most of the refugees, including our family, found that the food aid that we received didn't agree with us. Everyone grew weak suffering from diarrhoea and as winter thawed many refugees died. Wabu, my late sister's husband, became very ill with dysentery about four months after arriving at Pokhara and died soon after. He was in his late thirties at the time and we were all extremely grieved. Wabu had always been the sturdy one in our family — the hardy drogpa who collected the salt from the northern salt lakes and traded it in the southern markets. The one who brought back presents for all without differentiating between his own children and the rest of us. A quiet man who could not utter a single word apart from what he believed. His children, whom we thought of as our siblings, had now lost their father as well as their mother, my late sister Pendon. They must have felt an even greater loss than us.

Only a month or so after Wabu's death my mother became very sick. She was also suffering from acute dysentery, so soon after Wabu's sudden departure. We were all very worried about our mother. Every day as we walked back from school we feared that mother might have already passed away. And each day we found her alive, barely, and growing weaker and weaker; the dysentery was intensifying its hold on her. Soon she was so ill that she couldn't even recognise us. As she lay there with severe fever causing her to hallucinate, she repeatedly asked my older siblings, 'How are my children doing? Are Chope and Gyatso studying well?'

After hearing my mother, my resolve to study as well as I could became even more intense. One morning, about a week after she had become critically ill, my mother Choedon died. She was only forty-nine. The central fire, whose warm love had drawn our whole family together, was gone. Her sweet prayer songs would never again wake us up in the mornings. We would never again hear her stories about her family or feel her weathered hands wiping the tears from our eyes. Her warm embrace always put a smile on our faces, even during the harshest Chang-Thang winters. But when she had become weak we had been unable to do anything. We were condemned to helplessly watch her slip away from us. Once again we brought out the brave-faced masks and put them on. But in private we all knew that none of us could bear it. Except for Wangdrak, we were too powerless to hold back the tears that streamed from our eyes.

Despite the tremendous loneliness that we felt, this was not the prominent concern. As is the case with most Tibetans, the greatest concern we endured was for our dear mother's consciousness, which would be driven by the winds of her own karma to another life. Thus there was a glimmer of happiness, or at least consolation, in the fact that our mother had died in freedom rather than under the rule of sinful hands, invaders who called religion 'poison'.

We did not go to school that day. Ani Tenzin Choedon, brother Wangdrak and sister Lhamo burned lamps and called the very humble but well-respected Kanjam Lama to commence the phowa and other pujas. The lama and some of his monks carried out the prayers for the whole of that day and for a few days afterwards. And so as to live up to our parents' hopes and wishes, we attended school the following day. We did not want to waste another day in our pursuit to become learned.

During the morning break that next day, Gyatso and I walked about together, quite aimlessly. Neither of us felt like playing and running around with our friends. When I started to cry a little Gyatso also began to sob. As we were crying in a corner of the playground, one of my friends Chimae Tsewang and his little brother Sherab Lhawang came to console us. Our two families were very similar. They had a wonderful mother and a very intelligent and caring older brother, very much like our brother Wangdrak. They also had a kind and loving sister, just like our sister Lhamo. Searching his pocket, Chimae Tsewang pulled out a fifty-paisa coin and gave it to us. For us refugee children this was quite a decent amount, but it was not the purchasing power that was so moving, it was the act of giving to show their empathy with our loss. It was the melancholy look of genuine sympathy in the eyes of the two brothers as they gave the little silvery coin that we found so touching and helpful. They really made the day a little easier to scrape through.

A few months later Chimae Tsewang and Sherab Lhawang's mother passed away. Now it was our time to do the consoling. We gave them some coins, probably twenty-five paisas, just as they had given us, as they stood weeping in a corner of the school. Like ours, their mother was not old. I recalled that back in Tibet most people lived years past their middle ages, many surviving to the ripe old ages of eighty, ninety and even to over a hundred. Here in exile there did not seem to be much hope of surviving till one turned fifty, although our grandmother Mo Rinchen was still alive at the time. It seemed that loved ones were pulled away randomly. And in this game, neither age nor background mattered.

As the weeks and the mourning period passed, our grief did not subside. Even for a number of years following mother's death, we could never enjoy large gatherings. Every time we had to attend a community gathering, they felt more like tribulations rather than the celebrations they usually were. If we achieved something outstanding, there was no one we could share the precious news with. If we were suffering, there was no one in the crowd who would wipe the tears from our cheeks the way mother used to. We all wanted to be alone.

My brothers Jami and Jignam left to work in Kathmandu. Jami soon became a very talented cook at an established restaurant, and after a while Jignam also became an assistant cook at another restaurant. Following mother's passing away, Ani Tenzin Choedon went on a retreat for many months in a small bamboo hut attached to our family hut. During her retreat she carried out a series of pujas and fasted, and this was believed to be especially effective for relieving the fears and sufferings of the consciousness of the deceased person. It is thought that this could help the deceased person to a good rebirth, or even help the consciousness of the deceased to take rebirth in the pure land of the Buddha Amitabha which is beyond worldly existence.

Even though Wangdrak, Ani Tenzin Choedon and Lhamo were very kind and caring, I felt as if there was no one to return to after school. So I stayed away, studying on the hilltops with friends or running around with them, playing games. At least this took my mind off my memories.

The loss of my mother changed me deeply. For the first time in my life, I no longer wanted to think, I just wanted to run about and play and forget about everything. My thoughts criticised everything I came across. Understandably I hated the Chinese, who I believed had been the real source of all of my misery. But I even began to doubt the validity of certain religious practices. When my parents, Wabu, sister Pendon, or my little sister or nephew became ill, no amount of prayer or faith in the rituals and deities seemed to prevent their death. So what was the use of the prayers and the faith in the first place? And again, during the times when my parents had been sick, the divinations of the lamas repeatedly said that the protective deities were unhappy. So I became angry with the deities. What was the point of it all, if they didn't help us when we were weak and helpless?

I was unable to draw a distinction between the divinations and the deities, and the true Buddhist teachings of the law of karma and compassion. I was unaware that Buddhism was about interdependence and non-violence, rather than about worldly deities and spirits.

Despite my dissatisfaction and doubts, I still held my conviction in the Buddha and I still took part in the prayer sessions at school. I also read the old Tibetan books our family owned, as my parents had advised me to. While I read those books a true admiration blossomed within me and I felt that they could really make me a better person. During those days, there was a constant struggle taking place on the battlefield of my mind. A new part of me had emerged from a dark corner of my heart, the prodigy of tremendous loss and suffering. This part of me was engaged in a violent conflict with that which had been nurtured by the love and kindness of my parents and others. Both parts emphasised the necessity to become learned but they had very different motivations.

As I continued in school I kept up my relentless studies. Within two years I was promoted from year one to year six, the top class at the school. I was among the first batch of ten who were soon to be coached to take the School Leaving Certificate (SLC) exams. The SLC is the standard school graduation exam for year ten students in Nepal. If I had been able to take the SLC exams, I would have been among the first Tibetan refugee children to take the SLC exams in the Nepalese education system.

Despite my inner struggles, for the most part I managed to stick to the Tibetan ideals of being *yarab*, for which there is hardly any English equivalent. Being yarab includes, at the least, refraining from harming others and if possible, being kind and helpful. At the same time, one must have etiquette and humility. Thus, I quickly gained respect and friendship from most of my fellow students. I even gained a certain amount of respect from the teachers who made me the school prefect. I was very confident about my learning potential and believed I could handle any new knowledge that came my way. I really loved my time at school. It became an escape from the troubles in my mind, as well as a means through which I could fulfil the wishes of my parents.

At the time, the head of our settlement was a very kind Swiss man by the name of Schnurrenberger whom we called 'Sahib'. He truly cared about the plight of the Tibetans and was committed to the betterment of our education. Whenever he returned from Switzerland, he would bring back toys and books for the children to read and play with. In the evenings he would work untiringly, loudly typing on his typewriter as the Tibetan children shouted, giggled and sobbed as they played with the toys.

There must have been over forty children in the house each evening but I had been too embarrassed to go there. I only started going there regularly when the Sahib began to encourage and teach some of us older children to draw and paint. He also gave us some of his typed-up calculations to check from time to time. Then he would give us ten or fifteen rupees for checking his calculations. He really made the children of the settlement feel happier and useful.

As the prefect, it was my duty to blow a whistle at around half past five each morning — to call all the school children for the morning exercise session. Early one morning, I was woken up by a voice calling, 'Chope … Chope.' I opened the door to find a teacher looking troubled in the dawn's faint light. 'Don't blow the whistle today,' said the teacher, 'We will have to have a holiday.'

I was too sleepy to ask why so I went back to bed, drowsily satisfied that I would have some more sleep. I got up again well after the morning had brightened and warmed. I washed my face and stepped out into the sun. I was surprised to find the whole settlement outside, clustered in small groups.

'Oh dear, whatever shall we do?' some of them were asking.

Suddenly my heart stopped and my body froze. For a moment, I feared the unthinkable had happened. I tried to convince myself that something couldn't have happened to His Holiness, but I grew extremely anxious. I thought only something like that could cause such a reaction among the people. I rushed to the nearest group and asked them what had happened.

'What … you don't already know!' they exclaimed. 'The Sahib died last night.'

My initial reaction was relief. Then the sadness sank in. Yet another person whom I respected and held dear had died. The Sahib's hobby had been to collect snakes, and a very poisonous snake had bitten him while he was trying to pick it up.

The replacement Camp-in-Charge the Swiss Red Cross sent was a young hippie-like man in his twenties. He was a Peruvian with British citizenship. His name was Frank Baker. At first, it was quite hard to believe that this man was the replacement for Schnurrenberger. Frank Baker looked rather messy with his long, brown hair and hairy face. He was not tall either, whereas Schnurrenberger had been tall, bald and always looked organised. Frank Baker claimed to be a Buddhist, which must have made the Swiss interviewers in Kathmandu think him more suitable for the job than other applicants. Indeed, he must have had prior contact with Tibetans since he pronounced himself to be a follower of the Karmapa. He used to carry a spotted animal skin, perhaps a deer skin, with him wherever he went. He claimed this to be his meditation mat and he would often sit on it with his eyes closed.

Under Frank Baker the camp became increasingly disorderly. None of the children ever went to his house after school and he did nothing to encourage or teach us older ones, as our old Sahib had done. But still, Frank Baker would have a huge impact on my own education. A few months after he had taken charge a so-called 'drawing exam' was held. All of us tried our best in the exam and only later did we learn that the 'exam' had a different purpose. Whoever came first had to go and learn to become a silversmith. I had come first and I was devastated. This bearded man had so much power over our fate and was destroying my only hope and my only opportunity to fulfil my parents' wishes.

I cried and begged him to let me stay in the school when I was called to his office a few days later. Not only was I the school prefect, I was coming first in almost all of the subjects. He told me that I was too old to continue studying at a school. I was sixteen years old. I said that I would refuse to become an apprentice silversmith.

'If you do that, I will have to expel your whole family from the settlement,' he threatened. I did not reply. I was trapped and powerless. We had nowhere else to go and I couldn't ruin my younger relatives' chance of an education. How ashamed I would be if my family were expelled because of me. Frank Baker repeated this threat at a community meeting, 'Anyone who doesn't want to carry on one's own traditional arts deserve to be expelled from the settlement.'

Every day as the school bell rang I became miserable. I no longer wanted to comb my hair or keep myself clean. All of the roads to becoming learned and living up to the hopes of my parents had been blocked. All of the lamps under which my talents could shine were covered. Even when my parents had died, determination had not failed me. Now I had nothing. I began to smoke cheap cigarettes frequently. By today's standards, I would be considered an addict, and some days I would smoke as much as I could on purpose, hoping to find an escape from the situation.

Even though the skills of a silversmith were not the ones I truly wanted, I made sure I learnt everything the silversmith was teaching. The first items I made on my own were a brass spoon and a brass ring, decorated with a few intricate carvings. I gave the brass spoon to Auntie Pentso and the ring to sister Lhamo. They were very impressed with my craftsmanship and on the inside I was happy with my work. However, outwardly, I was completely unco-operative with my teacher. After a few months at the silversmith's, word about my lack of co-operation and my unhappiness must have been reported to Frank Baker. He decided that I would be allowed to go to school for half a day if I worked at the silversmith's for the other half.

One of the most memorable days of my life happened during this period. The Representative of His Holiness the Dalai Lama for Nepal (the de facto Tibetan Ambassador responsible for the welfare of the Tibetan community), and His Holiness the Dalai Lama's brother-in-law (a minister in the Tibetan Cabinet whom we referred to as Kungo Depon) visited our settlement. This was a most important visit by high-ranking Tibetan officials, and a wonderful opportunity for our community to show our talents and to share any worries or grievances. That day, we were all attending a class out in the open when the two officials stopped by.

'Are you all studying well?' Kungo Depon asked.

'We heard that you all did very well in the exam this year. Who came first?' asked the Representative.

My cheeks grew warm with embarrassment as I thought I would have to get up in front of everyone. But at the same time I was proud of what I had achieved. I topped the exam although I had missed much of the year, and even now I was only allowed to attend half a day of school. I was also thankful that the question was asked because I thought the officials might help me to attend a better school in India.

A great number of thoughts and feelings surged within me as if they were a thundering avalanche rushing down the white Himalayan slopes. The avalanche fell into a dark pit of shock when the teacher — who was also the headmaster — pointed to the boy who had come second and said, 'It's this boy.' I suppose I was not counted since I was not a full-time student.

I just didn't know what to do. My first instinct was to get up and tell the officials myself, but I realised that this would require enough courage to oppose my teacher in front of everyone. Even if I managed to do that, the officials would probably not believe me and I would just make a fool of myself. I just did not have the guts to speak in front of crowds let alone to speak to such important dignitaries.

That winter, anger and disappointment at my own weakness and the lack of integrity of others ate into my skin and kept me cold during the long nights. I was unhappy and could see my life wasting away as I watched on helplessly. My brother Wang-drak had gone north to carry out some business and did not return for many months. Our straw home felt empty. Without mother there seemed nothing to keep me home.

I wanted to run away — from the camp and Frank Baker whom I felt was holding me hostage. If I could somehow reach

Many families relied on relief aid. Tibetan children at one of the Tibetan settlements in Pokhara, Nepal, early 1960s.

Tibetan refugee children, Tibetan settlement, Pokhara, Nepal, early 1960s.

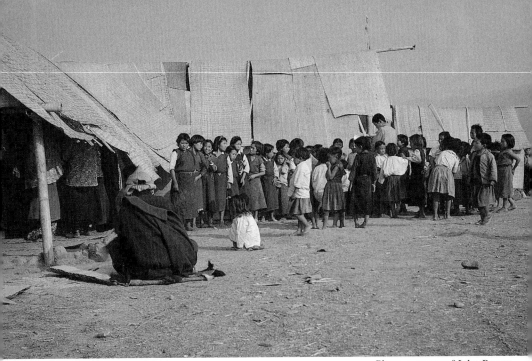

Tibetan settlement, Pokhara,
Nepal, early 1960s.

From left to right: Jignam, Chope, Wangdrak and a cousin, Nepal, 1963.

Chope attended the Eastbourne College and the
Eastbourne School of English, England, from 1968:
Chope (left) with two women from the society that
helped sponsor him, Roger Catchpole (centre),
and Karma (right).

Palden pregnant with their first child in Dhorpaten, Nepal, 1976. She is wearing a traditional Tibetan chupa, and a cardigan.

Palden with baby Tenzin Samdrup, Dhorpaten, Nepal, 1977.

India I would be accepted into one of the Tibetan government schools. Even if I was not accepted, I would be able to join the Dehradun Tibetan unit of the Indian Army. That way, I thought I would learn some military skills and somehow become the commander. Even if I died fighting, it would be more honourable than to waste my life in idle bitterness.

I often used to ask sister Lhamo, whether she and Ani Tenzin Choedon would be upset if I ran away. She would always reply, 'Never do that, Chope. We would be more than upset. Where would you go?'

Soon after, I received a letter from Wangdrak. I was very happy to have received it as he had been away for so long. He had become very ill and had to rest in a Tibetan settlement in northern Nepal called Dhorpaten. I don't know whether he'd heard about my inklings to run off, or whether the bond between two brothers had betrayed my plans, but he wrote saying, 'Chope, please abandon any plans to run away; whether it be to the Dehra Dun barracks or to other places in India. I asked Tahru Rinpoche (a very revered lama) to perform a divination and it advised that the future was bright if you stayed put.'

Not again! I thought. Divinations are again going to stop me from taking action. Bright future? How could there be any future here, I thought. Divinations and deities are going to be yet another reason for inaction. I felt pathetic. I was sick of life at Tashi Palkhiel. I believed with complete conviction that my life could be more useful elsewhere. But at the same time, I could never disrespect the words of my brother, Ani Tenzin Choedon and sister Lhamo. They had borne the hardest edges of our life so that the rest of us could fare a little better. They had carried the heavy loads, gone without food and stayed awake all night — all for us younger ones. How could I ever ignore them and set off on my own. That would be against the very values of karma that my parents had taught us: that one must see and value the kindness of others and return the kindness in whatever way one can.

A month or so later Frank Baker called me into his office, his face as bushy as ever. He had a new 'offer' for me.

'We need someone to go down to the airport on a couple of afternoons each week and record all the loads of aid that you refugees receive. Then the loads have to be assigned to individual Tibetans who will carry them back to the camp. The loads must be reported back to me when they arrive here. If you will agree to do this job then I will allow you to continue coming to school for half a day.'

I agreed. I didn't really have a choice. The work wasn't hard and I had most afternoons to do other things. Soon, some of the teachers wanted me to help teach at the school. I willingly obliged. I wanted to teach. I wanted to help make the younger children's futures brighter than mine. On my free afternoons I taught English, mathematics and geography to the lower classes and my students were only a few years younger than me. At the time an American Peace Corps volunteer by the name of Peter Thompson was helping at our camp. Because he was an independent volunteer he was free to teach anyone anything without obtaining Frank Baker's permission. I asked him to teach me some geography and he kindly agreed. Each day, in the mornings before school began or in the evenings after school, he would teach me on my own for about an hour. I really enjoyed those classes. Then when school started I studied with my class for the morning and then taught what I had learnt with Peter to some of the lower classes in the afternoon.

An education

Soon I heard that new evening classes for adults were being set up and that older students were required to teach those classes. I immediately volunteered and was chosen for the task along with a few others. I had found something that I could truly enjoy. It felt as though I achieved something enormously rewarding every time I was able to teach something new to the adults in our community. In those classes, I learnt that it was never too late to learn. Most of the adults were very keen and hungry to know more. Even the oldest had not lost their ability to learn.

16

The three Englishmen

As I was teaching one of the evening classes Frank Baker walked in. A cold sweat ran down my neck and made me freeze up. Three young Englishmen followed him into the classroom. To my relief Frank Baker did not speak to me. He just spoke with the three gentlemen while I taught my class of chupa-wearing, long-haired adults.

The next morning I was called to Frank Baker's office. My relief the evening before had been premature.

'You saw the three Englishmen yesterday evening?' he asked.

'I did,' I replied.

'They require a servant and they are likely to teach you new things. Will you go with them?'

'If they can help me improve my English and teach me other modern knowledge, I will go. Otherwise, I am happy with the present arrangements.'

'Then you will go. I will introduce you to them.' He paused, then added, 'If you go now and are unhappy with them, then I will send you to a college when you come back after a few months.'

'I will go and talk with them,' I said.

The following day I met them at the Annapurna Hotel and I learnt that their names were John Pearce, Roger Catchpole and David McPherson. The three had met His Holiness the Dalai Lama's sister, Jetsun Pema, at the Pestalozzi Children's Village in Sussex, UK, and she had suggested that they go to India or Nepal to help the Tibetans. They had then asked the United Nations High Commissioner for Refugees (UNHCR) to help them with their plan. The UNHCR had arranged for them to go as volunteers to work as a resettlement field team for the Nepal Red Cross. The three had then been sent to Pokhara to work with the Tibetans in the camp at the end of the airfield, known as the Pardi camp. This camp consisted of fifty or so bamboo-mat huts and was growing at a rather quick pace with the steady arrival of new refugees.

The three young Englishmen explained why they had come and asked me to go to the camp and draw a map of it as my first task. They all seemed sincere about their plans, so I went to the camp and drew the map as well as I could. When I took it back to the three Englishmen, they seemed happy with it. I made it clear to them that I had come because Frank Baker had said that they would teach me English and other things. They agreed to do so and I became their interpreter. In the evenings they would teach me English and I would also receive food and a decent salary of a hundred rupees per month, half of which they would save for me.

Soon we moved into a bamboo-mat hut built for us in the camp. The hut consisted of a cooking area, a common dining area, a bedroom for Roger, David and John, and a smaller one for my old friend Dhondup and I. Contrary to what Frank Baker had said, I was not going to be their servant or cook. Indeed, the three young men had never asked Frank Baker for a servant at all. But since we needed a cook I suggested that Dhondup, who had also moved from Jomsom to Pokhara, be invited. He accepted and moved into the hut with us.

For Dhondup and I, this was a life of relative luxury. We had our own little room and there was always food and money to buy clothes. But for my new English friends who had recently graduated from Cambridge University, this lifestyle must have been hard. This was in stark contrast to the lifestyle of Frank Baker and his predecessors at the Tashi Palkhiel camp. And this difference was partly due to the fact that my young English friends were on an adventure to help us Tibetans as volunteers. The Swiss appointees in Tashi Palkhiel were well-paid employees with great authority, representing a large international organisation.

I began to really enjoy the work with the trio even though I constantly worried that I lacked the English and Nepalese language skills to do the job satisfactorily. I felt as though I was part of something useful, something that could help my fellow Tibetans, and speaking with the three each day improved my English considerably. But after about a month or so there was just not enough time for my lessons. I had to get up at dawn when John and I, together with Penjung, the Pardi camp community leader, had to list all the Tibetan labourers who were going to work that day. Some labourers worked on the road that was being built between Nepal and India; others were employed at the construction site of the permanent settlement that was being built for them to move into.

Straight after breakfast I then had to go with David to the community clinic and help interpret there. After this I would help John while he organised and supervised the making of community handicrafts, and occasionally I helped Roger who concentrated on the settlement school. On top of all this I had to interpret during the meetings between the local community and David, Roger or John. My work only finished at dusk, by which time we were all too tired to hold the lessons. I also wanted some time to drink and gamble on domino games — a legacy of my anger after being expelled from school.

After my first month working with John, Roger and David, I received my first wage ever and was delighted to get the fifty rupees in cash. That weekend I went back to my home in Tashi Palkhiel, took the money and gave it all to brother Wangdrak, who had the hard time of trying to make ends meet for all of our siblings.

He smiled at me lovingly and said, 'There is no need to give it to me, you should keep it. The rest of us are fine. If you have any money left over and we need some, we will tell you.'

'There is a saying,' he continued, 'In the land of enemies, never trade life for sleep, in the land of friends, never trade your good reputation for ragged clothes … Why don't you go and buy yourself some new clothes? Wear better, cleaner clothes. Appearance cannot be neglected when one has to work within a society.'

Heeding my brother's advice I bought myself some new clothes and from that day I always had decent clothes to wear. Back then, everything was much cheaper. I could buy a good pair of trousers for twenty-five rupees and a proper shirt for perhaps ten rupees. By the 1990s a similar pair of trousers cost around two hundred rupees and a comparable shirt was about a hundred and fifty rupees.

Every evening there was a prayer session in the open space in the centre of the Pardi camp. There, after the prayers, the people would talk about their experiences in Tibet during the Chinese occupation. Many Tibetans had been beaten and killed. Some died after being forced to spend the coldest of Tibetan winter days and nights outside, kneeling on snow and ice with hardly any clothes on. Others were hung in the air from their hands, which were tied behind their backs. Their only crime was being a leader, slightly rich or resisting the Chinese occupation.

One tale that haunted me repeatedly was the story of an admired, respected and reportedly eloquent local village leader from a region in western Tibet. His name was Karchung. The camp-dwellers talked of how he had resisted the Chinese invasion courageously. When he was finally captured he was subjected to inconceivably inhumane torture. The torturers are said to have inserted small sticks underneath his finger- and toenails and even bits of his skin were said to have been cut off as he was interrogated. There were rumours that in the end Karchung had died after being skinned alive. This tale always made me shudder with pity, sadness and anger.

I used to listen to the Chinese radio broadcasts in Tibetan from Lhasa, on the wireless which John, Roger and David owned and which they used to listen to the BBC. It was almost amusing to hear the difference between the Chinese account of everything and the account of the Tibetan refugees. Every day the radio blurted out how happy the Tibetan people were after being liberated and how the Tibetan people had welcomed the People's Liberation Army with open arms. According to these news broadcasts, His Holiness the Dalai Lama and the Tibetan government were the real enemies, and the Chinese were the heroic liberators of the Tibetan people. We were meant to be grateful towards the Chinese. At first, these broadcasts unsettled me. But after a while I was so used to the propaganda that I learnt to either ignore it altogether, and only listen to the Tibetan songs they played, or to laugh at the shamelessness of these claims. They were telling complete lies — sometimes the exact opposite of what was really happening — to a world which I assumed knew that they were lies.

Saturdays were my holidays and I used to go back to my family in Tashi Palkhiel late on Fridays. I returned to the Pardi camp very early on Sunday morning or late on Saturday. It was a walk of around three-quarters of an hour each way between the two settlements. As the months passed by, I grew close to the three Englishmen and they began to feel like my English brothers. From time to time, one of them, Roger in particular, would come with me to my home in Tashi Palkhiel on Friday evenings.

One Friday evening, around seven months after I had begun working as an interpreter, Roger came to Tashi Palkhiel with me and Dhondup. There he bought hens for an experimental chicken farm that was going to be set up in the Pardi camp. Later that evening I met Dhondup who said, 'Roger told me that because we have to carry all the hens back, we don't have to return early in the morning.'

'That's great!' I replied, and that night I stayed up late, gambling, singing and drinking in the local Tibetan inn. On the Sunday morning I got up later than usual, well after sunrise. Dhondup and I set off together on a couple of bicycles with the poor hens hanging off our handlebars, arriving at the Pardi camp at around ten o'clock in the morning. To my surprise, I found Roger very angry. There must have been a misunderstanding between what Roger had said and what Dhondup thought he had said. Indeed, Dhondup's and my English was far from impeccable. Roger went on for quite a while, and when we met David and John, they were equally upset with us.

I was also very upset. I thought it completely unfair that Dhondup and I were being told off. We had returned carrying all the hens and our friends were still very angry with us for just one little misunderstanding.

'All these *inji* (English or Western) sahibs are the same. Frank Baker had expelled me from school. Now these injis are so angry about such a small matter,' I thought to myself.

'Let's go,' I said to Dhondup. 'We won't just accept such unfairness.'

We packed up all our belongings — a blanket each — and went to a little restaurant that a distant uncle ran close to the Pardi camp. Just as we were settling ourselves we saw Frank Baker riding a horse towards the restaurant. He halted, dismounted and walked in. He looked at us and sat himself on a nearby wooden bench and then said, 'Chope and Dhondup, you cannot return to Tashi Palkhiel. You have to stay here and help the three Englishmen.'

'Why can't I return?' I asked. 'You told me yourself that I could return if I stayed with the Englishmen for a few months. What's more, you said you would send me to a college when I do so,' I reminded him.

'If you stay here another three months then I will really send you to a college or to receive some other further education or training,' he said, 'If you don't, then I will definitely expel your whole family from my camp.'

The same threat, how many times was he going to use it? I had no answer. He held the power — I was just an orphan refugee boy who had nothing. I was determined not to return to work for my English friends. But Uncle Tamding, the wrestling and weight-lifting champion back in Namru, persuaded me to stay on.

'Chope, you only have to stay on for three more months and then Frank Baker has already said that you will be sent for further education. If he doesn't keep his promise I will speak out for you as a witness to his promise today. If you don't stay, don't forget the consequences for your family.'

Sadness and anger mingled and boiled in my mind for many

days. But I stayed on and so did Dhondup. He was willing to go along with whatever I decided. I demanded definite working hours from my English friends and for the next couple of weeks I worked as usual. But apart from the interpretations I carried out I hardly spoke a word to any of the three. At six o'clock each evening, I stopped whatever work I was doing and went back to the hut and slept and squandered my life. Other times I went to the bar and drank and gambled on domino games. These felt like the most interesting things to do to escape from a hostile world, and life again seemed meaningless.

One evening in our hut, I was sitting on a bench near Dhondup as he cooked. Roger walked into the kitchen area and sat beside me. All three of us were uneasy. I had not felt comfortable with Roger, John or David since that day I had been told off. Roger looked at me for a while.

'Chope …' he said gently. 'Why have you been so unhappy for the last couple of weeks? Is there anything we can do to help you?'

Roger meant what he said, he really wanted to help me and I could see it. I had also known him for long enough to see that he was a good-hearted man, sensitive towards the sorrow of others.

I did not want to speak, I still didn't think he would understand me. Besides, I did not even think I could put all that was in my mind into a foreign language. But I decided to give it a go. As I released all of my grief, tears ran freely down my cheeks.

'I don't have a country. I don't have my parents. What I need is education and I don't have the opportunity to receive schooling,' I sobbed.

'For being late just once, I was scolded so harshly. Now, if I want to return home to my siblings, I can't. If I do, Frank Baker will expel my whole family from Tashi Palkhiel. I have nowhere to go.'

Roger was listening closely to each of my words.

'I work from morning until night and I don't learn anything. Now what's the point of my life?'

I could feel his sympathy. He now really understood my dilemma. Through my own watery lenses I could see teardrops escape Roger's big eyes.

'What can we do to help you, Chope?' he asked.

'What I need is education. The opportunity to become learned,' I answered.

'If we can help you come to England to study after we go back, then will you be happier? Will you be able to be your old self again?'

'Of course I would. But how can I be sure you will be able to do that?'

'There must be a way ...' he said, thinking out loud. 'I will discuss it with John and David.'

The next morning Roger smiled at me and said, 'I think there is a way. We may only be here for less than a year, so after we get back to England, we will try to help you come over.'

Later on, I signed an agreement with Roger and Mr Sonam Wangchuk, the Tibetan government representative responsible for Tibetan settlements in western Nepal. This outlined that John and Roger would help me further my studies and that I would offer my services to the Tashi Ling community. Soon, we were all good friends again, just as we had been before that troubled Sunday. I began to enjoy my work again.

A few weeks later my brother Wangdrak came to see me as he often did. I had some spare time and we walked together to the nearby Pokhara airport. There we bought some mandarins and peanuts while we rested under the warm sun. We chatted for a while as we finished our snacks. Then as he got up to head back to Tashi Palkhiel an aeroplane boomed down onto the runway. This seemed to remind him of something.

'If there is anyone going to Kathmandu, could you let me know, I need to send some *ngoden* money with them, for Tahru Rinpoche and Dhabsang Rinpoche,' he said. Ngoden is a donation to a lama for performing prayers for the sake of a deceased person. I was slightly startled, I didn't know that anyone had died recently.

'Who is the ngoden for?' I asked.

'Oh, I am so sorry, I thought you knew. Because you didn't return home on the weekend, you must not have heard.'

Brother seemed quite surprised that I did not know what he was talking about. Then brother's voice grew a little quieter, 'Our Mo died,' he said.

I could not believe it. Our grandmother, Mo Rinchen, had died and I didn't even know about it. She had grown quiet with age in the last year or so. In stark contrast to earlier days, she had become very peaceful and contented. Sometimes, when I had gone home during the weekends, I would hardly be aware of her as she peacefully sat on her bed in a corner of our home, reciting mantras or spinning her mani prayer wheel. But despite her recent tranquillity, she had always been there, a warm presence that reminded me of the wonderful days in Tibet. Days when she used to take us onto green hilltops, tell us stories of local deities and make predictions for the future.

'Why didn't you tell me before?' I asked rather angrily. 'Did she become ill?'

'Seemingly not, it seemed as if she just died of old age,' he told me. 'For over a week before she died, Mo Rinchen hardly ate anything. Every meal time she would say, "Thank you very much but I am full. I have just eaten." For a number of days before she died, she kept repeating the conclusion and dedication prayers she used to say at the end of prayers.'

Grandmother Rinchen's death was more bearable than the passing away of my parents. At least she had lived a relatively long life of eighty-five years. Not only was she fortunate enough to have died in freedom, she had grown serene in her old age and had died very peacefully. This is usually considered a rather positive sign for the consciousness of the deceased.

That weekend when I went back home our bamboo hut seemed cleaner and emptier, as if something very important was missing. I learnt that Ani Tenzin Choedon was on retreat again, this time for our grandmother.

I managed to move on after grandmother's passing and contentedly continued my work with my three inji friends. A few months later John was going to go on a holiday to India, the place where our leader, His Holiness the Dalai Lama, was residing. I really wanted to go with John, and as the money my inji friends had saved for me added up to around eight hundred rupees we decided to go together.

John went to Kathmandu ahead of me, but before he left he and Roger gave me a hundred rupees. And on the day of my departure David came to see me off at the small local airport where he gave me a gift of fifty rupees. David also organised a friend of his — an Anglo-Indian pilot — to give me a lift to the capital. At the time, a small DC3 aeroplane transported goods several times each day between Pokhara and Bhairawa, a small city on the Indo–Nepalese border. That evening this plane was heading back to Kathmandu empty-hulled for the night.

I braced myself on a seat behind the cockpit and I watched the airport and the Pokhara region fall far below me as the loud roar of the propellers drove us on. We flew for a while with nothing but the majestic Himalayas on one side and blue sky spotted by the white islands of clouds on the other. Then we descended towards the Kathmandu valley.

After landing, I caught a taxi to the British Embassy where John was staying. I met John there and a friend of his drove me to where Dhondup and another friend Pema were staying. Dhondup had moved down to Kathmandu a few months earlier to study cooking to become a chef. I stayed with Dhondup and Pema for a couple of days.

From there John and I flew to Patna in India, and from Patna we had to travel by train in a third-class carriage to New Delhi. That was the first time I had ever travelled by rail and it wasn't a very pleasant experience at all. The train was hours late and then the carriage that we travelled in was so crowded, humid and uncomfortable that for the next few days I was very unsettled. During the trip, I met a Tibetan spice trader. He had a load of a spice known as *ying* with him. I found the smell of it, a disgusting fragrance not unlike the smell of manure, quite sickening. But the Tibetan trader was very happy about meeting a fellow Tibetan and I did not want to be impolite, so I conversed with him for quite a while. During those hours, the stench of the ying infected me and my clothes and I was unable to escape it until I had a shower and washed my clothes. Even then I was unable to get rid of a bit of the smell for a number of days.

In New Delhi we went on a sightseeing tour of the city. Until then the biggest city I had seen was Kathmandu, so New Delhi seemed immense. From New Delhi we went to Dharamsala in northern India. His Holiness the Dalai Lama and the Tibetan government, now unfortunately in exile, were centred at that hill station. By that time there was quite a sizable community of Tibetan refugees living in Dharamsala.

While in Dharamsala, I stayed with Gen-Jinpa, the old teacher of my older brother Jignam and the student of our old Genla. He was living in a very small, dark room. That very day Gen-Jinpa said, 'As you've come this far, you must at least see His Holiness the Dalai Lama.' So Gen-Jinpa and I managed to join a big crowd of Tibetans who were going to receive an audience with His Holiness. After a few minutes of waiting, as we jostled and stretched our heads — trying to see if His Holiness had appeared, there was a sudden hush and then sobs, tears and spontaneous prostrations surrounded me. I realised that His Holiness had arrived. And then for some time I saw His Holiness between the many heads swaying before me. His Holiness the Dalai Lama was smiling his completely sincere and loving smile, just like in the photos we owned. His Holiness smiled as he talked with some of the people in the front of the crowd. I was very happy to finally have had a glimpse of our true supreme leader and the hope of the six million Tibetans. I couldn't wait to tell Ani, brother Wangdrak, sister Lhamo and the others that I had seen His Holiness. Despite everything, I was struck by the weeping of almost everyone around me, including Gen-Jinpa. I didn't cry at all and I could not understand why they were all crying.

Meanwhile, John had a private audience with His Holiness and went on a camping trip up in the Dhauladhar mountains behind Dharamsala. Soon after, it was time for me and John to leave and I found that I still hadn't used up that much of my money. So before departing I managed to buy a Tibetan shirt and a pair of shoes for my wonderful sister Lhamo, and some other small gifts for other family members. Later I also bought a fine suit for Wangdrak from a Nepalese man.

After having experienced the discomfort of the third-class

carriages, we travelled to Lucknow and then to Gorakpur first class. This was the first time I had travelled in such luxury. The fact that I had also experienced the third-class carriages made me realise the vast differences in the lives of the rich and poor in India. From Gorakpur we travelled to Bhairawa on the Indo–Nepalese border. From there, John had to immediately fly off to Kathmandu after learning of his father's passing away. I felt very sorry for my friend. Having lost both of my parents I knew the loss he felt, but coming from a different cultural background, and with my limited command of English, I didn't know how to express my sympathy and condolences.

By the time I returned from India, the building of the new settlement had, by and large, been completed. Soon the community could happily move from their old bamboo-mat huts at the Pardi camp to the village of stone houses named Tashi Ling (Happy Place) by His Holiness the Dalai Lama. Finally, the people of Tashi Ling had proper homes, a school building, a clinic, a restaurant, a shop and a handicraft centre — all owned by the community. This settlement was now the home of around five hundred Tibetan refugees. It would provide a base from where they could preserve their identity, culture, arts and crafts, contribute towards the local economy and raise future generations as Tibetans, until a political solution to the Tibet issue is found.

Soon, it was time for us to farewell David as he was going back to England. It was sad to have to say goodbye to a close friend but I was happy that we would most probably meet again when I went to England. John and Roger stayed on for several more months to carry on projects in the new settlement. I continued working as their interpreter until it was time to bid farewell to

John and Roger as well. It was sad to have to part from them but I was happy that they would be able to return home and be with their families after being away for so long.

The people of Tashi Ling were also sad to see David, John and Roger go, and everyone was very grateful for their sincerity, kindness and friendship. I knew then that our friendship would be for life. They had worked from dawn till late into the evening for the people of the settlement. They discussed and argued among themselves in the evenings for the betterment of the living conditions of the people of Tashi Ling. They had achieved much in a relatively short time against so many odds. I was happy to have been able to make my own little contribution as a link between my inji friends and my Tibetan community, who on their part had kept their hopes and spirits high in all circumstances.

Young Tibetans who had studied abroad came to take over from John, Roger and David to help the people of the settlement, and I started work as a teacher at the Tashi Ling school, teaching Tibetan, maths, English and Nepalese. I enjoyed this work while I waited for about seven or eight months for John, Roger and David to finalise plans for me with the UNHCR to go to England.

Then one day we received a letter from Roger. It said that another boy could also be sent along with me. The conditions were that the boy should be from Tashi Palkhiel, so that the two of us could represent both settlements. The individual had to be willing to return to Tashi Palkhiel to work for the community after his time in England and he had to get along with me, as we would have to spend at least a year together in England. There were a number of possible candidates, but Karma Tsewang Tenzin was chosen by the settlement. I was happy that a very good friend of mine was selected.

Within a couple of months we had to set off for Kathmandu.

I said my farewells to my family and friends. Brother Wangdrak and my cousin Ami came to see me off at the Pokhara airport. Karma and I stayed for over a week in Kathmandu, in a room in the Representative's compound as our travel documents were being prepared.

At the time, a very kind man by the name of T. R. Onta was helping us prepare for our trip. He was the Tibetan Refugee Section Officer for the Nepal Red Cross. After a few days, Mr Onta took us to collect the one-page travel documents that would serve as our passports from the Nepalese government. From there, we went straight to the British Embassy to apply for a British visa. We had received the documents in an envelope, which we only opened just before reaching the British Embassy. To my horror the travel document stated that I was from 'The Tibetan Region of the People's Republic of China'. I was shocked.

I did not understand how complex and often dirty international politics was. I just couldn't believe that governments would lie so blatantly. I had read Nepalese history books and knew of many events that showed how Tibet had been an independent country for thousands of years. I had read how the Nepalese princess Brikuti had married the Tibetan king Songtsen Gampo during the seventh century. The books also included more recent histories of how the Nepalese had fought victorious battles against Tibet during the nineteenth century, and of the war indemnity of several hundred yak tails and silver coins they received annually. In fact, I have since met an old Tibetan official who had been to Kathmandu to make the payments as late as 1950.

'I'm not going with this document,' I said.

'I am a Tibetan, not a Chinese, why did the Nepalese government write down that I was Chinese? I won't go if I have to go as a Chinese!'

The truth was that Tibet was never a part of China and I

have never been Chinese. How could I identify myself with those who had robbed our land and suppressed our people?

Mr Onta looked straight at me and said calmly, 'You cannot change the policy of the Nepalese government. Now think carefully, and decide whether you want to waste this solitary opportunity. If you can't decide, consult the Representative of the Tibetan government in Kathmandu.'

I had made up my mind not to go, but after hearing Onta Sahib's words I realised that the decision should not be made so hastily. So we went to the Representative, Mr Serga, for his advice. It was extremely difficult for me to show the document to the Representative: the document which stated that Tibet was a Chinese region, right under my name. Now when I actually had the opportunity to pursue my goals, I would have to be identified as Chinese. It felt as though I was betraying myself, my country and my people.

I explained my predicament to the huge and very dominating Representative, who then looked at the document and sighed. Then he called in one of his secretaries who made a number of phone calls to Nepalese government offices. In the end we learnt that the document could not be changed. I was quite devastated.

'If I can't go as the Tibetan I am, I will not go,' I said, meaning each of my words.

'You should go,' advised the Representative in a consoling voice, 'You know you are a Tibetan and not a Chinese, now don't throw away this opportunity for further training in England.'

After more heavy sighs and more reflection, I decided to heed the advice of Onta Sahib and Mr Serga, but not without some doubts as to whether I was making the right decision. In the end, Karma and I applied for the British visa. The visa was granted the next day when we went with Onta Sahib to the British Embassy. Now, I was ready to set off for England.

17

Studying the world

Karma and I stepped off the plane with nothing but a small bag each. It was 18 August 1968, and I was nineteen years old. It was chilly, drizzly and foggy and I felt as if I was standing on a hill in Namru on a wet summer's morning. But I knew I was far from home. John and Roger were waiting for us and I was overjoyed to see them again. They looked so well — as if they were many years younger than when they had left Pokhara.

From London we drove straight to Lewes in Sussex. There, with Roger's parents, Joan and Jack Catchpole, we had our first-ever hearty, English breakfast. During those months in England I grew very close to all of Roger's wonderful family, and their kindness towards me is unforgettable. In the afternoon we drove to Eastbourne on the south coast of England where Karma and I were going to study for the next year or so. We were going to stay at Leyton Lodge with an elderly couple, Mr and Mrs Turner, as our friends had made arrangements for them to lease a spare room for the two of us, and also to provide us with breakfast.

Eastbourne College, the school that Roger had studied in, was going to sponsor our lunch and dinners. They were also going to sponsor a few classes for us at the college. But since our main subject of study was going to be English, our main place of study was going to be at the Eastbourne School of English. This was a school primarily for learning the English language, and whose students were mainly young adults from wealthy backgrounds. Eastbourne College was, on the other hand, a private British secondary school.

After meeting the elderly couple and dropping off our bags, Roger took us to the seaside. This was the first time I had ever seen the grey sea but it did not capture my awe. The great turquoise lakes of northern Tibet stretch into the horizon and are like small seas. On these lakes, long frothy waves would rush in from the distance, spurred on by the Chang-Thang winds, growing larger and larger before crashing against the rocky coasts or sweeping the stony beaches.

What did amaze me were the parking lots by the beach which were full of colourful cars, the mosaic of flowers that blossomed near the coast and the cleanliness of everything, everywhere. In Nepal and India the city centres were always crowded, but in Eastbourne it looked as if everyone was either at home or by the sea.

The Eastbourne School of English started within two days of our arrival. But Eastbourne College, the boarding school where we were to have our lunches and dinners, did not commence for another fortnight or so. Roger had left some money with us for our meals and on the first day we had had a lunch of fish and chips together. Roger said that the money should be enough for meals such as this, but he told us to let him know if the money ran out. So for the next few days, we bought fish and chips or just chips each noon and evening. We did not think our money would be enough for any other meal.

Being Tibetan drogpas we were not used to eating fish. I did not like fish and Karma couldn't bear it at all. He nearly vomited each time he tried it and so we were quite hungry for the first ten days. Roger would have helped us if we had told him about our little problem, but we were too embarrassed to trouble him.

When I was departing from Pokhara, my brother Wangdrak had given me the only silver charm box he had left. He had said, 'I don't have any money but when you get to the foreign land, you can sell it and buy something for yourself and Karma.'

I sold that silver charm box to one of the teachers at East-bourne College and it fetched a price of five pounds. So on the tenth day, I took the five pounds and I announced to Karma, 'Today, we will have a great feast! Something we have never had before!'

We went straight to the restaurant we always went to. When we looked at the menu, we realised that apart from the fish and chips, we couldn't recognise anything. None of the foods we knew from Nepal seemed to be on the menu. After a while of staring at the list I said, 'Let's order a big and expensive meal. How about it?'

Karma agreed.

We searched the menu for one of the dearest meals and found something that was over two pounds. This was quite a large amount for us at the time but we immediately ordered it. We excitedly waited for the delicious, big, warm meal we imagined we had ordered. We could already smell its satisfying aroma as we watched the waiters serve mouth-watering meals to the other customers. We had to wait for quite a while for the meal. This further increased our expectations and we smiled at each other in anticipation.

Suddenly someone put two very colourful things onto our table. It only took us a moment to realise that we'd ordered two painstakingly decorated, large cups of ice cream. The ice cream was mixed with chocolate sauce and lots of beautifully shaped cream, and on top of these small mountains were a flower and a miniature umbrella. I began to laugh unstoppably and I thought my body was going to burst. My laughing was made worse after seeing the gloomy expression on Karma's face. I thought he might cry with disappointment.

As we were leaving the restaurant, the manager — an Italian lady — came to us. She had been watching us since we had entered the restaurant.

'Are you students from overseas?' she asked with her friendly Italian accent. We replied that we were. 'How was the meal today?' she asked rather inquisitively.

'Not too good,' I replied, still smiling and remembering our rather amusing meal. I explained that it wasn't what we had in mind.

'Well ...' she said sympathetically, 'What is your budget?'

Our budget was only two shillings fifty, which wouldn't offer a great choice of meals. But the friendly lady thought for a moment and then suggested, 'Next time, ask for two small spaghettis and a Coke. That should be fine.'

After following the lady's advice the next day, we found the spaghetti more appealing and filling than the fish and chips. Until that day, we had just not been aware of what else we could purchase. In the days that followed, we were such spaghetti regulars that each time we stepped into the restaurant, the manager–lady would order for us, 'Two small spaghettis, please.'

Once Eastbourne College had commenced we no longer ate at that restaurant. The College was a respectable public school filled with well-disciplined, uniformed students from mostly upper middle-class families. Every day after the morning lessons at the Eastbourne School of English, we would rush to the College for lunch during the midday break. The lunches and dinners at the Eastbourne College were very filling, but during the first month of eating at the college, we found it quite embarrassing. The students at the school would throw away most of their meals, and we listened as the great leftovers were scraped off the plates and tipped into the bin with a thud. Karma and I left our plates rather clean and would always have some room for a few slices of bread after we had finished our meals.

Twice a week I attended the debating society at the College and this greatly improved my English. We discussed many issues of the time including Tibet, China, local British and Eastbourne issues, and particularly the Vietnam War. At first, whenever we debated on China, Tibet and other related issues, I couldn't help myself being completely drawn into the debate. So much so, that whenever someone argued that Mao Tse-tung was right, or that he was a great and wonderful human being, anger would flare up within. This anger was fuelled by the memories of the destruction of my country, the killing of hundreds of thousands of my people and the suffering of my own family. But soon I learnt to respect these views as the opinion of another person; someone who has an equal right to their views whether or not I knew or believed them to be wrong. These debating sessions were very enjoyable and rewarding. I made up my mind that once I returned to the Tibetan communities back in Nepal I would initiate a similar forum for the open exchange of ideas. I hoped that the same transformation that had taken place within me could also take place within the larger Tibetan community.

During the third month we began to grow quite homesick. Amid all the red, blonde and brown heads, whenever we saw someone with black hair sitting in a bus, or walking on the pavement, we would hope that they might be Tibetan. After school we used to catch the bus from the School of English to the bus stop at Meads, the local shopping area near Leyton Lodge. Every day the two of us would window-shop as we walked down the main street in Meads. There was a particular watch that Karma longingly inspected each day, while I stared at a special camera. We would each say, 'One day, I am going to buy that.' In fact I did buy that camera a few months later, by giving up smoking and saving up my pocket money.

One day after carrying out our daily inspection of our favoured items, we saw two girls who looked very Tibetan walking down the street. As we were discussing whether or not they could be Tibetan, we had to turn right down another street. The girls headed straight and it was too late to meet them. I said, 'Karma, I know those girls were Tibetan. They had Tibetan eyes.'

Karma giggled, 'Tibetan eyes? I've never heard of that before. I'm going back to have a second look.'

He had gone back just for a laugh. But as he reached the street corner, he nearly bumped into one of the girls who had come back to have a second look at the two of us. Soon I reached the street corner and so did the second girl. After the first few moments of silent embarrassment, one of the girls asked, 'So, where are you two from?'

'We are Tibetan,' we replied.

Suddenly, the two girls looked very surprised and excited. But before they said anything else we asked, 'Where are you from?'

'We are Tibetan too!' laughed the girls.

'Ngoney yinpai?' we asked in Tibetan, simply meaning, 'Are you really?'

'Yes, really,' one of the girls giggled in Tibetan.

Their names were Tsamcho and Choekyi and they immediately invited us to their cosy home, which they shared with two more Tibetan girls. They were all a little older than we were and had been sent to study in the Scandinavian countries by the Tibetan government. From there they had come to study and work as nurses in England. The girls invited us to have dinner with them that night, and when we returned we found the whiffs of *momos* (meat dumplings) and other Tibetan foods floating about their cosy apartment. Tsamcho and Choekyi introduced us to Dolma and Yeshi, their flatmates, and we had a wonderful dinner with the four girls. It felt like finding some long lost relatives.

Most of the other students at the Eastbourne School of English had wealthy backgrounds. There were quite a few students from the oil-rich Arab countries such as Saudi Arabia, and even a prince from Qatar. There were also students from European countries such as France, Switzerland and the Netherlands. The thing that struck me the most during my time at the school was the attitude of many of the students. In contrast to the uniformed students at the College, it seemed to me as if many of the students at the School of English had come simply to waste their time. They seemed more preoccupied with fashion, going out and romance than with studying.

At the time, Karma and I only had one pair of grey trousers and a black jacket each, both of which Roger had bought for us on the day we arrived. We also had some white shirts, a pair of shoes and an identical cardigan each. We used to wash our trousers every weekend and send the coats to be dry-cleaned every once in a while. There wasn't any choice of clothes each morning but we felt we had enough. Many of the other students seemed to wear brand new clothes every single day. Indeed, their ungoverned engrossment with fashion drove my thoughts to quite an ironic corner.

I began to feel as if the youth of the world were under the control of designers and business people. Whenever they created something new, the young would blindly chase after their creation, almost oblivious to priorities and rational thought. I felt the youth had lost their freedom of mind without being aware of it. I began to feel that they needed to be aware of the excesses of these forces and guard themselves from what could be termed 'capitalism'.

Back then I felt that in some ways Marxism could paint a picture of a fair and equitable society, particularly the idea of 'from each according to his ability, to each according his needs'. Indeed, the communist ideology of liberating the poor masses did not seem too far from the Mahayana Buddhist perspective of putting others (countless sentient beings) before the self (single being). The thing that I did not agree with was the constant class struggle to achieve these goals. Unfortunately I could not reconcile my feelings with China even though, if I were a true Buddhist practitioner, it should not have been difficult at all. Indeed, from a Buddhist perspective, to achieve perfect tolerance, one's enemy is one's best teacher.

I was caught in a corner, but I knew that education was the key to better understanding these ideologies and how they affect societies, and so I studied uncompromisingly.

This opportunity to study had been denied to me back in Pokhara. My country was in the hands of the Chinese. My people were suffering as never before in our long history. The advice and hope of my deceased parents was that I study and become learned and I was not about to shrink from this responsibility. I was not interested in many of the popular pastimes of the youth. My emphasis was so weighted on living up to these responsibilities that while I was in England I only ever went to a disco once. Karma and I went with the Tibetan girls we had met, and afterwards they commented that Tibetan boys didn't know how to have fun, and that we were always too lost in thought.

Looking back, I may have been the one who was more on the odd side. Being a drogpa child meant that I had spent my early childhood in a different world and I had spent much of my time quietly in the universe of thought. The death of my parents and the lack of opportunities to attend school meant that I didn't enjoy a normal childhood. Perhaps most importantly, I had been born into responsibility as a member of a race who had lost everything, and whose very existence was under threat. To me drinking, chasing after girls or even dancing seemed clearly pointless. So I did not enjoy dancing, nor did I believe I would be very good at it.

During our time in England there were celebrations of the centenary of Mahatma Gandhi's birth, and through these I gained an admiration for the British people. Everywhere I went there were genuine commemorations of Gandhi's life and his many achievements. One of his most important works was his prominent role in India's struggle for freedom from the British Raj. But here I was in Britain and the people were genuinely celebrating Gandhi's greatness. Programs on Gandhi were being splashed across the television and the newspapers, and the inspiring story of Gandhi's life and his wonderful virtues were repeated during public talks and on posters and pamphlets that were distributed on the streets. I became completely captivated by him and can honestly say that he was a true inspiration.

Soon after these celebrations a competition was held for students from all across the United Kingdom, to select attendees for a conference held by the United Nations Association of the UK. I was one of the two students chosen from the Eastbourne Borough, and following the competition a reporter interviewed me for the local newspaper. This strengthened my confidence that I could really achieve something if I reached the world stage. I told the reporter that I believed we would regain our independence soon and that we would be able to return to Tibet. I stated that I would be able to serve my people and work for peace in our world as a part of the Tibetan government.

On some weekends, Karma and I used to visit the Tibetan home at the Pestalozzi Children's Village near Hastings. The village housed orphans from many different countries and each country had their own home run by foster parents. The Tibetan government had sent a very caring and kindly couple, Mr and Mrs Druphok, to look after the children at the Tibetan home. The first time we went to the home was because one of His Holiness the Dalai Lama's two main tutors, Ling Rinpoche, was visiting. But soon I no longer wanted to visit the village.

As Karma and I were in a foreign land all the Tibetans we met felt like our siblings. But when we visited the Pestalozzi Children's Village, the children hardly took any notice of us. A few turned their heads to say a hasty, 'Hi', in English, but that was it. On our third visit we arrived late one morning and had planned to stay overnight. But by the afternoon I had had enough. It seemed to me as if the children were trying to be English, purposely shaking off their Tibetan values to become something they weren't. I was very upset. Many of the children were only a year or two younger than I was and I thought that they should be old enough to realise the gravity of the Tibetan situation.

'Let's go back Karma. I don't want to stay here any longer.' He agreed and we went to Mr and Mrs Druphok to take our leave. They asked why we had suddenly decided to go back.

I couldn't lie to them, 'I'm not very happy here. We have lost our country. I have come to England to study in the hope that I can help regain our country and serve our people, and I had also expected the children here to hold those same hopes, the same sense of purpose. Even if we were unable to help each other in any way, at the least we should acknowledge one another, and perhaps talk, speaking in Tibetan. That is why we come here.'

I had to pause, to take a deep breath. My voice was becoming rather shaky. It was not easy to let my disappointment flow out. The elderly man immediately replied in a gentle voice. 'Thank you, thank you son … there aren't many children who are as thoughtful as you. You must stay for the night. I will introduce you to the children. You must share your thoughts with them.'

So at the insistence of Mr and Mrs Druphok we reluctantly stayed for the night. In retrospect, I am no longer certain about the fairness of my perception. A number of the children from that home went on to become very sincere and active members of the Tibetan community.

After spending just over a year in Eastbourne and receiving the Cambridge Certificate in English we moved to London. For three months I studied teacher training while Karma studied accounting. During our time in London we stayed in Cambridge House, a hostel on the ill-reputed east side of the city. I became good friends with a Chinese girl who was also staying at Cambridge House. Her family had moved from mainland China to Hong Kong in recent years and she had come to study in London. She did not seem to know where Tibet was, despite all attempts at explanation on my part.

Then one day a Japanese adventurer became the first person

to ski down a slope of Mount Everest and the news appeared on the TV, radio and the newspapers. I was having breakfast with the Chinese girl and I tried to explain to her, 'Mount Everest — the mountain down which the Japanese man skied — half of it is in Tibet, my country, and the other half is in Nepal.'

She interrupted me before I had finished. 'See ... we are from the same country. Half of Mount Everest is in China. That's Chinese land. I now know where you are from.'

I felt that she said those last words rather degradingly. I tried to explain to her but she wouldn't listen. She was not budging from her insistence that Tibet was a part of China. I lost my patience at her stubbornness, 'What have you to prove that that land is China?' I shouted. 'I can prove that the land north of Mount Everest is Tibet.'

She could not prove that Tibet did not exist but neither would she listen to anything I had to say. The argument heated up and we lost our tempers. I thought her stubbornness and the baseless nature of her claims was representative of how the Chinese people seemed to have been brainwashed by government propaganda.

On the Tibetan New Year's Day that year, Karma and I were about to leave for Pestalozzi to celebrate the New Year with the Tibetans at the village. We met the Chinese girl at the doorway of the hostel. We had not spoken since the last argument. But that day she seemed particularly cheerful.

Smiling at us, she said, 'Hi Chope! Where are you off to?'

'I'm going to Pestalozzi,' I told her. 'For the Tibetan New Year.'

Immediately she beamed with satisfaction as if she had managed to prove a point. 'See! I told you,' she exclaimed. 'It's the Chinese New Year today. We're the same.'

She was still intent on proving that there was no Tibet.

'What the hell are you talking about?' I exclaimed. 'Do you mean to say that Britain is a part of Germany just because they happen to have the same New Year's Day?'

She didn't have a reply to my question. Then she said, still quite cheerfully, 'Okay, anyway, it doesn't matter. Don't talk about politics. Would you like to join us for our New Year's celebrations?'

'No, thank you!'

My stay in London was very important in shaping my future life, as it helped me reflect on my life as a Tibetan. One day while I was walking in London I was filled with a sense of awe as I looked upon the great buildings of the city and thought about the great technological advances in Britain over the centuries. These were the achievements of the British people. So what had we Tibetans, as a people, achieved? The answer immediately dawned on me. My people had not been idle.

While the rest of the world had been studying the outside world, the Tibetan nation had been studying the world within — the mind. Great men and women had spent their lives meditating and studying the mind. The geniuses of the Tibetan world had dedicated every ounce of their energy and every minute of their lives to it. Our whole race had been preoccupied with it for over a millennium, writing hundreds of thousands of books and developing diverse ways of studying this inner world.

England had all of the material conveniences and comforts, but there was a sovereignty of loneliness over many in the populace. I had shared this cold loneliness at times, and it was something I had almost never come across within the Tibetan society, even in the worst times. Perhaps, I thought, this may be thanks to our culture. 'I must find out,' I promised myself. Looking back, this was one of the most important lessons I learnt while in England.

At the beginning of 1970 Karma and I were ready to head back to India. I was eager to return and wanted to know how I could help the education of the younger Tibetans in exile. So before I returned to Pokhara I wanted to see for myself the state of the Tibetan schools in India and Nepal. I wondered if I could learn a few lessons from the schools in India that could help improve our school in Tashi Ling. I asked John and Roger to sponsor such a trip and they kindly agreed.

Soon Karma and I were heading back to India after a very interesting and fruitful time in England. The more I saw of the world and the more of life I lived, the more I realised the wisdom of my father's advice. Education was of the utmost importance for improving the lives of Tibetan children. Education was also a necessity if we were going to regain our homeland.

18

The essence of education

Once Karma and I reached India, we travelled to Dharamsala as soon as possible. There we were granted a personal audience with His Holiness the Dalai Lama.

As we entered the audience room, His Holiness came all the way to the door to greet us. I had no expectations of what His Holiness would be like. But like any Tibetan I had seen many photos of His Holiness, as these are placed on almost every Tibetan altar (but are now banned in Tibet by the Chinese government). I had also had glimpses of His Holiness during the public audience I had received with Gen-Jinpa. Nothing, not even the fact that His Holiness is believed to be the emanation of Avalokiteshvara, the bodhisattva of compassion, could have prepared me for the real audience.

The moment I entered the room with Karma there was a presence in the air. A maroon-robed Buddhist monk, His Holiness the Fourteenth Dalai Lama, greeted us warmly, with sincere humility. A tremendous humbling humility; a humility with unwavering dignity. I felt completely disconcerted and at the same time unmistakably serene. A sea of confusion raged within me, as if a great storm was passing over tumultuous waves; yet I felt assured that beneath the surface the clear waters were pristine, and everything was at peace.

His Holiness gestured for us to sit on the chairs prepared for visitors but I was so enraptured by the flood of feelings and emotions that I sat cross-legged on the floor. Beside me Karma did the same. I could not even manage to look up at His Holiness until I heard his resonant voice, fierce like the boom of thunder yet soft as the sweet song of a dawn bird.

'How was England? How did you feel there?'

I slowly looked up at His Holiness's face. His Holiness looked as youthful as an eighteen-year-old youngster in England, although I knew His Holiness was in his late-twenties at the time. For the whole time we were there I could feel His Holiness's curious and humorous eyes looking at us. Under this disarming glance I could only be myself, nothing more or less. I felt bare, as if my whole being had suddenly become transparent.

What was within me? The person who thought he could achieve as much as anyone, even as much as any lama? I knew the answer and it was far from satisfactory. I felt shame for the conceited thoughts I had since my mother's passing away. But despite the shame I felt a simultaneous joy. I felt soothed by compassion and suddenly the tears flowed out like two natural mountain streams. I had no control over them. Hundreds of thoughts raced through my mind in a spark of a moment, although I managed to gather myself enough to be able to speak.

'England was quite good but it seemed terribly lonely, especially for the elderly people,' I answered, speaking the first words that came to me. Once I was calmer I was able to build on the momentum of these first words. 'The youth seem to be quite intoxicated in pursuit of temporary delights. The moment people reach old age, they are on their own. They seem to only have loneliness as their companion.'

His Holiness nodded. The air in the room changed for an instant. I looked up and felt as if His Holiness had shared the loneliness of every being.

'Yes, it appears so,' said His Holiness.

The relentless tears did not subside, but now I was able to think. I wanted to be myself, to think clearly and talk about the question that had long been in my mind.

'I was born in Tibet to very kind parents who set me down the right track. But now I am very unsure of whether I am a Buddhist at all. From my own judgement, I think it is likely that I am not. Please confer on me any refuge blessings or initiations, so that I may become a Buddhist.'

His Holiness laughed a short natural laugh.

'I don't think you will need any further refuge blessings. You are a Buddhist … just saying such things shows you are a Buddhist.' His Holiness laughed again and there was a golden glint of humour in those incomparably alert eyes.

'Anyway,' His Holiness added, 'tomorrow is the conclusion day of the *Lam Rim Chen Mo* (*The Great Treatise on the Stages of the Path to Enlightenment*) teachings. During that teaching, you should offer some flowers to the seat of the Lama and pray well.'

His Holiness's words echoed from the four walls, resonating in the air and then inside of me. Suddenly my streams of tears turned into a great flood.

His Holiness talked with us about Tibet and about the hardship faced by Tibetan refugees in the settlements in southern India. I listened with all of my attention. I watched our leader through the tears in my eyes while His Holiness talked naturally, openly, as if with close friends. I told His Holiness about my plans and hopes for the coming years.

'I am very interested in education and teaching. Once I return to Pokhara I hope to start a debating society for the Tibetan youths. My hope is that it will increase their general knowledge and teach them to accept views other than their own.'

'That's a very good idea,' His Holiness agreed. 'But in our society, there seems to be a tendency for talks to remain unresolved. Unfortunately, this leads to some people bearing grudges against others. This is very unfortunate and purposeless. Individuals need to be able to speak when they should and discuss what they want to discuss, but leave talk at the debating table and not take grudges home. Such resentment will destroy happiness and harmony within the society. Thus talk and disagreements must be left behind on the discussion table.'

I have repeatedly reminded myself of these words throughout my life, and from that day forth I left behind all the bitterness of the past that was fuming inside me. In fact I became ashamed of all the venom I clung onto. So I left behind my anger and hatred towards the Chinese. I left behind my grudge for all the things Frank Baker had done. I left behind my resentment for all the big and small things that others had done that had made me suffer. It was as if a great burden was lifted and there was nothing weighing me down. From that day forth I have tried to consider all those who had affected me in any way, for better or worse, as a close friend or sibling. I cannot claim complete success but I always try my best.

In the audience room that day, the more I was in the presence of His Holiness the more my devotion grew. I realised that within this young man was unparalleled wisdom. Within this man was an unmatched, unconditional and universal love and humility. From whatever perspective I looked, whatever criteria I thought of, I came to the conclusion that this was as close to perfect as anyone could get. An elevating happiness lifted me high and I felt joy for my good fortune to have been born as a member of His Holiness's people. Joy for my six million countrymen and women. We had found the supreme leader; a true leader who could lead the Tibetan people through the two means to the two ends — to both material contentment and enlightenment. I now completely understood why all the people around me had been weeping helplessly the first time I had seen His Holiness, when on holiday with John.

Before we left the audience room, His Holiness said, 'Be happy and keep your spirits high. Do not lose your confidence and faith.'

His Holiness stood up and came all the way to the door to see us off. Once we were out under the open sky, my tears did not subside. For months after the audience, an invariable foundation of happiness held my days steady.

From Dharamsala Karma and I went to Manali, a popular hill station also in northern India. My niece Dolkar, who had been JoDol, my childhood playmate, was now married and living there with her husband. Dolkar and her husband Sampten owned a box of small items to sell to tourists. During the day, Sampten displayed the items for passers-by to see while Dolkar spent much of her time preparing food and grinding tsampa. In the evenings they rubbed and cleaned their box full of items until they sparkled.

The rest of my family had also moved to India from Pokhara. They were working with many other refugees building roads at a place called Pachang, which was a four-hour trek from Manali. Usually travellers hired porters but I didn't like the idea of someone else carrying my luggage while I walked ahead without a load on my back. At the same time that my siblings were working on the road just to survive, how could I waste money and not even carry my own luggage? So Karma and I trekked to Pachang on our own.

After a few hours of trekking, we could see a dusty hillside in the distance. As we got closer we could see the hundreds of perspiring Tibetan labourers digging and cutting into the hillside, preparing it for the road that was going to be built. We knew that my family was not with this group so we continued climbing up the hill within shouting distance of the nearest labourers. Suddenly, there was a shrill whistle. We turned to see all the workmen, women and children running down the hill eagerly.

I turned to Karma and said, 'It must be their lunchtime. You haven't worked on such sites, have you? I used to work at the Jomsom airport. This was exactly what we did at lunchtime.'

We walked on. We could hear voices but were too tired to hear what they were saying. When we looked towards the labourers gathered below the mountainside, quite a few of them were waving towards us and some were shouting audible but incomprehensible words. They seemed to be trying to tell us to come down towards them.

'See,' I said to Karma, 'they are inviting us for lunch.'

Why have lunch with strangers? We turned towards the distant workers and waved, trying to say, 'No, but thank you very much,' without words. Suddenly, everything shook. Two great explosions blew up a large part of the hillside before us, enveloping the sky with dust, as pieces of rock hurtled towards us. We turned around and ran and rocks fell behind us. When calm returned the shock clung onto us and the ringing in our ears remained. A few minutes after the explosions, someone blew a whistle again. All the dusty Tibetan labourers climbed back up the mountainside. It was not their lunchbreak just yet.

We passed another two groups of Tibetans before we came

to the group my family were in. Amid the grubby clothed labourers was my brother Wangdrak. I was very happy to see him again. I was also very sad to see him looking so weak; the roadwork had taken its toll and he had aged far more than the year-and-a-half that had passed. His skin was dark and the wrinkles on his forehead told me of the worries and hardship he had experienced while I had been away. We had a short talk but he had to stay at work as he was leading that group of labourers. His wife Choeying, who was also working with him, came to greet me. She was wearing an old cloth on her head and under the cloth was a frail and sickly face. My sister-in-law looked so different from the person who married my brother in Tibet. She even looked different from the one I had left behind in Pokhara.

Choeying led me towards a group of canvas tents. We reached the one in which my family was living and I stepped inside. I had known the conditions were bad in these places, but what I saw was very upsetting. There were a few flattened heaps of earth that were used as beds. In the middle was a dugout where the fire was lit and the meals were cooked. This was their new home. They had almost nothing.

That evening after Wangdrak returned my brother Jignam and cousin Ami also came back from the sites they were working at. They all looked exhausted. We all talked as the dinner, which was prepared as a special feast to celebrate my return, was cooked over the weak fire. It was rice with some potato stew. The next day Wangdrak took a day off work and stayed home to talk with me and keep me company.

I learnt that my Auntie Pentso and her family were living in the same group of labourers and I was very happy to have a chance to see them again. My sister Ani Tenzin Choedon had joined a nunnery at Telokpur, not very far from Dharamsala, while sister Lhamo was still in Pokhara. Lhamo had married and settled down with a local Tibetan man. My little brother Gyatso and nephew Guru had become monks and had joined a monastery established by Chogye Trichen Rinpoche in Lumbini, Lord Buddha's birthplace in Nepal. Our youngest sister Changchup and our nieces Urgyen and Sonam Wangmo had been admitted into the Mussoorie Tibetan Homes Foundation. This was a school in northern India set up to educate Tibetan children without parents, or whose parents were too poor to look after them.

I parted from my family on the third day after my arrival. Their health and living conditions were saddening but I found comfort and happiness in the fact that they were alive and somewhat contented with their lot. Before I left I gave Wangdrak a hundred Indian rupees; it wasn't much but I could not spare more. Then I headed off to Simla, the capital of the state of Himachal and the former summer capital of the British Raj in India. From there, I went on to the hill station of Mussoorie in the state of Uttar Pradesh. Both of these hill stations were popular summer retreats for the British while they were in India, and I was struck by how much they resembled English towns.

The Indian government had built schools for Tibetan refugee children in both of these hill stations, taking the cooler climate into consideration. These schools were administered jointly by Tibetans and Indians. Everyone was very welcoming and helpful and I was given the opportunity to sit in and observe the classes and to interact with students and teachers. This allowed me to get a general grasp of the level of education in those schools and how they were structured and administered. I was very impressed by the dedication of most of the teachers and their sense of common purpose for the cause of our nation.

After visiting Mussoorie I returned to Kathmandu, Nepal. I went to see Mr Onta in the Nepal Red Cross Office to see if I could work at the Tashi Ling school. He told me that I needed to see the representative of the UNHCR for Nepal, Mr Rizvi. Mr Rizvi led Mr Onta and I into a heated exchange about the qualities of Tibetans trained overseas and Mr Rizvi's respect for his Tibetan charges. Once the argument had calmed Mr Rizvi told me to come back to see him the following day. As I sat opposite him the next day he apologised.

'I am happy that you are able to stand up for yourself. I hope you will work at the Tashi Ling school.' He sounded quite earnest as he spoke and I still do not know whether his sudden and unexpected scolding of the day before had been a test.

So I started work at the Tashi Ling school and I truly enjoyed teaching. I believed I was helping the children of Tashi Ling to seek out a better future. After three months of teaching at the school, the Tibetan government's Education Department transferred the headmaster of the school, Gen-Gyaltsen, to head the newly established refugee school at Jomsom. At the recommendation of Gen-Gyaltsen, the Department appointed me as the new headmaster. Mr Rizvi and I now had daily contact and our mutual understanding and trust grew.

As the headmaster I had to draw up the annual budget for the school and organise scholarships for students who graduated from our primary school, and who were going on to study at the local Nepalese high schools. Knowing how tumultuous and unpredictable life could be I established a social service program within the school. I wanted the children to be able to cope with different circumstances, and so for one period every week the children took part in manual tasks including digging up earth, removing rocks, and other work that was needed by the community.

Unexpectedly I was elected the president of the regional Tibetan Youth Congress by the youth of both Tashi Palkhiel and

Tashi Ling. The Tibetan Youth Congress was a new political movement with the aim of preserving Tibetan culture and identity while in exile, and restoring the independence of Tibet.

In addition to political activities, we also took a strong interest in social work to improve the wellbeing of the communities within the two camps. One of the issues we promoted was hygiene, while others we tried to address were unemployment in the refugee communities and the working conditions of the Tibetans working as porters.

As the president of the Tibetan Youth Congress for Northern Nepal I attended the first-ever general meeting of the Congress in Dharamsala. But at this time I suddenly became unwell. I attended the meetings but once they were over I could not do anything but lie down on a bed. I sometimes thought death must be near. In Dharamsala I was nursed by my affectionate pen pal, Dhadon, who was studying to become a doctor at the Tibetan Medical Institution. I soon found out that I was suffering from tuberculosis.

I was advised to rest but my mind could not rest without returning to the Tashi Ling school to carry on my work. After returning, I became a little better in the next month, but soon I was very ill again. I wrote to Dharamsala informing the Education Department of my situation. The department advised me to go to Simla for treatment at a hospital that housed only tuberculosis patients. As I could not effectively work I took leave as headmaster of the school.

At the hospital I was amazed to again see my brother Jignam who was also suffering from tuberculosis. My sister Ani Tenzin Choedon and my cousin Achi Lhachoe were also in the women's ward at the same hospital. Altogether in our ward there were around sixty male Tibetan patients and twenty Indian patients. Much like a tsowa, the Tibetans had created their own community structure, with a leader to negotiate with the hospital on behalf of the patients, to settle disputes between patients and to send information to Dharamsala. Whenever we received clothes from the Tibetan government in Dharamsala, it was also the responsibility of the leader to distribute them fairly. The day after my admission the old leader was discharged after recovering and the patients were holding an election to find a new leader. Quite a few asked me to take on the work. I insisted that I did not want to be the patients' leader, and that I was only there for treatment. But the patients voted for me and I had to accept the role.

Since I spoke English well the doctors and the hospital staff were quite friendly and willing to compromise. During my stay at the hospital I managed to negotiate with the staff to allow the male and the female patients to meet. From that time on I was able to meet Ani Tenzin Choedon and Achi Lhachoe. I also asked the hospital to allow the patients whose TB was negative to visit the large library at the hospital. This was also granted.

Life was like a lottery in the ward: some people recovered while others died. No one knew who would die next until it happened. As the leader I had to call the hospital staff so that they could take the corpses away. I even had to attend the cremation of the bodies.

As the leader I also managed to see a list that the hospital kept which detailed which patients the hospital thought would die and which ones were likely to survive. I was in the survivors list but to my horror, brother Jignam's name was on the list of people whose fates were sealed. I was devastated. I could not even bear to think about his death, although I knew that indeed it was likely that he might soon die. If I had to watch my brother die, I thought that I too would die of grief.

At the time both Jignam and Ani Tenzin Choedon were

urging me to leave the hospital. They both knew that my TB was not too serious. They also knew that my TB had been negative all along — meaning it was safe for others to be in contact with me. But my position as leader of the Tibetan patients meant that I was constantly interacting with all of them. Therefore, brother Jignam and sister Ani Tenzin Choedon feared that I might somehow catch a terminal positive TB from the others. The doctors also believed that I could be discharged, so there was no reason for me to remain at the hospital, and I soon left. Ani Tenzin Choedon also soon recovered, and a few months later Jignam took leave from the sanitorium against the advice of his doctors and friends. He went straight to Bodh Gaya, the place where the Buddha gained enlightenment. Jignam's TB was said to be terminal and although he had never responded to any treatment, at Bodh Gaya he carried out a hundred-thousand prostrations and somehow was cured.

I returned to Dharamsala from Simla where I was able to gain another audience with His Holiness the Dalai Lama. I expressed my wish to study further and gain a degree, perhaps by joining the Tibetan University at Varanasi.

'Teaching is a very good and useful job,' His Holiness said. 'You can help create a better future for others. If you hold the right motivation, you can greatly benefit society. Continue teaching; teach your students to be good people and keep a compassionate mind. Even adults, if they will listen, tell them to be kind-hearted and compassionate too. That is the essence of education isn't it? Carry on teaching. If you are unhappy over there, then you can work here if you want to.'

I again felt reinvigorated after the audience. My sense of purpose and direction felt sharpened and there was tremendous joy in my heart. After the audience, I went to see the Minister of Internal Affairs and Religion, Mr Tsewang Tamdin.

'How was the audience?' the minister asked.

'Wonderful,' I said.

'Was there any advice?'

I told the minister what I had said to His Holiness and His Holiness's advice. Tsewang Tamdin-la listened to my words carefully and thought for a moment. Then he seemed to remember something and said, 'We need a Camp-in-Charge for the settlement of Dhorpaten. We require someone who can speak English and is able to communicate effectively with non-Tibetans. We haven't found anyone else. Would you be willing to go?'

Dhorpaten was the remote settlement in northern Nepal where brother Wangdrak had fallen ill while the rest of the family were in Pokhara. I was unprepared for such an offer and told the minister, 'I am sorry, I cannot decide right now. I must consult Chogye Trichen Rinpoche. I will meet him soon. I am going to Rajpur where Rinpoche is residing, straight from Dharamsala.'

In Rajpur I consulted Chogye Trichen Rinpoche. I had met Rinpoche several times since he had visited Namru when I was a little boy. Rinpoche had served as the Secretary of the Department of Religion and Culture of the Tibetan Government-in-Exile. Rinpoche was always warm, kind and extremely wise. He also never seemed to age! That day Rinpoche's eyes were a little red and looked slightly tired. I learnt that he had had only two hours of sleep each night for the last several months, as he was preparing and giving *Lamdre* teachings to Sakya Trizin, the head of the Sakya branch of Tibetan Buddhism.

Rinpoche's divination proved very favourable. Therefore, soon afterwards, I sent a letter to Minister Tsewang Tamdin informing him that Rinpoche's divination was favourable, and that I would accept the appointment to Dhorpaten.

I was happy to be able to help, but I did not want to stay in a remote part of Nepal such as Dhorpaten for too long, and I made it clear that if I was posted there, I would not serve for more than two years.

19

Breaking down barriers

Dhorpaten was situated on a plateau surrounded by hills and mountains on all sides. Not too far away to the north were the Himalayas behind some lesser mountains. These closer hills were either green with grass or covered by trees. A large river rolled across the plateau dividing it into two almost equal halves and the settlement was situated on a small slope overlooking the river and the flat plain, to the north of the river. Thousands of flowers grew in the wild on the grassy fields and during the spring the beauty was mesmerising. Just like the Chang-Thang, wild animals roamed freely on the mountains surrounding Dhorpaten, and in the valley on most days there were hundreds of cows, sheep and horses grazing. Dhorpaten looked like a serene settlement in a forgotten part of the Swiss Alps. Indeed the Swiss Red Cross had helped to build this settlement for the Tibetan refugees, and altogether there were around three hundred Tibetans living here.

Dhorpaten was primarily an agricultural settlement, but the only major crop was potatoes. The Tibetans of Dhorpaten lived by bartering their potatoes for salt in southern towns and then bartering the salt in exchange for other foodstuffs in lower-lying Nepalese villages to the north. These northern Nepalese villages used to get their salt from Tibet before the Chinese sealed the border. Each family in Dhorpaten owned a few horses and the menfolk were seasonally away on trading trips. In fact, during the winters, Dhorpaten was almost empty and therefore all the community meetings had to take place during the spring and summer months.

As a single man I did not have many belongings with me when I arrived at the small Dhorpaten airport. I only owned a few small pots and pans, and had sent these ahead of me on horseback. With these few possessions I was going to start my new home. Mr Rana, a Nepalese man who was the representative of the Swiss Association for Technical Assistance (SATA) for Dhorpaten, had come with me. When we arrived no one came to greet me, but there were a few dozen curious onlookers who rushed to the airstrip to see who was coming and going on the small Platus Porter aeroplane. One of the few people I knew in Dhorpaten was my new neighbour Pema, the young Bhutanese man I knew from Jomsom. He had led us to Pokhara to carry back loads of rice for the Red Cross, and had since married a Tibetan girl from Tashi Palkhiel.

Back in Pokhara, the school staff had a common kitchen and our own cook. Here, I only had my own hands, my pots and pans and a very poor knowledge of cooking. During the first day I visited Pema's house where I had some tsampa pak. I did not have any other meal and as the afternoon matured, I began to grow hungry. Hoping to bake a type of bread, I went to buy some flour from the only local store.

That evening, I lit a wood fire to bake my bread with. It had been a long time since I had stayed in a room where anything was cooked on a wood fire and my eyes began to itch. Then the itch grew into pain and it was a struggle just to keep my eyes open. But still, I managed to prepare some dough with tears streaming down my face. Then I poured a bit of cooking oil into a pot, put the dough in, put a lid on and left the pot to be heated on the fire. I waited for quite a while with nothing to do. Then I opened the lid expectantly as some steam danced towards the ceiling. Despite my itching eyes, I wiped my tears and gawked at what I hoped would be properly cooked bread. The dough was still wet and it was not appealing at all. I flipped the bread over and was startled to find the other side completely black! It was disappointing yet quite funny and I laughed on my own.

Whether it was burnt or uncooked, this bread was all I had for dinner, so I put the lid back on and waited. The room was quiet except for the crackle of the fire. My eyes were still hurting badly, and I lit a candle to dispel the growing darkness and sat beside the fire.

I heard a knock at the door that startled me. Before I could get up and open the door, in walked an old man. He was very dark and looked even darker with the night sky at his back. His dark, greasy face was smiling a friendly grin.

He was completely bald, like a monk. But he was wearing a dark shirt, black trousers and a pair of black, Tibetan, cloth boots.

'Ah … the new settlement leader. So what might you be doing?' the stranger asked, inspecting my belongings.

'Just lit a fire,' I answered.

'So, you're cooking … what is it?'

With that, he grabbed the lid off the pot.

'Yuk!' he exclaimed. 'That looks awful! You poor boy. What sort of food is this? How can anyone eat this?'

The peculiar stranger wasn't very polite, but at least he was honest.

'No one can eat that!' he said loudly, and left.

'What an annoying man,' I thought to myself.

A while later, there was another knock on the door and in came the old man once again.

He handed me a large piece of raw meat.

'Take this. It's for you,' he said.

That evening, thanks to the old man, I had some fried meat for dinner, with some tsampa that I found in my luggage.

Later I learnt that this man was Acu Tempa Gyaltsen who owned the small local store and a small inn.

During my time in Dhorpaten I kept His Holiness the Dalai Lama's advice close to my heart. I always did my best to be kind and to help the people of this remote settlement without bias or prejudice. I truly cared about the settlement and felt joy that I was in a position to help others, and that I'd taken on the responsibility. I could now share what little knowledge I had and use it to better the lives of other people.

The people of Dhorpaten were both Buddhists and followers of Bon — an ancient indigenous religion in Tibet, and the populace was from widely distant parts of Tibet so that accents, clothing styles and habits were quite varied. When the Chinese had begun their invasion of Tibet, many Tibetans from the east had run out of food and had forcefully appealed for food and other necessities from the people of other regions. Due to these and other reasons there was still some distrust between different factions of the community.

I took on the full responsibility of leadership and believed that it was my duty to break down these barriers and to promote sincerity and confidence between the people of Dhorpaten. Drawing on my experience as a teacher and headmaster I did my best to improve the school. There was also a small health clinic within the settlement and through this clinic it was my hope that I could help to improve the health of both the Tibetans and the local Nepalese.

I also placed great importance on the harmony and understanding between the Tibetans and Nepalese of the locality. Personally and through my influence within the community I tried to build a genuine friendship with the local Nepalese. During my first year, through a Nepalese charitable organisation called 'Paropakar' ('Help Others'), I came in contact with an American economist by the name of Ross Anthony. We discussed how his foundation could help Dhorpaten and our small medical clinic in particular. In the end, a Canadian medical doctor whom we called Doctor Steven, his wife Mary-Lynn, another Mary, a helper, and Michael, a young wood craftsman, joined Ross in coming to Dhorpaten.

In Doctor Steven we had a fully qualified and experienced world-class doctor in this remote part of Nepal. We were able to help not only the Tibetans but many local Nepalese as well, and for over two years the doctor and his sponsoring team's work was a great help for everyone in the locality. But in the end, for some strange reason, some local Nepalese leaders did not like them and that resulted in them having to leave Nepal falsely accused of being American spies.

I was twenty-five and, at times, my only friend in Dhorpaten seemed to be my radio and the BBC broadcasts, which kept me informed about what was happening in the world. There were no libraries to satisfy my boredom and sometimes I was lonely. Although I was the leader of the community and I never really had any affection for romance, I soon got caught up in the circle of youth within our community. Because of my education and background there were many attractive young girls in the community showing their affection towards me. But unfortunately, the only girl I was really fond of didn't seem particularly interested. Her name was Palden. She was a young woman with calm eyes and long hair that glistened red under the sunshine. She was known to be kind and honest, although she was rather reserved towards those she was not familiar with. I did not know whether my silent affection for her was reciprocated, but the more I knew of her, the more my affection grew.

One day as I was passing by the local watermill, I saw a young woman sitting by the river calmly combing her hair. As I got closer I recognised Palden. She was alone and I joined her by the riverside. I found her friendlier than I had thought and as we shared the beautiful day I learnt that we also shared an affection for each other. After that day our relationship bloomed.

During this first year at Dhorpaten I realised that the community was not able to work efficiently with the assets belonging to the community co-operative society. The co-operative society owned a small shop and a small restaurant, both of which were not doing as well as they could. Most of the profit and benefit seemed to slip into private pockets. Thus I knew there had to be an overhaul of the way in which these assets were looked after. I read up on all the Nepalese government laws and regulations concerning such community ventures. Then I read all the laws and regulations of the Tibetan government concerning such ventures. Making sure that I did not infringe either of them I devised a new system for our community. A new council for the co-operative society was set up, the members of which were elected by the local community. It was the responsibility of these elected members to run and look after these community assets and they were accountable in the case of any mismanagement. It was my hope that the new equity and accountability that was established would allow the co-operative society to become more productive and profitable.

The community elected a young man to manage the co-operative society. With the help of the Swiss he had completed secondary schooling, and was known to have also received business management training. He seemed like the logical choice. This young man was a very friendly and good-natured person, but we did not know that he was not at all able to manage money properly. Whether his motivation or intentions were at fault, or whether he was just incapable of fulfilling the requirements of his role, he was nonetheless unable to keep a clean balance sheet.

This young man did not have a permanent home at first, and as he was an elected local leader I allowed him to share my house. As time passed, the state of the community assets became worse and worse. Within a year it became clear that the manager was completely unable to keep track of money. Some members of the small community began to tie my hands together with his. Gossip was spread that I had conspired with the young man to take some of the community money. Unfortunately, this rumour was given extra meaning by the fact that Palden was related to him. As someone who always hoped and meant the best for the local community, I found these rumours upsetting.

I called a meeting for all the leaders of the community. I invited them to my house and I told them that for the next ten days we should read all the talks and speeches given by His Holiness the Dalai Lama since 1959. Then in the evenings we would all gather and discuss what we had read.

During the evening gatherings we asked ourselves, 'What can we learn from each speech? How does this help us to be better people? How does this help us in our fight for freedom for our country? What would improve the wellbeing of our community? What could help in the education of our children?'

For the first two days everyone attended the sessions. On the third day, however, hardly anyone turned up. I immediately wrote a letter to all those participants who were absent.

'It is improbable that you disagree with His Holiness's speeches, therefore, did you not attend the session because it was me who organised them? Whatever the reason may be, you must let me know. I will send your reasons to His Holiness's office and to the Cabinet.'

The next day everyone came to apologise. 'We somehow just never got around to coming,' they said, and for the rest of the ten days, the attendance was extremely good. At the conclusion, we all gathered together and discussed what the underlying themes of the speeches were. In all the speeches we discovered at least one common theme. No matter who the speech was given to or when, the theme was that one should be sincere and help others, and at the very least one should not harm others.

'I believe I have kept true to this underlying advice of His Holiness the Dalai Lama,' I told the community leaders gathered in my house. 'And I will keep true to this in the future. I will be sincere towards the community and will do my best to help our community in any way. As the leaders you must also do likewise.

'There have been rumours that I have somehow been involved with the manager of the co-operative society in the disintegration of the common community assets. Tomorrow, we will hold a session where everyone in the community will pledge before the protective deities that we have not taken even a single coin from the co-operative society. We will also pledge that we will heed our own promise to serve the community and help others as much as we can.'

The next day, as the community gathered, I led the session by pledging in front of pictures of the protective deities. But most of the community members were unwilling to follow straightaway.

'I have a long-forgotten axe,' one person said.

'I forgot to repay the hundred rupees I borrowed,' said another.

'Oh, I forgot to pay for the bag of rice I bought the other day,' said yet another. Soon there were lots of things returned to the co-operative society, including a great deal of money, and quite suddenly the community enterprises became a great deal wealthier.

I always tried my best to develop religious harmony in Dhorpaten. After arriving I earnestly tried to gain a better understanding of Bon and I read Bon scriptures, met Bon lamas and began to develop genuine respect for the religion. I began to feel that the only major differences between Choe (Buddhism) and Bon were in the empty names. Since I respected and was not apprehensive of Bon, the Bon followers within the community trusted me.

The people of Dhorpaten were also fortunate enough to have an extremely kind and humble Buddhist lama called Lama Choedhar residing there. Lama Choedhar spent most of the year on retreats but for three months during the summer Lama Choedhar would pause his retreats to hold *nyung-nae* (fasting). A set of nyung-nae takes two days and the participants only eat a vegetarian lunch on the first day and fast on the second. During my years in Dhorpaten, Lama Choedhar completed his one thousandth set of nyung-nae. Although he was our community's spiritual master, he had no pride at all and he taught everyone the consequences of destructive evil deeds and the benefits of kindness and compassion. Lama Choedhar was a great asset to the people of Dhorpaten and I always felt the small community was incredibly lucky to have such a lama with them.

Out of the five years I was in Dhorpaten it took most of the first year for me and the community to size each other up. I was able to undertake fruitful work during the second year, and unfortunately the third year was disrupted by misunderstandings and disharmony within the community, caused by those who had a vested interest in social disharmony. During the fourth and fifth years it was as if we had reached an unobstructed road to development and everything went smoothly. The people of Dhorpaten were happy and I was content that my sincerity and efforts were not wasted, and that I was really able to help.

During my years in Dhorpaten, I was also able to initiate a number of small projects which were quite beneficial to the community in the long run, including the planting of apples (with the help of Ross Anthony) and the breeding of mules. Mules were very useful in carrying heavy loads to the distant markets and apples have since become a major produce of that area. Certain members of our community were not very supportive of these projects but, in the long run, those who participated were able to reap substantial rewards.

At the time, Tibetan resistance fighters in Mustang were being disarmed and disbanded by the Nepalese government. This guerilla force had initially been established with the help of the CIA and the tacit acceptance of the Nepalese authorities. But with the change of US policy towards China, specifically after the visit to China by President Nixon, the CIA dumped the Tibetan guerilla force and Nepal also changed its policy.

With the disbanding of the resistance movement Tibetans were depicted quite negatively within the Nepalese press. There was no freedom of the press under an autocratic monarch and most editorials had to reflect government views. Those people within towns and villages who had an interest in politics and inclinations towards communism, as well as those who disliked people of other races, caused problems for us. In a number of the newspapers at the time, articles appeared saying that Dhorpaten was harbouring resistance fighters and arms hordes, and that they must not be allowed to remain. They alleged that many weapons had been amassed near the Tibetan border and that the fighters had caused problems for the Nepalese authorities. These calls were getting louder and louder, and this quite baseless anti-Tibetan sentiment seemed to be gathering momentum rather rapidly.

That year, in 1976, I was meant to go to the annual Tibetan Government-in-Exile's general meeting that was being held in Dharamsala, but Palden became pregnant with our first child. With the growing pressure from the small but loud anti-Tibetan camp in the media, I needed guidance from His Holiness the Dalai Lama and from the Home Affairs Ministry. I decided I had to go.

As soon as I reached Pokhara on my way to India, I suddenly became very ill. The cause seemed to be a cup of Tibetan wine I had drunk that day. It was so painful that I knew I was in very real danger. That night amid an uneasy sleep I had a very special dream. As I noted in my diary, I dreamt that if my child had been born on that day, this child would be someone extraordinary. My health rapidly improved and I was able to go to Kathmandu within a few days. I remained in Kathmandu for about a month and at the end of this time I heard that Lama Choedhar had come to Kathmandu and that he was looking for me. When I met Lama Choedhar he gave me a letter telling me that Palden had given birth to our first son on 6 January, almost a month premature, the very night when I had had that particular dream.

From Kathmandu I went to Dharamsala and during my audience with His Holiness I asked about what course of action I should take regarding the new developments in Nepal. His Holiness advised me that he did not think the Tibetans would have to leave the region and that I should work to allow the Tibetans to remain in Dhorpaten. I also met the Home Affairs Minister who told me that I would be transferred from Dhorpaten before the end of that year. By then that was welcome news to me. Before leaving Dharamsala I requested a name for my newborn son from His Holiness, and he was named Tenzin Samdrup.

I was so eager to see both Palden and our newborn son, and so worried about their wellbeing that I took leave before the general meetings had concluded. I returned to Dhorpaten as quickly as possible. As I stepped off the light plane in Dhorpaten I was welcomed by Palden. A few moments later Palden's father arrived carrying the little bundle that had turned him into a grandfather. The baby Tenzin looked at me with his large inquisitive eyes. He was so small and furry. I was too embarrassed to look at him. I had become a father! I slowly peeped at my son, overcoming my embarrassment. I saw the baby more closely and he looked like one of my own siblings!

The life of a father felt very different and the responsibility of love felt immense. Sometimes I truly agreed with the saying, 'One's children cause more worries than one's enemy.' One can avoid the enemy, but you cannot avoid your own children. If a child starts crying in the middle of a meal, a parent's love for the child makes them run to them. If the child cries in the middle of a peaceful sleep, both parents wake up and care for the child. If the child becomes sick, both parents are overcome by worry. Parents go through so many difficulties because of their love for their child that the old Tibetan saying, 'That enemies who are unable to fulfil their vengeance take birth as one's child', seems quite believable.

Our baby Tenzin was at first very small and furry due to his premature birth. But as the months wore on his skin cleared and he lost his furry look. By this time my post at Dhorpaten was concluded and I was transferred to Kathmandu as the Secretary at the Representative's Office. On our way to Kathmandu, as we trekked through the Nepalese countryside, Nepalese village women would run up to us upon seeing Tenzin and pray for children as cute as him.

I left Dhorpaten with even less belongings than when I had first arrived. Most of the old pots and pans were too old to take. But I now had two new precious companions, Palden and our little son Tenzin.

Chope hanging a khata at a mountain pass in Tibet, 1984.

Chope's children in Kathmandu, 1988: Tenzin Samdup (left),
Shenphen (centre) and Tenzin Lhadhar (right).

As the Representative of His Holiness the Dalai Lama, Chope (centre) leads the Tibetan community during the celebrations for His Holiness's birthday, Boudhanath stupa, Kathmandu, Nepal, 1987.

Chope and his sister at the holy lake, Tso-Pema, India, 1996: Ani Tenzin Choedon (left) and Chope (right).

Chope and four of his siblings, 1999. From left to right:
Jamyang (Jami), Lhamo, Changchup, Jignam, Chope.

Above and below: His Holiness the
Fourteenth Dalai Lama of Tibet
with Chope (background left),
Budapest, Hungary, 1996.

20

Remembering impermanence

Although we had not officially married, Palden and I were effectively husband and wife. We used to say that the day Tenzin was born was the day we were married, because it was then that we realised we would be spending our lives together. Palden's parents did not demand a proper marriage and I wasn't very keen on such formal ceremonies either. I was embarrassed at the prospect of having to endure a traditional Tibetan wedding. Moreover, we could not really afford all the expenses of a wedding ceremony.

My job as the Secretary was very convenient as the offices were in the same building as our living quarters. Also, having faced the politics and friction of the small Dhorpaten settlement, some normal office work was a relief. For the first year or so I was able to have a relatively enjoyable time, but as my days at the office wore on I became somewhat dissatisfied. I was unable to take the initiative — if I ever thought of anything that could help the community, all I could do was to let the Representative know about it.

During those years, many of the old Tibetan resistance fighters were imprisoned in Nepalese jails. Due to this, the Representative was constantly out negotiating for their sake with the

Nepalese authorities, and on some days he would only come to the office for an hour or two. As the second-ranked staff member at the office, I found myself doing most of the work that was usually the responsibility of the Representative.

Unfortunately the staff members of our office could not get our salaries from the Representative on time. Most times I wasn't given my salary until at least two or three months after it was due, and without borrowing money Palden and I found it difficult to meet the daily necessities for our son and ourselves.

Meanwhile, the economic situation for the 16,000 or so Tibetan refugees living in Nepal had improved thanks to the far-sighted efforts of the Swiss aid agencies and the Tibetan Government-in-Exile. They had been able to utilise and foster the unique skills of Tibetans, such as weaving rugs. In fact Tibetan rugs had become one of the biggest foreign currency-earning industries in Nepal. But great hardship remained for the Tibetans in the more remote parts of Nepal, and they still lacked proper opportunities for healthcare and education. In fact there was a whole decade when the Nepalese government nationalised the education system. Under this system, even Tibetan schools in the settlements could teach neither Tibetan nor English during the primary school years.

From 1979 the Tibetan political situation seemed a little more hopeful. With Deng Xiaoping leading the Chinese Communist Party, Tibet was opened up and representatives of His Holiness the Dalai Lama were invited to visit Tibet twice. Many Tibetans from within Tibet were also allowed to visit their relatives in exile and it was the Tibetan Representative's office that assisted the Tibetan visitors to proceed to India and elsewhere. Many of these Tibetans hoped to receive an audience with His Holiness the Dalai Lama, and I was delighted to be able to help our fellow Tibetans in any way. Each of these Tibetans felt like my own family members who had long been imprisoned, and finally after so many years we had the opportunity to hear about our brothers' and sisters' lives.

During this time I received a letter from my own brother Wangdrak in Kollegal in southern India. He had terminal throat cancer and wrote that, 'It was unlikely that we would ever meet again. Even if we don't, don't worry, there is no need. Work diligently, and always have faith in the Three Jewels.'

I was devastated. My grief was acute. Not only had Wangdrak been a brother, he was like a second father to all of the younger siblings. He had looked after us and made sure we had everything we needed. It was intensely difficult to face the prospect of him passing away and my initial reaction was to set off straightaway for southern India. But as I thought about it, I was not sure about the wisdom of my reaction, which was so highly influenced by emotion. I decided to consult a lama in Kathmandu about whether I should go. The lama gave me a time frame and said, 'If you go before so and so day, you will meet your brother. Otherwise you will not.'

In short, according to the lama, if I headed for Kollegal within the next three months or so, I would be able to meet my brother, otherwise it would be too late. Once I got back home, I sat quietly, weighing up my options.

Palden had recently given birth to our second child and was quite weak and ill. Nor did we have money to spare for such a trip. If I decided to go, I would have to borrow some money. When I reached Kollegal, I would meet brother Wangdrak, but due to the time restraints placed by my work I would not be able to care for him until his death. We would part after a brief reunion and this would mean more suffering for him, as well as for me. There was no point in going.

I wrote to my brother saying I would not come to Kollegal

and that whatever happened to him, it would just be a change of the physical body. I wrote that consciousness is something that cannot be killed or destroyed, even if the whole earth and sky rose against it. Since the consciousness cannot die, all that we can take with us are the footprints of our own actions, the remnants of our good or bad thoughts and deeds, our karma. I advised him to seek teachings from an experienced lama whom he had unwavering trust in; as we witnessed at our father's passing away, such practices were infallible.

I would save the money it would have cost for me to visit him and the moment word reached me that he had died, I would offer that money to all the major monasteries around the Great Stupa at Boudhanath as ngoden (prayers for the deceased). As the Three Jewels and his positive karma would not let him down, I wanted him to have no fear for his future and have no attachments and worries for those who remained behind.

I later heard from my sister Ani Tenzin Choedon that my brother was extremely happy to receive my letter. Ani Tenzin Choedon cared for Wangdrak before and after his passing away, performing and overseeing all the necessary religious ceremonies.

Although Palden did not suffer any complications during the birth of our second son, afterwards she became thinner and weaker. She was constantly ill. Even so, Palden not only looked after our two very young children but also wove Tibetan rugs from dawn till dusk. As I never received my salary on time, her weaving was our main source of income. We felt trapped as Palden's health was deteriorating, yet her income was so important for our young family. I took her to see many well-reputed Nepalese physicians but they could not diagnose her illness. Then I went to see many lamas about Palden's poor health. Their diagnosis was almost unanimous, they said that there was a clash of protective deities.

As Palden's illness seemed to be caused by the supernatural we decided to go on a pilgrimage to Tso-Pema, the 'Lotus Lake' in northern India. Tso-Pema is a renowned pilgrimage site for Tibetans where Padmasambhava, the great Indian Buddhist master, performed the miracle of turning a great bonfire into a holy, lotus-filled lake when the local king had tried to burn him alive. His Holiness the Dalai Lama was due to give teachings there soon during Losar, the Tibetan New Year.

I took leave from work and we somehow managed to put together enough money to pay for our trip. Altogether it took six days to reach the auspicious lake and we travelled by train for much of the way. At the crowded Lucknow railway station we struggled onto one of the packed third-class carriages, where I saw a child severely ill with measles. I immediately pushed our way through to the next carriage.

Upon arriving at Tso-Pema, both our children became very ill. They had measles. And by the time His Holiness the Dalai Lama's teachings had begun, Palden was critically ill and she was rapidly losing her sight. Tenzin, my older son, was so ill that he was completely mute, and although my younger son seemed better for the first few days, his illness worsened and he suddenly died. My younger son, who had always seemed the stronger one, was suddenly gone.

Remembering the Buddhist teachings on the impermanence of all physical phenomena helped me to cope with the agonising loss of my second son. Indeed, from one perspective, my son was only my son because of my attachment to my self and therefore to him. From one perspective, although he had materialised with Palden and I as the cause, he was just another person we had known for a year. I carried out a number of pujas for our deceased son.

At this time my sister Ani Tenzin Choedon was living at Tso-Pema and she helped us tirelessly. Money was also not a great problem since my niece Dolkar owned a shop in Manali and came to help us with generous sums of money.

The agony I felt due to the loss of my son was coupled with the growing fear I felt for the lives of Tenzin and Palden. Every day I ran to and from lamas and doctors seeking their advice. One day Tenzin was extremely ill and I ran to a local lama to seek his advice. His name was Gelong Kunchok. He said, 'We must perform a body and name change puja ceremony, immediately.'

Gelong Kunchok came with me straightaway. He cut a lock of my son's hair, gave him a new name, Kunchok Tsering, and performed some prayers and blessings, giving him a yellow shirt to symbolise his ordination. As the prayers were concluding my son's eyes twitched and he began to cry. I was happy and grateful beyond expression. My son had returned from the clutches of death. From then on my son's condition improved, and within a few days he was able to walk about and keep me company while we cared for Palden.

No matter what medicines Palden took or how many prayers were said for her, she did not get better. I used to often go to see an old ascetic Tibetan lama. During one of my visits he carefully carried out some divinations and said in a gentle voice, 'Prepare some tsampa, I will come soon to carry out a puja.' He talked to everyone lovingly as though we were all his children.

I prepared the tsampa. When he arrived I was expecting him to carry out a long puja session but he just made a little human figure from the tsampa and said to Palden, 'Alright daughter, now give him something.' Palden struggled to get a little hairclip from her hair and put it beside the little figure.

'Now son, go and put it somewhere quite far away. Beside the road should do. Leave it facing Kathmandu.'

I did as I was told. When I returned, the ascetic lama turned to me and said, 'The puja is over. Now you don't need to carry out any more.'

I was amazed. The puja was so different from the usual. But the next day it seemed as if the puja had worked wonders and Palden seemed a little better. Then on the seventh day I met a Tibetan doctor we knew from Kathmandu. I went straight to the ascetic lama, 'I have met a doctor from Kathmandu, what should I do?' I asked.

'This is very good, you must seek his help and do as he advises,' he said. So I asked the doctor to visit Palden.

'Oh … Oh dear!' exclaimed the very worried doctor. 'This is very dangerous. You are in danger of becoming blind! We must carry out a moxabation immediately.'

Palden and I consented and the moxabation was done; this was a traditional medical treatment that involved the controlled 'burning' of small areas of certain parts of the body. We did not have much of a choice. That night she was able to relax a little and sleep longer than usual; she could also see a little. Palden took some medication that was left for her and over the next week she slowly but steadily got better. That week I went to the bus station and found someone who was going to Dharamsala. I told him that I was an employee of the Tibetan government and about my situation. I requested him to ask the Internal Affairs Department to send me some medication for Palden.

The next day a jeep arrived — the vehicle had been sent by the department and the Secretary sent a message that we must come to Dharamsala for treatment as soon as possible. I went to thank the ascetic lama, and then Palden, Kunchok and I went to Dharamsala by jeep. The department had prepared living quarters for us and arriving in Dharamsala was like leaving behind all of the pain and suffering of Tso-Pema. It was as if a great dark cloud had dissolved and now the warm sun was shining again.

We were also granted an audience with His Holiness the Dalai Lama, and just being in His Holiness's presence brought me great hope and strength. I now knew that everything would be fine. We told His Holiness about our little son, how he had died and how ill Palden was. His Holiness blessed Palden's eyes, and then His Holiness held our folded hands in his and consoled us, advising us to see a Western doctor.

'I will carry out some divinations tonight to see if Western medicine would be of more help,' said His Holiness.

The next day someone from His Holiness's private office relayed His Holiness's advice that Palden continue her treatment with Tibetan medicine rather than start taking Western medication.

After the forty-ninth day of mourning had been held for our son, Palden and I decided to move on. We had stayed in Dharamsala for about a month and I was looking forward to returning to my work in Kathmandu. Since the changes in the stance of the Chinese in 1979, my work had become more interesting and rewarding. But I soon learned that I had been transferred while on leave, fighting to save my wife and two sons at Tso-Pema. My next post would be at the remote Tibetan camp of Shapruk near the Tibetan border, but I declined the offer due to my family's difficult circumstances at the time. The Tibetan government was kind enough to reconsider my transfer and reinstated me at the Representative's office in Kathmandu.

When we arrived back in Kathmandu we had no money at all. I did not know how we could manage. Upon arriving at the Representative's compound we met the cook and he told us that someone had been looking for me. Then he shouted to a Western lady who was about to leave. This lady came to us and said, 'Do you know a friend of Steven Bezruchka's by the name of Chope?'

'That's me,' I replied.

'Steven has sent you a thousand rupees.'

With that money we were able to buy our necessities. I was so grateful to Doctor Steven, the Canadian doctor who had worked in Dhorpaten, but despite our situation, we had never worried much about money. We always felt that things would be all right, and they usually were.

Soon after arriving in Kathmandu I went to see Chogye Trichen Rinpoche. I asked him to come to my home to carry out pujas. A few days later, Rinpoche came and in the middle of his pujas, he paused and said, 'You two should wear your best clothes.'

We wore our chupas, the ones that we usually wore on important days. Then Rinpoche drew a sacred symbol on the carpet with rice and told us to sit on it. Placing a very long khata (a Tibetan ceremonial scarf) around our necks, Rinpoche said, 'Now I have married you two. You will prosper.'

We had never told Rinpoche that we had not had a formal marriage ceremony, but somehow he knew. I later learnt that the clashing of the protective deities resulted from not having had such a ceremony. With the kindness of Chogye Trichen Rinpoche this was finally resolved.

While in England a deep admiration for the Tibetan Buddhist culture had been born within me. This led to a craving to learn and practise more of my culture at a deeper, more profound level. Immediately after returning from England I listened to and received the great *Lam Rim Chen Mo* teachings, commonly translated as the 'Stages of the Path to Enlightenment', from His Holiness the Dalai Lama. While teaching in Pokhara I came to the conclusion that the essence behind the great teachings was the need to know and understand your own mind. One day my desire to learn about my mind was so forceful that I took leave for the day and went to see a lama called Drubsing Rinpoche, who lived in Tashi Palkhiel.

'I cannot stay idle without understanding the mind. Please give me a teaching,' I requested.

'Very well,' he said and gave me a short teaching focused mainly on the nature of emptiness and the law of interdependence. I can still clearly remember him pointing to the low Tibetan-style table before him.

'You believe this to be a table,' he said, 'But I can argue that this is not so. Indeed, "table" is only a name that you have created and attached to something. In fact, it is pieces of wood that have been put together with nails. It required woodworkers and all of their tools. In turn, for these causes and conditions to come together, the wood would have needed countless different conditions of the elements to become the way it was. When all these countless causes and conditions come together then this table is created. Otherwise, "table" is just an empty name, there is nothing which is inherently a "table".'

This teaching was very helpful and increased my hunger and curiosity to learn more. I had also read a number of books and attended other teachings by many great lamas. Through these masters I had grown to respect and admire all the different branches of Tibetan Buddhism. My faith had grown with each teaching, and with each new step I took in my life I had a basis upon which I could develop these practices.

After my first-hand experiences of impermanence, through

the experiences of my life and through the teachings of a number of great lamas, I wanted to build on my practices. Therefore, after receiving a teaching from Dudjom Rinpoche, one of the greatest lamas of Tibet, I decided to carry out a three-month retreat. Unfortunately, two months into my retreat, Palden became very sick again. I had to prematurely end my retreat and care for her and our son Kunchok. Meanwhile, I also received news that I had been transferred to Dharamsala. After our return from Tso-Pema we had managed to build a manageable and relatively content life. With the encouragement and help of an American friend, Kunchok was attending a very good local English school. Now we had to leave this life in Kathmandu and head for Dharamsala.

Palden, Kunchok and I arrived in Dharamsala in 1982. I was appointed as Deputy-Secretary of the Department of Education. As the most senior of the three Deputy-Secretaries it was my duty to chair all the meetings of our department and finalise any decisions that had to be made, whenever the Secretary was away. The staff at the head office were all very sincere and enthusiastic towards their work. The office was filled with the cordial atmosphere of our shared goal — to improve the education of Tibetan children in any way that we could, so that they could effectively build a free and prosperous Tibet.

Education had always been my prime interest and I was very happy during the two years I worked for the department. I visited many schools and met both teachers and students. I had the opportunity to plan and supervise the initiation of new schools and the expansion and improvement of existing ones. Every time I met the students my heart filled with joy, knowing that I had been able to do something to improve their future. But the nature of my work meant that I was often away from Dharamsala, and both Palden and Kunchok found my long absences difficult at times. Indeed, I was away visiting schools so often that I was in Kathmandu when our third child Tenzin Lhadhar was born. Kunchok was very happy, as ever since our second son died at Tso-Pema, Kunchok had been praying for another little brother.

21

A mountain of ashes

Since becoming a refugee I had longed to return to Tibet, but this was just not possible. While I was working in Nepal this feeling intensified with the arrival of each new visitor and refugee. With a slight shift in the cold Chinese attitude towards Tibet during the early 1980s, I realised that this was my best opportunity to visit my homeland. This 'shift' meant that China was opening up to the outside world, and contact was established with an envoy of His Holiness the Dalai Lama. If I did not go back to Tibet soon I might not have the opportunity for a long while, as Chinese policy in Tibet was known to change at any moment, without notice.

I told my family, friends and relatives of my plans, but almost everyone was against the idea. Palden was especially worried, thinking that such a trip was just too dangerous. My decision was made even harder because Palden and I did not have the money to pay for such a journey. I would also have to seek leave from work and get permission from the Tibetan government because of my status as an employee.

My older brother Jignam had been back to Tibet twice in recent years and his help was a necessity. But such a trip for two people was going to be expensive — according to my brother's estimate it would cost 10,000 Indian rupees each. I borrowed 10,000 rupees from a friend in Manali, and with that money I bought goods from Delhi that could be sold in Lhasa. My plan was to then buy goods from Lhasa to sell in Kathmandu on the way back. I hoped that the profit would cover the costs of the trip — it did, and I was able to return the borrowed money after my return.

This trip provided a number of 'firsts' in my life. It was the first time that I was going to carry out a profit-making business. It was the first time that I had borrowed such a huge amount of money. It was the first time I was going to risk my life by going into Chinese hands. And most importantly, it was going to be the first time that I would set foot in my homeland since the Chinese occupation.

In July 1984, myself, my brother and some other fellow travellers reached the Tibetan border. We had walked for two-and-a-half days to reach the Nepalese checkpost; we then had to walk for another half a day to reach the Chinese checkpost. As soon as we reached the other side the emotion I felt was overwhelming. One of my fellow travellers and I dropped down. We touched the soil of Tibet, held it in our hands and then kissed the brown earth. We were back.

We found the road that led further into our country. This was still being built by Tibetan road labourers, and the dust from the roadworks and the poverty of the workers reminded me of the Tibetans in exile in the sixties, working on road construction sites in India and Nepal. Even in our homeland, Tibetans had become road construction labourers working under foreign control.

Many of these labourers came to us in large groups enthusiastically asking for blessed pills, and threads blessed by His Holiness the Dalai Lama and other lamas. I had brought many of these things into Tibet but I had to hold back — I could not give the labourers what they wanted. Handing out such things would have been inviting trouble from the Chinese authorities before we had even left the border area.

The huge red national flag of China was flying over the checkpost and customs office. It was flapping rather uneasily — as if it did not agree with the Tibetan winds. Neither did the sharp-red look comfortable in front of the vast, unique deep-blue backdrop of the Tibetan sky.

Just entering the customs office was rather intimidating. Everyone was speaking in Chinese, even the Tibetans who were working there. The coarse language and the untamed rough-ness of the officers echoed off the blank walls of the office. We were uneasy and afraid. One of the officers asked, 'Have you anything to declare?'

He was referring to such things as radios, cameras, watches and other contraband. My brother and I declared the six watches we had brought. We knew that we were each allowed to take ex-actly three watches, a tape-recorder/radio and any number of cameras into Tibet. We declared all such items and then one of the officers searched my brother's bags.

The Chinese officer was very thorough with his search, check-ing every corner of the bags, and opening every book and piece of paper. Then the officer took out my brother's diary. Now we were extremely nervous. My brother was keeping small Tibetan flags hidden in the back of his diary. The officer flipped through the pages, and surely … the flags fell out. The officer fumed with anger and stamped his feet on the floor.

'You know that this is very anti-national,' he shouted like a madman. 'You are risking your life, you know that. Do you want life-imprisonment or the death-penalty?' This was translated for us by a nervous Tibetan officer.

We quietly watched as the Chinese officer threatened my brother and then led him down a flight of stairs. A short while later a customs officer of Tibetan origin came to confirm with me that Jignam was indeed my brother. He was as coarse and rough as any of the Chinese officers, and suddenly he began to behave very forcefully.

'Show me your other belongings!' he shouted. I pointed out my luggage to him. Inside one of the boxes I had a huge portrait of His Holiness the Dalai Lama.

'What's in there?' he shouted again, pointing at that box.

'There is nothing but a portrait,' I answered.

He leaned towards me and quickly whispered, 'Is it a portrait of His Holiness?'

'Yes,' I replied, startled by the sudden drop in the volume of his voice and his use of 'His Holiness'. Then he went back to shouting.

'Open the box!' He pointed at the rolled-up portrait of His Holiness. 'What is this?'

'It is a portrait of His Holiness.'

'Let me see,' he cried sternly, but with a tone of eagerness in his voice. He looked at it for a while. I don't know whether he was praying with an inner voice or just satisfying some curiosity, but he held the portrait high and scanned every inch of it. He then handed it back to me rather carefully before continuing his shouting.

'You are a very good man,' he said. 'You declared all that you have, and you only brought one portrait of the Dalai. The policy of the Chinese government is absolutely good and lenient. Whatever is allowed is allowed and whatever is disallowed is disallowed. You may take what you have. Close the suitcase!'

The officer quickly marked that he had checked all of my belongings including the ones he had not even touched, and I realised that this Tibetan officer was helping me. He had to shout and put on this charade to deceive the Chinese officers. I was grateful but also rather sad. In order to survive and succeed in our homeland Tibetans had to be what they were not.

Once everyone else had been cleared by customs my brother finally reappeared, and we were allowed to proceed to the hotel where we were going to stay. We were tired and hungry but we could not sleep; worry about what tomorrow might bring kept us awake. Suddenly, around half-past midnight, someone kicked open our door and marched into the room. It was a Chinese army official in his green uniform. He demanded our permits and passports, although these had already been taken by the authorities and were being kept at the reception office so that we could not go anywhere. After intimidating us and a fellow Tibetan roommate, he left. The next morning I found out that this treatment had been directed especially at us, in all probability, because of the Tibetan flags my brother had brought with him.

That day we had to go to the Immigration Office with our permits. We were made to fill out a form that recorded every detail of who we were and what we had been doing since 1959. We even had to fill in details of our family and relatives, including their names, ages, and other personal information. I did not like it at all. I felt as if I was somehow betraying my family and relatives by giving their details to the Chinese. When it was my brother's turn to fill out the forms, the official overseeing us stopped him and said, 'Sorry, there is something wrong with your permit, you should come back this afternoon.'

We knew that this was not normal. We left the office and slowly walked back towards the hotel. I knew I had to do something. I told my brother to return to the hotel while I went back to the Immigration Office. When I arrived I found a Tibetan in uniform pacing around in the office. This man looked like a visitor and not a local officer. I went to the desk of some lower-ranking officers.

'Who is the most important person in the office?' I asked them.

'Why?' they asked suspiciously.

'I have something very important to tell,' I told them.

'Talk to that gentleman,' they said, pointing at the official pacing around the office. I decided to play on the psychology of the Chinese officials — knowing how much they loved flattery of any sort and how keen they would be to gain a staff member of the Tibetan Government-in-Exile on their side. I told the official that I was a staff member from Dharamsala. They probably knew this anyway. Then I bent the facts for both my brother's sake and mine.

'My brother has been to Tibet twice already. He was the one who convinced me to come with him and to return to my birth-place. I did not want to return to Tibet unless it was completely independent ... this was my aim in living abroad. But my brother insisted that I should visit Tibet. He told me that things had changed. That there were positive developments. Only because he wanted to show all this to me did I change my mind.

'Despite my faith in my brother and the words encouraging our return by the Chinese leadership, I have experienced so many difficulties in just twenty-four hours that I do not wish to proceed any further.

'My brother has been threatened with execution and life im-prisonment just because some Tibetan flags fell out of his diary. Secondly, a Chinese army officer marched into our hotel room well after midnight without even knocking on the door. I am only at the border with Nepal and I have already faced so many difficulties. I am bound to meet more problems and hostilities if I proceed any further into Tibet. Therefore, I do not wish to go any further. I am also going to take my brother back with me because you consider him to be a troublemaker. From my point of view, my brother is a traitor to me, as he was the one who encouraged me to come on this journey at all!'

The official hesitated for a moment, then he said, 'I am very glad that you told me the truth. I am very happy that you decided to at least visit this country. It is very good of your brother to have persuaded you to come this far.

'I will use my powers to facilitate your visit to our country,' he said. 'Don't return from here, I give you my word that you will have a happy journey. Please proceed further. Just tell your brother to return here at three o'clock. Nothing will happen to him, I guarantee it.'

I was not happy that my brother would still have to return to the office at three.

'Do you promise?' I asked.

At three o'clock that afternoon Jignam wasn't even asked the usual questions. He just had to fill out a form similar to the one I had filled out, but before he was allowed to leave he had to go to another office with a uniformed Chinese officer. There he was told about the seriousness of his crime. He was also told that he had been forgiven and he was congratulated for convincing me to come to Tibet. The lecture continued for quite a while before my brother was allowed to leave.

Despite us being seemingly free I was very uneasy. I was suspicious and felt that the police were watching us wherever we went. We had to wait for a bus to Lhasa but it wasn't due for another few days. On the fifth day after reaching the border, the official with whom I had talked came to our hotel. He wanted to know how we proposed to travel from the border-post. I said that we were leaving on the bus that was meant to come the following day.

'You won't need to take the bus, there will be a jeep coming to fetch you two from Lhasa,' he told us.

'From Lhasa?' I was surprised and suspicious. It could not be a good sign to have official vehicles from Lhasa come to fetch us.

'Oh no,' he replied, looking as if he had said something he had not meant to. 'No … from Shigatse, not from Lhasa. I am sorry. The reception committee from Shigatse decided to send a jeep especially for you as you are an official from Dharamsala.'

I was not eager to travel in a government jeep with official escorts watching everything we did.

'But I have already booked seats in the bus,' I replied. 'I would rather go in the bus even though the jeep has been sent.'

'No, no, no, the jeep will be here by five o'clock in the afternoon.' He was sterner this time. I knew we did not have a choice.

We hurriedly packed our things and a member of the police force accompanied us in the jeep from the hotel. That afternoon we drove past two to three thousand Tibetans working on the road. Their tired faces looked up at us as the jeep drove past. I could not even look into their eyes. Most of the labourers wore clothes that were patched up so many times that I could not tell which was the original cloth or what was the original colour. The shabby small tents the workers had erected by the roadside reminded me of my own family's experience near Manali on my return from England. But in India we were refugees and free. Here the labourers looked bleak and sad and without energy.

That first night we were put up in a tent with one of the labourer families — the security official diligently stayed with us too. That evening, as I sat in that small tent, I took out my prayer books and started my evening prayers. The family's small child who was about three came to me and took my rosary. He folded it in his small hands and then stumbled over to the officer. Then the child put it on the man's head saying '*Om mani padme hum*' — the mantra of compassion that almost every Tibetan recites. Then the child put my rosary on his own head, and then his father's and his mother's heads while still reciting the mantra.

Because it was a Sunday night, the father was dead drunk. But even in this state he was very patriotic to the Tibetan cause. He kept saying, 'If only I could see His Holiness return to Tibet … nothing else matters.' Then he would point at the official and say, 'I know you will tell this to the authorities tomorrow.'

This made my guard–guide very embarrassed, perhaps because he was a Tibetan who had studied in China. In his uneasiness he tried to explain, 'The supreme policy of the Chinese government is completely pure. There will be no repercussions for you. Whatever you say today will be of no consequence tomorrow.'

The poor mother of the little child became visibly anxious although she tried to hide it. She seemed very worried about the consequences of both her son's and her husband's actions.

'His grandmother has absolute blind faith in the religion and this boy, this very naughty boy, is again following his stupid grandmother's bad example.'

The young woman was pretending to curse her own mother, but I think in her heart she was happy that her son acted as he did. Her use of the words 'blind faith' was important since they were the words used by the Chinese authorities to describe religion.

As we travelled through the ever-changing landscape of Tibet, a few things didn't change. Overlooking almost every village and town was a dominating ruin; these were the remains of old Tibet. They used to be great monasteries or grand buildings such as the district headquarters; they were places of authority — focal points for the local people. Places where the people could come together and satisfy their spiritual needs, or places where they could settle disputes and seek justice. These places were all destroyed during the Chinese invasion.

Another thing that didn't change was the poverty. In all the villages and towns the majority of inhabitants looked unbearably poor. I really believe that they were much poorer than almost any Tibetans had been when Tibet was still independent.

I learnt that the Chinese claims of building many schools, hospitals and roads also seemed rather baseless. The 'road' from the Nepalese border to Lhasa was a long stretch of dirt, and I counted only three schools between the border and Lhasa, only one of which looked presentable from the outside.

I also learnt that the 'hospitals' where Western medicine was practised could not possibly deserve such a name. Most of the doctors who claimed to be qualified surgeons only had a meagre three to six months of training in China before being sent to remote places in Tibet.

Fortunately, Tibetan medicine was still practised, and need-less to say it was much more popular. In old Tibet, although we did not have designated hospital buildings, every village had their own doctors. But after the invasion, most of these doctors were forced into labour camps where they perished. Now, very few were left. In Namru, before the invasion, there were two doctors in my tsowa alone and the district had over twenty-five respected doctors. Now, in this same district (which is much larger today than it was in my childhood due to the Chinese redrawing of maps), there was only one Tibetan doctor and one of the three-to-six-month Chinese-trained doctors.

While I was travelling between major towns and cities in Tibet every vehicle I saw on the roads was owned by the People's Lib-eration Army or the police. Out of the few inter-city roads I travelled on only the Lhasa–Nakchukha road was sealed, and that had only happened the year before. This is hardly surprising, being part of a national highway connecting China and Tibet. But even on this highway, there was hardly any traffic. Later during my time in Tibet, when I travelled on this road, the only vehicles I saw were three convoys of army trucks, each with over eighty trucks. Except for these huge convoys I never saw a private car, and not a single bus. Traditionally the roads between Lhasa and Nepal were very important trade routes. But on this important route there was only a solitary bus service, and to catch this bus, travellers had to wait for two to three weeks. This can hardly be called a bus service!

The Western media, even at the time, used to say rather confidently that the Chinese invasion had brought modernity to Tibet — that there were now roads, hospitals and other modern necessities. There was hardly any mention or attention paid to the quantity, quality and purposes of these 'modern' things. Neither was there any real analysis of whether Tibetans — the people to whom this land belonged — were better or worse off.

Since then, there has been tremendous infrastructure development accompanied by unprecedented economic growth in Tibet. But this has only accelerated the government-encouraged mass migration of the Chinese into Tibet which has further marginalised the Tibetan people. With the exception of a few, the Tibetans are unable to take part in this rapid economic growth due to the fact that the Chinese language has become predominant in all facets of life in Tibet. Besides, Tibetans do not enjoy the official 'back-door' connections which seem to be very important for any success. Rather, Tibetans are treated with suspicion as potential 'splittists'. Therefore we Tibetans are fast becoming a disadvantaged minority in our own homeland and the Tibetan culture and race could face annihilation. The strategic railway linking China and Tibet will further accelerate this end.

When we reached the district headquarters in Namru we found that it was now some two kilometres away from the original buildings. In the old district headquarters we had a temple and a big library for Buddhist texts and biographies of great lamas and people of the area. There was also a two-storey stone building for the district commissioners. Except for feelings and memories, there was nothing there but remnants; everything had been destroyed. In its place, at the new site, the Chinese had built new, long, tin-roofed, one-storey buildings, surrounded by a high wall. It looked like a military barrack or a prison camp: isolated, saddening and cold.

After staying there for a night we travelled to our aunt's home. As with everywhere we went, the Chinese came to us and asked if they could help us in any way. We always declined this seemingly polite offer. This was because any assistance would mean sending a 'guide' with us who would watch over us the whole while.

Our aunt used to be very wealthy before we escaped to India. It was said that her family had enough barley in their granary to feed them for at least two years. They had owned a huge house, a big chapel of their own and had a huge black tent pitched permanently near the house. Most importantly, they had many, many horses, sheep and yaks — the symbols of wealth in the land of the drogpas.

All these had been confiscated and the buildings had been demolished. After the Chinese invasion my aunt's family had been labelled as 'rich' and a 'landlord'. In the years that followed not only had the Chinese robbed them of everything they had owned but they had forcibly divided up my aunt's large family into four smaller families.

When we reached our aunt's house there was only ruins and a very small, ragged tent. My aunt had died many years ago. Now her eldest daughter and her family were living in that small tent. I was so happy to meet her, but so sad and shocked to see my cousin in such a state. I felt as if I could not even stay there a moment longer, but I had to. We had come all the way from India, putting our lives at risk, primarily to see her and our surviving relatives again. I had to stay with them.

I travelled around Namru for fourteen days visiting relatives, friends, well-wishers and even the families of people I had never seen, but whose parents I had known. Everyone had suffered, everyone lived in terrible conditions, everyone had grown poor. Still, many of these families invited us to their homes. They considered our visit a blessing just because we had come from the headquarters of His Holiness the Dalai Lama. They felt that His Holiness's blessing was somehow with us.

When I was a child, even an average drogpa family had a large, strong tent that could house ten to fifteen people comfortably. Now only one family in the region had a tent that could house more than five people. None of the Tibetan families in my locality had more than fifty Chinese yuan, so they had no money to buy anything. Even if they did have money there was hardly anything to buy. In old Tibet, if someone had money they could purchase treasures brought from Kham, Kalimpong or Lhasa. They could buy anything from guns to sweets. But now there was absolutely nothing. Indeed, it had only been a year since they were even allowed to sell their own wool. Until then, the government had even taken that. How were the drogpas expected to survive?

Not only had the lives of the people of Namru changed tremendously, even the landscape had changed. The Chinese had forced the local people to build walls around mountains and across thousands of miles over the Chang-Thang plains. On top of all the hills and mountains the Chinese have erected high iron pillars. Over hundreds of years Tibetans had carved and painted the mani, as well as other such mantras, on rocks on the slopes of mountains. But now the Chinese had carved or painted huge Chinese characters praising Chairman Mao and exalting the Communist Party. These ludicrous praises had also replaced the mani on the walls near every family home in my area.

The Chinese had forced our people to destroy the great stone mani walls which their own families had accumulated over many generations. The Chinese even forced the Tibetans to use these stones for sacrilegious purposes. They were made to use mani stones to cover the floor of their homes and to build bridges over rivers. No one would ever step over a mani stone in old Tibet; even now they would never do that if they lived in freedom and had the choice.

During this time in my region I didn't see wild animals roaming the great plains. Most of them had been killed off. My children, Tibetan children, Chinese children — no one would be able to see some of those amazing animals that I had seen in my childhood.

The Chinese even stole the names of our tsowas and districts, replacing them with their own. Namru was now called Pago-shen and Ringpa had been changed to Phuwo-chu. For us exiles returning home, the whole district of Namru and my own tsowa had completely disappeared. None of the younger generations in our region knew about the old names, and they did not even exist in the memories of most people in the area. The older generations had not dared to mention the old names for fear of being prosecuted for harbouring counter-revolutionary thoughts.

While in Namru, Jignam and I reluctantly went to visit the place where our house used to stand. In the green valley between four small mountains and two clear sparkling streams, there was nothing. Our family home had been keenly destroyed by the Chinese because my father had been the elected garpon of the district. The generations-old thangkas and statues were destroyed. The 108 volumes of the teachings of Lord Buddha were destroyed too. The wall of our large family tent was destroyed. Everything was gone. The only things that testified that a family had lived there for many generations were the stone pillars to which we tied up our mastiff dogs, and the mountain of ashes. And even the heap of ashes, with grass growing from it, looked ancient and as if it had always been a part of the land.

On our way to Namru from Lhasa the Chinese sent an emissary to us. This happened to be someone my family knew, and he came to us many times trying to persuade us to return for good. He told us how wonderful it would be in the future, despite the past mistakes made by the Gang of Four — the radical members of Mao's inner circle who were later purged and imprisoned after Mao's death. Every time I had to tell him the same thing, 'After the Gang of Four, there would be another group who in turn would be blamed. So, until the whole question of Tibet is settled, I am very reluctant to accept any invitation.'

Each time I repeated this I could see that he felt a little uneasy about my straightforwardness, having lived in an authoritarian society for decades, but there was little he could say in return.

While in Tibet I could not fail to see the determination of the majority of Tibetans to secretly fight in their own ways for their nation. I met a number of people, including several high-ranking officials, who made their feelings plain to me. When word went around that a staff member from Dharamsala was visiting, many

Tibetans came to me to say that I was wrong to have come at all. Others came to me hoping that I would be able to inform His Holiness of their plight. Many asked me to convey to His Holiness that he should never return until the Chinese had vacated our country. Even among the Tibetan members of the Communist Party there were many who had strong feelings for their country and for what the Chinese had done to it. Whenever I spoke with these people, they never used the word 'Chinese', rather they just said 'our boss'.

The division between the Tibetans and Chinese was very clear. In Lhasa, for instance, the Chinese lived in newly built, decent, clean areas, while the Tibetans were still in the old Tibetan houses. The sanitation in the Tibetan quarter was very poor. The few public toilets had no roofs and were only shielded from public view up to the hips. Of course, in the Chinese quarter, they had proper public lavatories.

In Lhasa, around the Jokhang Temple, the heart of the old Tibetan capital city, there were almost no Chinese in sight. I don't think they dared to go there alone as they were very suspicious of Tibetans. And in the Chinese quarter there were only a few trusted Tibetans. Lhasa had become a city divided in two, but the Chinese quarter was growing at an increasingly quick rate, while the Tibetan quarter was shrinking as the authorities demolished age-old buildings.

Since the Chinese invasion Tibetans have suffered incalculably. But the force and inhumane treatment of Tibetans has led Tibetans to resist in any way they could and to remain united despite all efforts by the Chinese. It made them long for the leadership of His Holiness the Dalai Lama and for the independence of Tibet. But the introduction of more lenient policies by the Chinese during the 1980s has relaxed the attentiveness of every Tibetan. And the Chinese seemed to be using more subtle methods to destroy the Tibetan identity. For instance, I noticed that the Chinese were discreetly bringing a large number of televisions into Tibet and selling them at amazingly cheap prices. While most Tibetan families had television sets they did not have the choice of viewing anything apart from the Chinese programs. Most of those programs were hardly more than Chinese government propaganda, and I feared this might be a very effective and subtle form of brainwashing.

The one positive effect of the more lenient policy was that Tibetans were now listening to radio broadcasts from overseas. These broadcasts would have helped to broaden their views and to develop an understanding of the real world beyond the government propaganda they are fed in Tibet.

There is no balance to the positive and negative effects of the Chinese occupation, and at the end of my travels in Tibet the sadness in my heart settled permanently. Certainly, having seen my homeland, I returned to Nepal with a reinforced resolution to work even harder for my people. But as I crossed the border I looked back to my country again and again, and sent a wish to the heavens that I would be able to return to a free Tibet, my rightful homeland, before the end of my days.

22

The Representative of His Holiness the Dalai Lama

Upon my return from Tibet I learnt that I had been transferred from Dharamsala back to Nepal as the Education Officer, to oversee the Tibetan government schools. The decade of nationalised education in Nepal had ended and my appointment was in conjunction with this policy shift.

An important outcome of my work was to achieve a consensus on the meaning of 'education'. I believed that without a firm grasp of the meaning of this word, the teachers and government officers in Nepal could not hope to effectively educate the Tibetan children. Therefore, I organised a week-long seminar for the headmasters and teachers of the Tibetan schools. At the conclusion of the seminar we agreed that we must aim to cultivate three qualities within each student by the time they graduate. Firstly, the individual must uphold kindness and compassion as a means to serve and interact within society. Secondly, as a Tibetan, our graduates must uphold a love of Tibet and the Tibetan cause. Thirdly, we aimed to provide our students with a modern education that would equip them with the skills to face the inevitable challenges of life. At the conclusion of the seminar, all the participants agreed to strive towards these ideals and hold them close to their hearts when they carried out their jobs as teachers, headmasters and administrators.

During that time I took part in the planning and building of a new secondary school for the Tibetan children in the Himalayan kingdom. Simultaneously, I raised the wages of the teachers to attract new, better-trained professionals. To cover the pay rise I initiated a small school-fee system. I feared that there might be an outcry from the parents who may refuse to pay the fees, but fortunately I was wrong. The majority of parents were more than co-operative and took greater interest in the education of their children and the results their children achieved. This further motivated the students to study and developed a healthy sense of competition between the schools, as many parents chose the higher-achieving schools over others.

Within two years the performance of the fifteen or sixteen Tibetan schools in Nepal had dramatically improved.

At the time, Palden and I joked that our first child was the son of the Dhorpaten Camp-in-Charge and our third child was the son of a Deputy-Secretary in the Department of Education, whose son would our fourth child be? Towards the end of my second year as the Education Officer, that question was answered. I received a letter that appointed me the new Representative of His Holiness the Dalai Lama for Nepal. The title was simply overwhelming. In truth, I do not have any qualities to represent His Holiness in any way, but I did my very best as an ordinary Tibetan to uphold the dignity and duty that came with it.

In November of that year, 1987, my fourth child was born — the son of the new Representative for Nepal. On the day of his birth the two older children excitedly jumped about the house shouting, 'Shenphen Dorje is here! Shenphen has arrived!'

I didn't know what they were talking about.

'Who has arrived?' I asked my sons.

I had forgotten that I had half jokingly given a name for my fourth son many months before he was born. *Shenphen* means 'to help others' and I had used that particular name to remind my sons of the value attached to those words. I had not particularly intended to name our youngest son.

Palden was uncomfortable with the fact that our new child's name was given by his father instead of a lama, so a few days later we went to see Chogye Trichen Rinpoche. Rinpoche asked what we called him now. He said that Shenphen Dorje was a very good name and added 'Tsering' to it which means 'long life'. Therefore, our fourth son became Tsering Shenphen Dorje. My older boys continued to call him 'Shenphen'.

Although Nepal is a small nation, due to its strategic geographical situation it is one of the most active stages upon which the struggle between the Tibetans and the Chinese is played out. From that perspective the responsibility that I took on was quite heavy. But as the Tibetan saying goes, 'When carried, half a container of water splashes about more than a full container', and after having worked in the little settlement of Dhorpaten nothing felt too difficult.

The major responsibility of the Representative was to look after the general welfare of the Tibetans in Nepal. That included the education and health of the public, and ensuring there were no misunderstandings and disharmonies between the Nepalese and the Tibetan refugee communities. I was also the chairman of many of the industries which the Tibetan community had built and, therefore, partly responsible for their efficiency, productivity and the wellbeing of their employees.

Another important responsibility was helping new refugees

from Tibet, and the few who were allowed to visit their relatives in exile. Keeping their faith in His Holiness the Dalai Lama deep within their hearts, the refugees had endured enormous hardships on their treacherous journey across the Himalayas, and Nepal was the door through which they entered a new life. The majority were teenagers and younger children who had come for the education opportunities — to freely learn their own language, culture and to practise Buddhism. Therefore, a sizable share were young nuns and monks. As the representative of His Holiness the Dalai Lama and the Tibetan Government-in-Exile, I considered it of utmost importance to receive these new refugees and visitors sincerely and warmly.

Although the United Nations High Commissioner for Refugees (UNHCR) had an office in Kathmandu and was heavily involved with Tibetan refugees during the 1960s, this assistance completely ceased once the People's Republic of China gained membership to the United Nations in 1971. In fact, under Chinese pressure they decided not to even recognise Tibetans as refugees and their office in Kathmandu was closed. While there had always been a steady trickle of Tibetan refugees fleeing Chinese persecution, following the 1988 and 1989 protests, and their brutal suppression in Lhasa, several hundred refugees escaped into Nepal every month. And none of the international aid organisations, including the UNHCR, would assist them.

I came to know that the UNHCR, through the UNICEF office in Kathmandu, were assisting about half a dozen Chinese refugees following the 1989 Tiananmen Square tragedy. I approached the UNICEF officer for the protection of five recent escapees from Tibet, who were also wanted by the Chinese authorities for their political activities. I was told that the UNHCR does not recognise the existence of Tibetan refugees because they do not believe there to be a conflict in Tibet. I told the representative that the Tibetan escapees were escaping from the same repressive authority as the Chinese students. If they had two policies — one for the Chinese and one for the Tibetan refugees — it was either discrimination against Tibetans or recognition of the fact that Tibet is a separate country. I demanded a letter explaining the case. Two days later, the UNICEF representative called me and said the UNHCR regional office gave her permission to give protection and a small financial allowance to the five Tibetan escapees.

At the time the Nepal government was pressing for a UNHCR office to be set up in Kathmandu for the sake of the Nepalese refugees expelled from Bhutan. This had become a contentious issue between the two neighbouring kingdoms and Nepal wanted the involvement of the international community. I was able to privately meet the three-member delegation from Geneva, and they later pressed that the UNHCR office in Nepal should process any legitimate refugee cases, including Tibetan cases as well. The UNHCR re-established its office in Kathmandu and they processed and recognised thousands of Tibetan refugees in co-operation with the Tibetan Refugee Welfare Office — the official title of our office in Nepal. I was very happy that my quiet lobbying had paid off.

In October 1989 a great wave of joy swept across the Tibetan community the world over. The Nobel Committee had announced the awarding of that year's Nobel Peace Prize to His Holiness the Dalai Lama. We all felt that His Holiness's leadership of the Tibetan struggle for truth and justice through non-violence had been recognised at last. As a Tibetan this has been one of the most joyful occasions of my life.

Working in Nepal was often a delicate and problematic task. After the Chinese occupation of Tibet, Nepal was sandwiched between two competing giants, India and China. The kingdom has had to tread carefully in its international relations, but appears to be fostering closer political and economic ties with China. The kingdom often seems to take India's open-mindedness and its political culture of democracy for granted. Taking too much consideration of Chinese sensitivities, Tibetan refugees often fall victim to the kingdom's efforts to keep China happy.

Consequently, with growing pressure on the Nepalese government from the Chinese, more and more restrictions were placed on the activities of the Tibetans in Nepal. Although we had no obvious political activities, Tibetans always celebrated important Tibetan national days such as His Holiness the Dalai Lama's Birthday (6 July), National Uprising Day (10 March), Tibetan Democracy Day (2 September) and Tibetan New Year's Day. The Nepalese government always attempted to curb these events through the offices of the Zonal Commissioner, the Chief District Office and the local police departments. Many times I was summoned to these offices to be warned that if any anti-Chinese sentiments occurred I would be held responsible, and that there would be severe consequences.

In October 1987, almost a year after I had taken on the position as the representative, Nepal hosted the Summit of the South Asian Association for Regional Cooperation (SAARC), which included India, Pakistan, Bhutan, Bangladesh, Sri Lanka, the Maldives and Nepal. All the heads of states were to be in attendance. In anticipation of the pressure that the Nepalese government would place on us, we decided not to carry out any Tibet-related political activities and to assist the government in any way we could to make the event a success.

Ten days prior to the commencement of the summit I met

the Secretary of the Home Affairs Ministry and the Kathmandu Zonal Commissioner. I assured them that the Tibetans would not carry out any Tibet-related political activities and offered our sincere wish to assist in making the summit a success. I also requested the release of a Tibetan businessman who had been arrested by the police two days ago. In those days there was a draconian law enabling local authorities to arrest and hold people in detention without having to charge them for nine months. Both the Secretary and the Commissioner denied knowledge of the businessman's arrest and promised to look into the case. They also expressed their gratitude for our assurance and willingness to help make the summit a success.

A few days after my meetings, I was met by a casually dressed police officer who saluted me and asked me to come to our local police station. He told me that the director of station wished to meet me at his office. The officer did not know the reason, but I hoped that the station director was going to release the Tibetan businessman who was arrested there. Accompanied by the officer, I went to the police station. Upon arrival the officer saluted his superior in his very serious fashion and reported, 'Mr Tsering is here, sir.'

The station director asked me to sit down. After a short while, I was surprised to see Phenpo Gyaltsen, another Tibetan community leader, also coming through the door with a police escort. He was asked to sit beside me. I began to feel suspicious but the station director was still very courteous and respectful. He told us that the Kathmandu central police station had asked us to see them.

With a police inspector beside me and with Gyaltsen in the rear seat I drove my car to the central police station. As I drove I felt that I was going to be detained and Gyaltsen confirmed my suspicion. He had been detained in a similar manner a couple of times before. When we arrived at the central police station some officers asked us to confirm our details and then led us to a heavily guarded gate and said, 'Please walk in.'

This gate led us into the most notorious detention centre in Nepal.

'I will not …' I protested, 'without an explanation and a warrant.'

'It is orders from above, please don't argue … get in,' said one of the officers as he pushed me past the gate.

I was locked into a small dark cell where Gyaltsen was already sitting. About an hour later our cell door was opened and Wangchuk Tsering, another Tibetan community leader, joined us. His wife had also been arrested and was at a women's detention centre. It was now obvious that the Nepal government was rounding up the Tibetan community leaders as an overly cautious precaution for the SAARC summit. A few minutes after Wangchuk Tsering's arrival, bedding and food sent by our three families was given to us by a warden.

The following morning one of my senior staff members was allowed to meet me briefly and he told me that he had already informed the Tibetan government in Dharamsala of our arrests. That afternoon at around three o'clock we were told to pack up our bedding. Our belongings were returned to us and we were asked to sign a couple of documents. We were then put into a high-security police van, with an armed escort, and taken to the central jail. Compared to the notorious detention centre, the jail seemed quite pleasant at first. Prisoners were strolling about in a large, open courtyard and around this sunny courtyard there were four, two-storey prison blocks on each of the four sides. I was told that each of the blocks could house up to fifty prisoners. The whole complex was surrounded by high walls crowned with barbed-wire fencing, police watchtowers and searchlights. There were about five hundred prisoners there, the majority of whom were convicted murderers serving life sentences.

I was kept in that prison for the next eleven days. Every day Tibetans in the dozens came to meet me bearing plenty of food and fruits. Many of them were people I had never personally known; Tibetans from all walks of life. Many of them broke down as they saw me, the Representative of His Holiness the Dalai Lama, behind bars. I tried my best to comfort them but that was all I could do. One young woman even became uncontrollably emotional — she pushed and tried to scratch the faces of the prison guards as she screamed, 'Arrest me if you dare!'

Most of the detainees who were detained due to the SAARC summit were released a few days after its conclusion. But there was no indication that we, the Tibetan prisoners, were going to be released. Although the excuse for our arrest seemed to have been the SAARC summit, I feared we were being held for a more sinister reason. Indeed, former Tibetan guerilla leaders had been held under this same act for over six years. Therefore, I planned to launch a hunger strike if we were not released after the completion of the second week.

The boys and Palden came to see me. I gave Kunchok and Lhadhar some packets of biscuits and asked them to be strong. I asked Palden to take good care of herself if I was held for long. I was happy to see them for the first time after my arrest, and somehow felt it could also be the last time. But Palden told me that my staff had met Nepalese officials and there were indications that we could be released soon. I did not believe this as it is a common promise made by Nepalese government officials.

Forty minutes after Palden and the boys had left, as I was walking around the barren courtyard in my pyjamas, slippers and a shawl, my name was called again from the gate. I walked over wondering who had come to see me this time. There was nobody. A warden opened the gate and the guards pushed me out saying, 'You are released.'

I was a free man again — at least, as free as a stateless man can be.

Epilogue

In June 1992, His Holiness the Dalai Lama was visiting Hungary, having been invited to mark the 150th birthday of the world's best-known Tibetologist: the Hungarian national hero, Alexander Csoma de Koros. As the designated Representative of His Holiness the Dalai Lama for Eastern Europe, I was a member of His Holiness's entourage and following the visit I remained behind in London to initiate discussions on establishing a representative's office in Hungary. At the time, the Office of Tibet in London covered the Eastern European countries as well. Subsequent to the agreement I formally returned to Budapest — as the Representative of His Holiness the Dalai Lama for Eastern Europe, and remained there for the next six years.

During those years I was inspired by the winds of new-found freedom and the optimism shared by the people, as their societies were transformed from rigid communist states to countries that embraced democracy and the market economy. From the Baltic States in the north to Albania in the south, the nations I frequently travelled to had been under the shackles of an oppressive system; the same system that now brutally rules my own country. I could see a positive trend towards the disintegration of this system and at the time this gave me added hope. The people of these countries could truly understand our plight, and I particularly valued the genuine sympathy and understanding of the people of Eastern Europe. Whenever we told them of how 1.2 million Tibetans perished as a direct result of Chinese occupation, leaving not even a single Tibetan family untouched, and how thousands of monasteries and temples had been destroyed, they understood us completely because they had been through similar experiences. In most Western countries, and even in Nepal or India, it is much harder for people to understand or accept these facts. In some cases, with the Western media in particular, our experiences are viewed as only a one-sided perspective, and they often seem to work hard to seek out the Chinese government's version of each story. Our truth is therefore sometimes overwhelmed by Chinese propaganda. I find this very disturbing.

There is a real belief in the countries of Eastern Europe that the issue of Tibet should be resolved peacefully, while His Holiness the Dalai Lama is guiding the Tibetan people with his message of peace and love. Otherwise the situation in Tibet has the potential to become violent and unstable, like any prolonged situation of oppression, as in the Balkans. The genuine sympathy of Eastern Europeans has translated into strong support for the Tibetan cause by parliamentarians and civic organisations such as the Helsinki Foundation for Human Rights in Warsaw, and other similar groups. Through the United Nations Commission on Human Rights (UNCHR) in Geneva these countries have annually supported censure motions against China for human rights violations in Tibet.

While in Eastern Europe I worked with the people of this region who still felt the trauma of decades of brutality. I wanted to share our unique expertise: how to achieve peace of mind.

Through His Holiness the Dalai Lama's numerous visits to the region and by organising the creation of sand mandalas and teachings by Tibetan masters, our office worked hard to achieve this goal.

Following my time in Eastern Europe my family moved to Australia, where I served as His Holiness the Dalai Lama's Representative for the Oceania Region for four years. My family and I love life in Australia. We love the beauty of the vast land, the 'fair go' nature of the people and how Australians tend to support the underdogs, just as Tibetans do. We love the wonderful multicultural spirit of the nation and decided that this country would be our home until the issue of Tibet is resolved.

Tibet is fortunate to have true friends within the parliaments of both Australia and New Zealand, and to have strong public Tibet support groups such as the Australia Tibet Council and Friends of Tibet, New Zealand. The substantial membership of these support groups and their presence in most regional capitals reflects the public's sympathy and concern for my country's plight.

During His Holiness's last visit to Australia and New Zealand in May 2002, more than 120,000 people directly participated in the public talks and teachings in Australia and another 50,000 in New Zealand. Buddhism is reported to be the fastest growing religion in Australia, and these figures indicate the level of appreciation for His Holiness the Dalai Lama's philosophy of non-violence and compassion, as well as indirect support for Tibet.

Both the Australian and New Zealand governments encourage the People's Republic of China to resolve the issue of Tibet through dialogue with His Holiness the Dalai Lama. Australia maintains an annual human rights dialogue with China, and human rights issues in Tibet are important items on their agenda.

The fact that the issue of Tibet is an international matter is clear, and sooner or later this issue must be resolved. The Tibetan struggle is not the struggle of a person, an elite group or even a generation. It is the struggle of a nation and its people.

While the world is blessed with the presence of His Holiness, who enjoys the confidence of every Tibetan, be they in Tibet or in exile, it would be foolish for the Chinese leadership not to have the political will and courage to seriously engage in a meaningful dialogue with His Holiness. Unfortunately, so far in the past, the Chinese leadership has been blinded by suspicion and a chauvinistic complexity. Whereas the new Chinese leadership has had direct experience of Tibetan sentiment and culture. I sincerely hope that they will have the courage and wisdom to see the sincerity of His Holiness's proposals.

A solution based on His Holiness's Middle Way proposal could offer a unique opportunity for the Chinese leadership to legally include Tibet as a part of China. Tibet and Tibetans could share our generations of experience and expertise in cultivating inner peace and social happiness; while China and the Chinese could share their development skills in the material sphere. The two communities could happily complement each other's well-being while maintaining their own way of life in their own regions within one international boundary.

However, if the Chinese leadership believe they can find a lasting solution to the issue of Tibet through suppression and force, they are wrong. So far, the Tibetan people have heeded His Holiness's advice and followed His Holiness's path of non-violence. Tibetans have not taken their hatred to the Chinese people, although their anger has surfaced against the policies of suppression and the suppression itself. However, if this repressive situation continues for too long the Tibetan struggle will not be the same.

Despite the difficult and critical situation we are presented with, I am observing a very positive development in the Tibetan diaspora. An extremely dedicated and highly educated new generation of Tibetans is emerging. They are equipped with the best knowledge and skills characteristic of their adopted countries, and yet they are still passionately Tibetan. My generation can soon confidently hand over our responsibilities to our children.

In the course of my job over the last sixteen years, I have been privileged to have had the opportunity to meet and exchange thoughts and views with thousands of great ordinary citizens, as well as presidents, prime ministers, diplomats, writers and artists. But the greatest honour has always been my association with His Holiness the Dalai Lama as his Representative, and to serve the Tibetan cause under His Holiness's wise leadership.

As I think back to the days when I was the son of a drogpa, living a simple but contented life in peace and freedom, caring for yaks and sheep, I am grateful for many things.

When I think back to when we were forcefully driven into exile and when I was deprived of the opportunity for an education — the days when I was driven to the verge of despair — I am grateful that I never lost my determination and self-confidence. I am grateful for the love and kindness of my parents and my siblings, when all we had was each other. I am grateful to the teachings of the Buddha that I absorbed from my parents and gurus, which taught me that whether 'good' or 'bad' all things are by nature impermanent, and that with perseverance and a good heart there will always be light at the end of the tunnel. Above all, I am grateful to His Holiness the Dalai Lama for his supreme leadership in guiding us to a life of peace, compassion, hope and dignity.

Glossary

amdrak The chest pocket created by the overlapping of the chupa cloak when tied up around the waist. *See* chupa.

ani The Tibetan word for 'nun', an ordained female practitioner.

Avalokiteshvara Known as 'Chenrezig' in Tibetan, Avalokiteshvara is the bodhisattva or Buddha of compassion. *See also* mani prayer.

bardo The bardo state is the intermediate state that the consciousness exists in between death and rebirth. In the bardo the consciousness of the deceased takes a 'mental' body which is projected by the person's previous karmic tendencies. *See also* Bardo Thoedrol.

Bardo Thoedrol The *Bardo Thoedrol* which is translated as *The Tibetan Book of the Dead* is traditionally read during the forty-nine days after a person's consciousness has left their body — after they have 'passed away'. The book may also be read to a person who is dying to prepare them for what occurs during and after death, especially when the consciousness is in an intermediate state or 'bardo'. *See also* bardo.

bodhisattva A bodhisattva possesses the aspiration to achieve enlightenment for the benefit of all sentient beings and the mind of enlightenment. Having embarked on the path to enlightenment a bodhisattva passes through ten stages or levels (bhumis). Many Mahayana sutras state that a bodhisattva foregoes final enlightenment until all beings have been liberated.

Bon The ancient pre-Buddhist religion of Tibet.

Boudhanath Known to Tibetans as Jharungkhashor, and commonly called 'The Great Stupa', the stupa at Boudhanath is a major Buddhist monument in Kathmandu, Nepal, which contains relics and other sacred items. It is an important pilgrimage site for Buddhists.

Buddha, The (c. 485–405 BCE) Siddhartha Gautama, the historical Buddha, also referred to as Shakyamuni Buddha, was born a prince, around 485 BCE, in Lumbini, in what is now the Kingdom of Nepal. After witnessing an old man, a sick man, a corpse and a renunciate, he renounced the world and became a religious mendicant. He had two teachers, but after six years of studying with these ascetics he renounced the path of austerity for the 'Middle Way'. Through following the Middle Way he gained enlightenment at the age of thirty-five in Bodh Gaya, which is in present day Bihar, India, and became a Buddha. After his awakening he was requested to teach, and his first teachings became known as the Four Noble Truths and he began to turn the Wheel of Dharma. He established a monastic order, the Sangha, and continued to teach the Dharma for another forty years. He passed into parinirvana at around the age of eighty. The Buddha is the first of the Three Jewels of Buddhism. *See also* the Three Jewels.

Chang-Thang plains The great northern and central plains of Tibet.

Chogye Trichen Rinpoche (1919–) His Eminence Chogye Trichen Rinpoche is the lineage holder of the Tsharpa lineage, a branch of the Sakya lineage of Tibetan Buddhism. He is the most senior Sakya lama living today. *See also* Tibetan Buddhism.

chupa The Tibetan national dress worn by both men and women. Men and women wear a different style of chupa.

circumambulations Pilgrims and Buddhist practitioners circle clockwise around stupas, temples and holy objects as a practice of veneration, homage and the creation and sharing of merit. *See also* merit.

Dalai Lama, His Holiness the Tenzin Gyatso the Fourteenth Dalai Lama was born in Tibet in 1935. He was the spiritual and temporal ruler of Tibet. In 1949 the People's Republic of China invaded Tibet and in 1959 the Dalai Lama went into exile in northern India where the Tibetan Government was re-established in exile. In 1989 he received the Nobel Peace Prize in recognition of his consistent adherence to non-violence for the Tibetan struggle and his constructive proposals for international conflict resolutions, human rights issues and environment protection. He accepted the prize on behalf of oppressed people everywhere, for those who struggle for freedom and work for world peace, and for the people of Tibet. He is considered to be the emanation of Avalokiteshvara, the Buddha of compassion.

Dégé An area of Kham, in eastern Tibet.

Dégé Khandro A female lama from Dégé.

deities Deities or buddhas such as Tara and Avalokiteshvara are embodiments of enlightened qualities which inspire and inform the positive actions of Buddhist practitioners. *See also* bodhisattvas, Tara and Avalokiteshvara.

Dharma The second of the Three Jewels of Buddhism. The Dharma is the Buddha's teachings. *See also* Three Jewels.

Dharokha In Namru, Tibet, the dharokha was the highest leader of a tsowa. The dharokha of the tsowa enjoyed a tax exemption. *See also* tsowa.

divinations Divination was practised widely throughout Tibet to foresee the outcome of events or decide which course of action would be most auspicious or successful. Various methods of divination were employed including consulting a protective deity.

Drepung monastery One of the three great monasteries of central Tibet, Drepung monastery is west of Lhasa and was built in 1416. It was partially destroyed during the Chinese invasion, but prior to that it had as many as 10,000 monks.

drogpa 'Drogpa' means 'animal farmer' or 'nomad'. Many Tibetans throughout Tibet including most living on the vast Chang-Thang plains were drogpas. Most of the drogpa families of Namru lived permanently in the same place, many in houses. While they moved their herds seasonally for better pasture, many drogpa families of Namru had settled in the same place for generations.

Ganden monastery The foremost monastery of the Gelug lineage, founded in 1409 by Lama Tsongkhapa. It was completely destroyed during the Chinese invasion but considerable restoration has since been undertaken.

garpon The garpon was the highest local authority who was indirectly elected by the people of Namru. (The Namru district had several levels of local leaders, including the Namru Garpon.) During his tenure the garpon enjoyed the rank of a cabinet minister of the Tibetan government. As such he had all the official costumes and ornaments of this rank and these items were handed over from the old to the new incumbent. One of the garpon's privileges included an annual audience with the Dalai Lama.

genla A 'genla' is a teacher or monk-teacher.

gompa The Tibetan word for a monastery.

guru 'Guru' simply means 'teacher', but particularly refers to a qualified spiritual guide or master.

inji The colloquial Tibetan expression for 'Westerner'.

ka kha The 'ka kha' is the Tibetan alphabet, which begins with these two consonants.

karma In Buddhism 'karma' is the law of cause and effect. Karma means 'deed' in Sanskrit, and in Buddhism it is understood as how actions bring forth results or consequences which can affect this life and future lives.

Karmapa The sixteenth Gyalwa Karmapa, Rangjung Rigpe
   Dorje was the head of the Kagyu branch of Tibetan
   Buddhism and was one of the foremost masters of his
   generation. The seventeenth Karmapa currently resides
   in northern India after a dramatic escape from Tibet in
   the year 2000.

Kham An eastern region of Tibet.

khata A khata is traditionally white or yellow in colour and
   is often made of a fine fabric. It is traditional for Tibetans
   to offer a khata to visitors, dignitaries and Buddhist
   masters, and once offered the khata can then be returned
   to the giver as a blessing by placing it around their neck
   and shoulders like a scarf.

Lam Rim Chen Mo The Tibetan title *Lam Rim Chen Mo* is
   translated as *The Great Treatise on the Stages of the Path to
   Enlightenment*, which was composed by Lama Tsongkhapa
   in the fifteenth century.

lama A 'lama' is a Buddhist teacher or qualified spiritual
   guide.

Lamdre The Tibetan title *Lamdre* means 'the path and
   its result'. It is the central teaching and practice of the
   Sakya lineage which encompasses the entire range of
   teachings from the Buddha, and also contains teachings
   on Tantra, especially the *Heyvajra* Tantra. The crux of
   the *Lamdre* teachings is the inseparability of the worldly
   existence (Samsara) and enlightenment (Nirvana).
   The *Lamdre* teaching is given by an officially recognised
   lineage holder over a period of around six weeks. *See*
   Chogye Trichen Rinpoche.

lhakhang The Buddhist 'chapel' or shrine room.

Lhasa The capital of Tibet, situated in the south.

lineages *See* Tibetan Buddhism.

Mahayana Buddhism Mahayana is Sanskrit for 'great vehicle' and refers to this tradition's emphasis on Bodhicitta or the 'mind of enlightenment'. Tibetan Buddhism includes Mahayana Buddhism, which was also traditionally practised in Vietnam, Korea, Japan and China.

mani prayer The mani prayer or mani mantra OM MANI PADME HUM is loosely translated from Sanskrit as 'homage to the jewel in the lotus'. It is the mantra of Chenrezig known also as Avalokiteshvara, the Buddha of Compassion, and is depicted in Buddhist images, thankgas and carvings throughout Tibet. *See also* mani stones and Avalokiteshvara.

mani stones These are stones or rocks which had carved into them the mani prayer or mantra OM MANI PADME HUM as an act of merit and a homage. *See also* mani prayer.

mantras Mantras are composed of sacred syllables or sounds that are attributed with the power to purify and bless the consciousness of those who recite them. Each deity has a sacred mantra and often there are short and long mantras which, like prayers, can be recited as meditations or as part of a Tantric practice. *See also* Tantra.

Mao Tse-tung (1893–1976) Chairman Mao Tse-tung was a founding member of the Chinese Communist Party in 1921 and became its leader. He developed his own revolutionary theories stemming from Marxist-Leninist philosophy.

Many of his military theories and philosophical ideas are summed up in what has become known in the West as 'The Little Red Book', which is a collection of quotations excerpted from Mao's speeches and publications. After 1945, during the Chinese civil war, Mao and his movement overwhelmed the Nationalists and proclaimed the People's Republic of China on 1 October 1949. Two of his initiatives, the 'Great Leap Forward' and the 'Cultural Revolution', resulted in widespread oppression and death. He along with his Communist Party colleagues engineered the invasion and occupation of Tibet.

meeser 'Meesers' were 'subjects' who paid tax to a monastery or directly to aristocrats in Lhasa, in contrast to 'tralwas' who paid their tax directly to the government of Tibet. *See also* tralwa.

merit In Tibetan *sonam* means merit or virtuous karma, which is synonymous with virtuous activity.

Milarepa Known as the greatest yogi of Tibet, Milarepa searched for a master who could help him absolve his guilt after he used sorcery to bring about the death of many people, including his uncle. His life story is one of the most revered and popular biographies of Tibetan Buddhism.

momos A traditional Tibetan meat dumpling.

Monlam The Tibetan Buddhist annual prayer festival.

Mount Kailash The sacred mountain in western Tibet, revered by Buddhists and Hindus alike.

Mustang A small kingdom within the Kingdom of Nepal that is culturally Tibetan and has its own monarchy.

Nalanda monastery The monastery of Chogye Trichen Rinpoche.

Namo Buda Known as Takmolugen to the Tibetans, this hillside in the Kathmandu valley is believed to be the place where the Buddha in one of his previous lives sacrificed his body to feed a starving tigress and her cubs.

Namru A large district on the central plains of Tibet. *See also* drogpa.

nirvana The permanent state of complete peace and knowing; a state of existence free from suffering.

Nyenchen Thangla A mountain range in central Tibet which is believed to be the residence of one of the protective deities of Tibet by the same name. The Nyenchen Thangla protective deity is believed to be committed to protecting the Buddhadharma and practitioners of the Dharma. Nyenchen Thangla is one of the protective deities of Tibet known as the Nine Deities of Existence, which are believed to have existed ever since the birth of the Tibetan land. He is depicted as a handsome young man riding a white horse and wearing white apparel, including a white woollen hat. With his right hand he clasps a horsewhip high in the air, while his left hand bears a spear with a white banner attached to it. His turquoise hair is divided into five portions on his head and he is said to have three hundred and sixty attendants. He is thought to have received teachings from Lord Buddha himself and to have taken a vow before the Buddha to protect the Dharma when it arrived in Tibet.

Padmasambhava The eighth-century yogi known as Guru Rinpoche who was a great tantric master. Padmasambhava was instrumental in introducing Buddhism to Tibet from India, during the reign of King Trisong Detsen. His name means 'lotus-born'.

parinirvana The final or highest nirvana; the state of nirvana that is entered at death.

phowa The practice or technique for the transference of consciousness at the time of death.

Pokhara The second largest city in Nepal. At an altitude of 827 metres above sea level and 200 kilometres west of Kathmandu valley, Pokhara is part of the once vibrant trade route extending between India and Tibet. It is the site of four major Tibetan settlements in Nepal.

prayer beads Known as 'malas', prayer beads or rosaries are used to count mantras and other repetitive devotional practices. Prayer beads are often made of precious stones, seeds or wood and are usually blessed before use.

prayer wheel Prayer wheels can be made of wood or metal, and are usually carved with sacred symbols or mantras externally. They contain mantras, sutras or sacred prayers which are rolled and placed within the wheel which, when spun, rotate in a clockwise direction thus repeating the merit of the practitioners' practices many times over and spreading their benefit to other beings.

prostrating Prostrations are performed as a physical act of homage and devotion to purify the practitioner and increase their faith in the Three Jewels. This is a preliminary everyday Buddhist practice.

puja A form of worship, offering or homage to devotional deities or the Three Jewels. A puja can be conducted privately or publicly, by an individual or a group.

rebirth In Buddhism the concept of rebirth is based on the idea that a being is an aggregate of both physical material and mental consciousness that has arisen as a result of past karma. When the conditions for the present life expire, the consciousness then takes rebirth in any of the six realms according to the karmic conditions brought about through past lives. Consciousness is not considered to be a result of physical phenomena, therefore its cause for existence is the immediately preceding moment of consciousness. Thus the consciousness existed before the formation of the present physical body, and will continue to exist after the disintegration of the present physical body.

rinpoche The Tibetan word 'rinpoche' literally means 'precious one'. It is used as a respectful title for many reincarnated lamas and highly regarded teachers of the Buddhadharma.

Risol A one-day festival held in midsummer each year in Namru. Risol was literally 'the ceremony to praise the mountains'. This festival was dedicated chiefly to the protective deity Nyenchen Thangla. *See also* Nyenchen Thangla.

Sakya The third oldest school or lineage of Tibetan Buddhism, headed by the Sakya Trizin, who is one of the foremost living Buddhist masters.

sand mandalas These sacred diagrams made of coloured sand are used for initiations and for meditational practices. Common to the Tantric practices, most mandalas contain a host of deities as well as other sacred items. They are said to exist in several planes of reality. Sand mandalas are created to be impermanent and are destroyed or 'dissolved' shortly after their completion. *See also* Tantra.

sang The Tibetan currency prior to the Chinese invasion of 1949.

Sangha The third of the Three Jewels, the Sangha is the community of Buddhist practitioners, especially the ordained Buddhist practitioners but also the lay community.

Sera monastery One of three great Buddhist monasteries of central Tibet, Sera monastery was founded in 1419.

Seven Thirang Siblings The pinnacles of rock in Namru that marked the place where the borax mine was constructed after the Chinese invasion.

six realms The realms of hells, hungry ghosts, animals, humans, demi-gods and gods.

stupa A religious monument created to commemorate a Buddha or other enlightened being, which contains relics and other sacred items such as texts. Small replica stupas are often used as reliquaries.

Swayambhunath stupa Situated on a hilltop overlooking the Kathmandu valley in Nepal, this stupa is a sacred site for Buddhists.

Tantra Tantra is often referred to as the 'secret doctrine' of the Buddha's teachings. Tantra refers to the teachings of the Vajrayana or 'diamond vehicle' of Tibetan Buddhism. Tantric teachings and practices are part of the esoteric path of Buddhism, in which initiations and practices are passed to the student through a lineage and guru.

Tara The buddha or bodhisattva Tara is depicted in female form as the embodiment of enlightened activity and compassion. To Tibetans she is the 'saviouress' and 'protector'. The blessing or initiation of White Tara represents long life, while Green Tara is the protector who defeats evil, cures illness, averts natural disasters and remedies many other afflictions.

Tashi Lhunpo monastery The seat of the Panchen Lama.

thangkas Tibetan scroll paintings depicting Buddhist images of buddhas, bodhisattvas and other deities.

Three Jewels, the The Three Jewels of Buddhism are the Buddha, the Dharma and the Sangha. The Buddha's teachings are the Dharma and the Sangha are the practitioners who uphold the teachings.

Tibetan Buddhism Tibetan Buddhism has four main schools or branches, which are Nyingma, Kagyu, Sakya and Gelug.

tralwa In Tibet 'tralwas' were taxpayers who paid their taxes directly to the government of Tibet, in contrast to 'meesers'. *See also* meeser.

tsampa Tsampa is a type of flour that is traditionally made from roasted barley. It can be kneaded into a dough to make 'pak'. Pak is made by adding a liquid such as tea to the flour, to which butter may also be added, after which the the dough is kneaded. Tibetans normally make pak with a little bit of dried cheese dust, a lump of butter and some Tibetan tea. Pak can also be made with just cheese dust and butter added to tsampa.

tsog Tsampa cakes used as offerings. *See also* puja.

tsowa In the district of Namru, in Tibet, a 'tsowa' was a sub-grouping of the district, rather like a village. Namru had thirteen tsowas, each with its own name. The highest leader of each tsowa was called the *dharokha*.

Zamling Gyalchi Tibetan name for the United Nations.

zong The vast territory of Tibet was naturally divided into several districts. The Tibetan term for 'district' was 'zong'.

zongkhang The zongkhang is the district house.

zongpon Each 'zong' or 'district' of Tibet was administered by two zongpons (district commissioners) — one a lay person and the other a monk. *See also* zong and garpon.